THE LOST GENERATION OF 1914

The Menin Road

The
Lost Generation
of 1914

REGINALD POUND

Illustrated With Photographs

Coward-McCann, Inc.   New York

RP

CONTENTS

*A section of photographs
follows page 128.*

c.2

Author's Note

RESEARCH FOR THIS book has been greatly helped by the facilities available at the Library of the Imperial War Museum, the London Library, and the Guildhall Library. To their staffs I am indebted for services courteously rendered.

For help of a more personal kind, I thank Lady Salmond, who allowed me to read the private journal of the Grenfell family; and Sir Rex Benson, whose recollections of contemporaries who fell in the First World War supplied valuable material.

I thank Mrs. John Drinkwater for lending me Rupert Brooke's letter on page 89 and Sir Geoffrey Keynes for giving me permission to publish it; Lord Rothermere for the extracts from the letter written by his brother, the Hon. Vere Harmsworth (page 264); Mrs. C. Browning (formerly Mrs. Harold Chapin) for allowing me to quote from the letters of Harold Chapin on pages 241–243; Mrs. Peter Pound for access to the war diary kept by her father, Captain Neville G. Chamberlain; Mr. R. R. Calkin for notes and privately printed memoirs; Mr. Bernard Slater, M.A. (Oxon) for information from the files of *The Portcullis*, the magazine of Emanuel School, London, S.W.; Miss Jelly d'Aranyi for her reminiscences of F. S. Kelly and for showing me letters from him; and Messrs. J. M. Dent & Son, Ltd., for permission to quote from *Everyman at War*.

Although present-day publishers discourage the compilation of those intimidatingly long lists of authors' acknowledgements, I seize the opportunity of thanking, also, Signora Patricia Volterra; Mrs. Beatrice McPhillamy; Miss Peggy Simpson; Mr. Hugh Miller; Mr. A. E. D. Anderson; the General Secretary, King Edward VII's Hospital for Officers; Army Records Centre; Sir John Elliot; Major T. Baxter Milne; Mr. T. McColl Smith; Mr. D. Lyall Grant; Mr. W. A. Roberts; Miss W. Gwyn-Jeffreys; Messrs. Sidgwick & Jackson, Ltd; Mrs. Rolanda Ronald; Mrs. M. Hottinger; Mr. George Vincent; Dr. Patrick Shackleton; and the National Book League Information Bureau.

To many others from whom the theme of the book has evoked an equally generous response I reaffirm my appreciation.

R. P.

Welbeck Street,
London, W.

THE LOST GENERATION OF 1914

CHAPTER ONE

A Party for the Shooting Season

1

A LOVELY SUMMER was bringing ripeness to the kindly fruits of England. Nature presciently imposed herself with double splendour on the senses of a people whose patriotism, like their poetry, derived its most powerful impulses from their countryside. Gorse blazed like solar flares on the hills. Down and wold and moor rolled towards horizons that were never more enticing. Daily the sun went down out of cloudless skies that were wine-coloured at dusk and at night a carnival of stars.

As a bonus of beauty, a new English rose, Paul's Scarlet Climber, raised at Waltham Cross, made its début to grace garden walls, as it does these fifty years after. A new sweetpea, Mrs. E. Wright, "the colour white ground, washed and edged with blue, a most exquisite novelty," (*Country Life*), was carrying off first prizes at the flower shows. The poppies in the cornfields were not yet dyed the deep compassionate red of the next year's harvest.

Over the August Bank Holiday, coastal England was crowded down to the watermarks. At some seaside places mixed bathing was still an innovation in sex freedom, a spectacle for straw-hatted *voyeurs* lining the promenade railings. At a few resorts men and women still bathed in separate preserves, splashing one another with sensuous pleasure over dividing ropes. Decaying bathing machines,

11

derelict among the tamarisks, were museum-pieces of a prudery that continued to govern the design and wear of bathing costumes. At most coast towns bathers whose figures were insufficiently draped were liable to be reported by vigilantes of the local watch committees.

Public behaviour between the sexes in England in 1914 still conformed to the pattern and proprieties of the waltz. Walking arm-in-arm was the limit of affectionate display out of doors. Only a formal engagement permitted a man to be seen with his arm round his fiancée's waist. Walking hand-in-hand, now common enough, would have been thought a nursery reflex. There were no signs of the public endearments that meet the eye today in every street and on all the leading football grounds. The effeminisation of England had hardly begun. Meanwhile, the inhibitions were the price of a certain dignity that no longer graces sex relations in our country.

Far out on the sparkling sea white yacht sails leant against the sky. Paddle steamers threshed like ocean pachyderms towards the pierheads, where penny-in-the-slot machines clanged and clattered incessantly and where the "glad eye" was the unspoken language of romance. England was on holiday. Gay abandoned laughter was the common denominator of the popular mood. Most of the people, nearly all of the people, would be going home after the annual fortnight to a standard of living unthinkable today and now only a memory, like the gay abandoned laughter.

The sardonic objectivity of our latter-day school of historians can neither penetrate nor dissipate the golden haze of that singular time. For all its rampant injustices, its soaring unearned incomes and its wages barely keeping abreast of prices, its abounding wretchedness, its drunkenness galore, the people knew a kind of untainted happiness that has since gone from the world. Doubtless with no intention of baffling the sociologists, an East End housewife told *The Times* in 1964: "Years ago it was marvellous here."

Grandfathers who saw the last stage coaches, the first railway trains, the first telegraph wires, were taking the air in the last Bath chairs. The fathers, middle-aged promenaders cherishing illusions as foolishly fragile as the toy balloons bursting about them, had seen Victorian idealism come to fruit in the Education Act of 1870. They had seen the rise of the popular press, due largely to the proliferation of those telegraph wires; and the beginnings of a technology that would "process" not only breakfast foods but thoughts and ideas. They saw electric light brought from the street into the home. They saw also the first tentative movements of organised labour, provoked by a Board of Trade report on the Whitechapel sweatshops.

Their sons, buoyant with the promise of an unprecedented age but still obedient to the gravitational pull of the family, were there in the crowd, sporting blazers and the broad-striped socks that were *le dernier cri* in 1914. Three generalisations could be made about them by a possibly eccentric sociologist. They were the last representatives of the race to be breast-fed in significant numbers, the last to play with tin soldiers before they were displaced by mechanical toys, and the last to be brought up in sailor suits.

Their most dynamic epithet was "bally" (rhymed with valley: "you bally idiot, you!"). "Damn" was impermissible in polite company. "Bloody" was the password to hell. "Rotter" was the currently preferred synonym for cad or bounder. "Decent" was the commonest ethical adjective. "New," "quick," "cheap," were not the keywords that they have since become.

Among their heroes were Fry and Ranjitsinjhi in county cricket, S. F. Edge on the motor racing track,

13

Grahame White in the air, Max Linder on the film screen, Sherlock Holmes in fiction. They laughed at politics and were not much more serious about love. For them, of all the generations, had been reserved the transcendent excitement of seeing the first men to fly. They had already witnessed the advent of the motor-car, that major propellant of the twentieth-century momentum. They had seen the first moving pictures, the greatest cultural force of the era. They heard the first radio signals, cheeping like a fledgling lost in outer space.

No heirs of the ages had been granted a more triumphant sense of the human potential. Science was about to set men free and so make them happy. Despite the enervating effect of a widely read novel, *When It Was Dark*,[1] which struck at the roots of their formative religion, they had an exhilarating assurance of receiving the title deeds to a fabulous future, of being favourites of destiny rather than puppets of fate. They were the last of our English youth to be brought up in a state of fatuous innocence. The ironic gods never had more wicked sport with any generation.

2

They came of age in a calm of history that still has the power to stir insidious longings in those who remember it. They were not rehearsed in violence, as their successors were to be. There were no raving dictators, no vast credulous crowds endorsing demands for revenge in the monotone chanting of mass hypnosis. What since 1898 had been building up as "the German menace" was hardly more than an occasionally jarring discord in their lives, an intermittent tingling of the nerves.

Alsace-Lorraine, that bitterness from 1870; Pan-Slav

[1] By Guy Thorn.

14

agitation; German naval expansion: those persisting bedevilments of European diplomacy never took away their appetites as the Munich conference of 1938 did ours. Was it because, as an eminent surgeon later remarked, they had "more beef in their blood"? One cannot imagine the display of hysterical relief in the House of Commons on September 28, 1938, occurring in Asquith's time.

At Wellington College speech day, 1909, Lord Rosebery, the ex-Prime Minister, said that "the stress that patriotism will have to bear in days not far distant, and perhaps imminent, will be greater than has yet been known in the history of this country. (Hear, hear)." It was not recorded that the boys dispersed with dread in their hearts. Twelve months later, the head of the Beacon School, Sevenoaks, wrote privately to the headmasters of the leading public schools begging them to prepare their pupils for the possibility of war. He explained that he had spent the long vacation of 1910 with French professors whose estimate of the European situation compelled him to believe that the breaking point would come in 1914. Sitting on a Mendips hillside one August day in 1911, the year of Agadir, Winston Churchill "could think of nothing but the perils of war."

Lord Roberts toured the country, trying to rouse the people, who rarely filled the halls he spoke in. Critics of his campaign for national service said that it was discouraging recruitment for the Territorials, for whom Lord Haldane had planned a leading role in the country's defence if war came. Prophetic articles were published in the *United Service Magazine*, which incorporated the titles of two defunct Service journals, suggesting a declining professional circulation. The works of Bernhardi, Treitschke and Von der Goltz were no doubt seriously regarded at the military academies of Sandhurst and Woolwich, where it may also have been noted

15

that new books on war as a science were coming in exceptional numbers from German publishing houses. An invasion play, *The Englishman's Home*, quickened the pulses of old ladies who never saw it. In 1909 and 1912, Charles M. Doughty, author of *Travels in Arabia Deserta*, published two poetic dramas that were derided for their theme of war with Germany. They contained remarkable foreshadowings of wartime experiences. Robert Blatchford, a Socialist editor, wrote for the *Daily Mail* a series of articles about Germany's dreams of conquest which the Liberal *Daily News* dismissed as "ravings." In 1913, a future Chief of the Imperial General Staff, General Sir William Robertson, told the Officers' Training Corps in camp in Salisbury Plain that war would come soon.

The sombre pronouncements, the high-pitched warnings, did not disturb a generation beguiled by the brazen new rhythms of *Alexander's Ragtime Band*. True, many colleges and public schools had an O.T.C. tradition, their contingents miniature Sandhursts in zeal and efficiency. At Oxford, military history was given its own professorial chair. The implication certainly was not that young Englishmen were susceptible to martial propaganda, still less that they were "howling impatiently . . . for immediate war."[1] They thought of war as they thought of death, as a far-off event. Nor were they distracted by the Irish turmoil, the dockers' strike at Liverpool, suffragette militancy, or Futurism; since unconvincingly interpreted as "a sign that men were wearying of peace."[2]

As for the precariousness of the human situation in general, they had been sufficiently reminded of it by the

[1] *The Unlovely War*, by Michael Howard, *Encounter*, January 1964, apparently prompted by the tendentious statement to that effect in the Lloyd George *Memoirs*.
[2] A. J. P. Taylor: *Englishmen and Others* (1956).

16

headlined horrors of the Messina earthquake (1908), the sinking of the *Titanic* (1912), and the worst of all Welsh mining disasters (1913). To young tennis players, leaping and skipping on lawns trellised by pink Dorothy Perkins roses under those memorably blue skies, such mischances were too remote to spoil eager dreams, high hopes, great expectations. Not with supercilious conceit, rather as believers in luck, they were proud to be English-born, transmitters of a political maturity that honoured the nation and mankind. Heedless of the claustrophobic discomfort of the land-bound peoples of the Continent, the islanders continued to relax in the immunity guaranteed them by several seas and the great navy that kept watch and ward over them.

3

On the European mainland the war theme was endlessly perpetuated in bronze and stone: in the mausoleums of conquering heroes; in captured cannon rusting in city parks. Every German town had its memorial to the dead of '71. The French bowed the head before the empurpled panoply of Napoleon's tomb and cherished bloodstained uniforms at the military college of St. Cyr. Conscripts in the streets were living testimony to hatreds that endured.

In England, sheltered by a tradition of inviolability, youth was not in thrall to the associative oppressiveness of such symbols. The museum of the Royal United Service Institution in Whitehall was not besieged by sightseers. Trafalgar Day, October 21, was a Royal Navy occasion. For the public, Nelson's Column was a directional aid rather than a reminder of sublime victory. Wellington lay unregarded in his rococo sarcophagus in St. Paul's. Until December 16, 1914, there were no war-

17

scarred buildings in the kingdom, except one or two in Limerick and Londonderry that Cromwell's cannon balls had knocked about a bit.

This English generation was less enamoured of the past than any that had gone before. More schooling, more libraries, more journalism, enabled them to see through the sham glories of history, including recent history in South Africa. They were not seized of the imperial idea that exhausted Jubilee emotions in 1897, when they were very young. Rudyard Kipling was not their laureate. Cecil Rhodes seemed to them a less heroic figure than Baden Powell, whose Boy Scouts were unlikely to involve the nation in complications abroad. Free of the loud peremptory "Sit still!" discipline of the Victorians and of the *fin-de-siècle* neurasthenia, they believed that they stood on the threshold of a new age blazing with the promise of enlightenment and significant change.

The optimism had deeper sanctions than the exuberance and warmth of spirit that are renewed with every generation. Along with the scientific advances, which had made their boyhood so much more wonderful than any other, there were new educational opportunities to make young hearts leap. Higher education was at least a practical hope for thousands. There was a more generous largesse of scholarships. The secondary school population was rising. More grammar school places were available.

While the public schools were still enclosed orders, their least typical product trained minds and their most typical an uninspired amateurism, there were inspiring university developments. Leeds, Sheffield and Bristol were added to Birmingham, Manchester and Liverpool as university centres. There was an increase in the number of university colleges and technical institutes. The university extension lecture network had spread and given birth to the Workers' Educational Association, which by 1914 had 179 branches. Multiplying correspondence courses reached out to large numbers of lower middle class students who were obliged to leave school at 14 to earn a living. They were the public for the *Harmsworth Self-Educator*, a fortnightly part-work so popular that copies were snatched from the bookstalls as soon as a new issue appeared. The indiscriminate journalism of Newnes and Harmsworth was an immeasurable influence in the lives of the masses, providing mental stimulus far beyond the scope of the Board and Church schools and, indeed, most others. In spite of the pathos of so much wistful endeavour, which, as Lady Bracknell would have said, was only "remotely connected with education," youth was uplifted by the belief that a richer life was within the grasp of many more who aspired to it than ever before.

4

"The position in Europe," *The Times* reported on Tuesday, August 4, 1914, striking an unexpectedly dramatic pose, "is one of breathless anticipation of the beginning of hostilities on a large scale."

At Welbeck Abbey, the Duke of Portland's tenants, assembled for their annual agricultural show, waited while His Grace considered whether it might decently be allowed to proceed. He gave a decision in favour, although "many men of the house party were called away by the exigencies of the situation," among them Lord Annaly, "who usually judged the horses." (Local paper.) Privileged visitors, invited to look over the Abbey, noticed displayed in more than one of the rooms a framed *pronunciamento* of the Duchess's guiding principle in life: "I expect to pass through this world but

19

once. Any good therefore that I can do," etc.

Canterbury Cricket Week opened with the season's return match in the ancient rivalry between Kent and Sussex. In some of the private marquees champagne corks popped with unabated gusto. Tents reserved for the Buffs (East Kent Regiment) and the Carabiniers were deserted. At the Oval, London, there was a good attendance for Surrey *v.* Nottinghamshire, in which J. Hobbs (later Sir Jack) made 226, reaching his 800th run in first-class cricket and winning an ovation from the stands. Late that afternoon, as the crowd streamed through the exit gates, word was passed along that the Oval was "being commandeered for military purposes." At Old Trafford, Manchester, where Lancashire was playing Yorkshire, another historic match, "Mr. A. H. Hornby had to leave the ground at 1.30 in response to a call from the War Office," (*Daily Mail*), which momentous summons resulted in his appearance shortly afterwards with the modest rank of captain in the Remount Department. The immortal Rhodes remained in the game, with Hirst, Hayward, three Tyldesleys and *Mr.* R. H. Spooner.

In *The Times* for August 4, additions to the population were announced from The Elms, Wargrave; 24 Staverton Road, Oxford; "Orleans," New Barnet; 44 Rusholme Road, Putney; 8 Atholl Crescent, Edinburgh; Crofton, Ashtead, Surrey; The Dene, Great Shalford, Cambridge; Oteley, Ellesmere, Cheshire; Monkton Vicarage, Isle of Thanet. The Personal column contained hints of more complex human activities.

"To J.B. – I have discovered that your legal ferrets and your private detectives are watching my movements, but I can assure you that you are wasting their time and your money, especially as I expect to be returning to America soon, for good, so please forget me. M.B." There was a trumpet blast from an anonymous patriot:

"To All Who Call Themselves English Gentlemen –
Are You Drilled and Armed Ready to Defend Your
Country?" Donations to the Flying Accidents Fund were
acknowledged: $28.00 from Lady Forbes-Robertson;
$1.87 from the Officers' Mess, 3rd Battn., The Middlesex
Regiment (Duke of Cornwall's Own).

In the same place, Austrians and Hungarians exiled in
England were resoundingly notified that "His Imperial
and Royal Apostolic Majesty has ordered a General
Mobilization of all men liable to serve in the Army and
Navy. They are instructed to proceed home at once to
their respective depots for obtaining equipment." The
charge for that last-hour civility between impending
enemies was 28¢ a line.

Sweating, singing, cursing, watering their horses at
village ponds, stripping cottage plum trees as they
passed, long columns of men in dusty khaki, recalled from
the summer camps on Salisbury Plain, wound through
southern landscapes lush with harvest promise. They
were on their way back to Aldershot, Shorncliffe and
Lydd. Cries of sunstroke delirium rang out from the
swaying Red Cross wagons in the rear. The old Regular
Army was marching for the last time on the rolling roads
of England. Soon it would be fighting its last and greatest
battles. Soon it would win back tenfold the esteem be-
grudged it during the years of the Liberal ascendancy.
Soon Tommy Atkins and his quiff would disappear into
the archetypes' limbo.

Presumably with no occult promptings, Peter Robin-
son, Ltd., the Regent Street fashion house, advertised
themselves in the newspapers that month as "Mourning
Specialists." The Social column of *The Times* contained
the announcement that "Mrs. A. Sassoon has arrived at
Tulchan Lodge, Elgin, where she will entertain a party
for the shooting season."

21

CHAPTER TWO

Unready but not Uninsured

1

PRECEDED BY the briefest chapter of diplomacy in European annals, war came with the climacteric force of great drama for the middle-aged and with the crashing swiftness of a thunderbolt for their sons. Overnight, youth's gay and easy stance stiffened into the postures of the barrack square. White flannels, blazers, cricket bats, tennis rackets, club ties, were flung into the lumber room of time.

A future Socialist Chancellor of the Exchequer, then 27 and reading for the Bar, was "deeply shaken and sharply astonished."[1] "England suffered a shock. All things were changed in a day or two."[2] *The Nation:* "It paralyzed the minds of men." A celebrated observer of the contemporary scene wrote of his "recovering consciousness after the first shock of the war."[3] It was "a severe shock" to a subsequently famous historian.[4] The editor of *The Economist*[5] noted in his diary that the outbreak of war "submerged our artificial world as Herculaneum and Pompeii were buried by the eruption of Vesuvius."

The shock wave was registered in a more frivolous

[1] Hugh Dalton: *Call Back Yesterday.*
[2] Sir Philip Gibbs: *The Soul of War.*
[3] H. G. Wells: *Experiment in Autobiography.*
[4] Professor Arnold Toynbee: *Encounter,* April 1964.
[5] F. W. Hirst.

milieu. "It just doesn't seem *possible* that only a week or two ago those of us who amuse ourselves were – well, amusing ourselves! The veil has been torn from our eyes very suddenly, and it's rather stilled and startled us, the glimpses of blood and sweat and agony, the ugly things and the grim realities of life."[1]

Not for a hundred years had England fought in Continental Europe. Despite Moltke's comment when it was suggested to him that the English were not a military race: "No, but very warlike," the warrior spirit had been alien to them as a people far longer. It disappeared with the tribes, since when it had been treated as an anomaly in human affairs and the German version of it as something of a joke. Prussian spiked-helmet conceit in particular seemed to Englishmen to partake of pantomime, with goose-stepping its loudest laugh.

As for England's unpreparedness in 1914, reprehensible as it seemed to her Allies and to the military critics, it did not finally detract from her moral stature in the court of civilised opinion. No other nation was so demonstrably unready that its officers were obliged to advertise in the newspapers for Webley service revolvers, Mauser pistols, field-glasses, prismatic compasses and wrist watches.

Late in the evening of August 4, Army depot commanders in the United Kingdom received the telegram that had long before been drafted for the emergency that had come at last: *Mobilize stop acknowledge.* Practice mobilisations had been a feature of the Army's training for several years. In spite of the sense and appearance of all-round and sometimes desperate improvisation, in the inner councils more foresight had been shown in broad outline than the public could conveniently be told. Out of Lord Haldane's reverberating Army reforms of six years before had come other

[1] *The Tatler*: Letters of Eve, August 18, 1914.

23

measures of importance when the storm broke. Some were specified in the War Book compiled by Colonel (later Lord) Hankey, Secretary of the Cabinet, a highly confidential set of plans, draft projects, orders and proclamations to meet the more obvious emergencies of a declaration of war. It was designed to supply government departments with directives that would obviate flurry and indecision. It specified compulsory billeting and anti-espionage measures. It provided for the immediate dispatch of an Expeditionary Force of 160,000 men.

Commanding officers received instructions that were certainly not the result of hurried decision. The time-tables for troop movements by rail were minutely exact and obviously the outcome of long prior consultation with the railway authorities. In one day eighty trainloads of troops and supplies were run into Southampton without a hitch. The Engineer and Railway Staff Corps, dating from the Crimea, had functioned with secret success. The arrangements worked so well that shortly after the despatch of the last Expeditionary Force soldier and gun, the Great Western Railway advertised the resumption of its weekly excursion services "to the charming resorts of Dorset, Devon, Cornwall, Somerset and the Wye Valley."

Unready, but not uninsured: that would have been fair comment on the situation of the country in those days of patriotic turmoil. The Royal Navy was in splendid trim. The Army that was about to be landed in France was a superb fighting machine. On August 14, five years after Bleriot's famous flight, people at Dover and Folkestone saw the exciting spectacle of 37 aircraft in the Channel sky. Mostly B.E.s and B.E.2cs, they were under secret orders to rendezvous at Amiens. All arrived safely, though only a few of the pilots had flown the Channel before. They had been preceded by a stream of single flights. Others kept the flow going for several days after. At Spithead, the Royal Naval Air Service was standing by its 20 machines, awaiting the call to action.

Some English sensibilities were aroused by the prospect of horses being involved in fighting on the Continent. As soon as it was known that cavalry formed a large part of the Expeditionary Force, the Royal Society for the Prevention of Cruelty to Animals was urged to make sure that "no unnecessary suffering was caused to horses on the battlefield."

2

A busy black-and-white artist, Alfred Leete, one of the quieter wits of the Savage Club, was hastily commissioned to re-design the front cover of *London Opinion*, a popular weekly paper which was about to go to press. Recruiting was the obvious topic. Leete drew a bold cartoon of Kitchener, whose pointing forefinger stressed the message: *Your Country Needs You*. Within a few hours of its appearance on the bookstalls later that week, the War Office secured the right to reproduce it in poster form. Soon it was displayed on every hoarding in the land. It was the prototype recruiting poster and has since served as a documentary illustration in many histories of the First World War.[1]

The Army Reserve and Special Reserve—formerly known as the Militia—were called up immediately, to the number of 200,000. No absentees were reported. About 260,000 Territorials were under canvas in the summer camps and they also were called up. On August 5, the House of Commons authorised an increase of the Regular Army by half a million men with an age

[1] In 1917–18 the United States recruiting authorities used Leete's idea and design, substituting Uncle Sam for Kitchener.

limit of 19–30 and a minimum height of 5ft 6ins, the maximum demanded since the Crimea. The Army, with the Reserve and Special Reserve, numbered 450,000 men. Of those, 118,000 were garrisoned in India and elsewhere overseas. On August 7, Kitchener's call went out for the first 100,000 of a new army to be enlisted for the duration of the war.

Compared with the leading Continental armies, those figures of immediate British manpower resources seemed woefully small. Doubt and fear were kept at bay by the supreme faith of the people in the power of the Royal Navy to stand between them and whatever might befall. Aid and comfort were coming also from the Dominions. New Zealand had immediately offered a fully equipped contingent. Canada signalled her readiness to help. An Army corps was on the move in Australia.

There was an almost dramatic and certainly a welcome curbing of political rivalry at home. The parties sank their differences to form the Parliamentary Recruiting Committee, which undertook the business of telling the nation about war needs and stimulating the flow of men into the recruiting offices. In a few days, Tyneside raised ten local battalions, Manchester eight, Glasgow, Salford and Hull four each. On August 28, Lord Derby addressed a crowded meeting at St. George's Hall, Liverpool, inviting the clerks of that city to form their own battalion. In three days two battalions were raised and before the week was out, a third. The kindling spark was the suggestion that men would enlist more readily if they could be sure of serving with their friends and neighbours. Lord Kitchener saw the point and sanctioned the formation of "Pals" battalions, raised either by municipal authorities or individuals. A total of 172 battalions of infantry was raised on that basis of sentiment, plus 84 units of artillery and 48 of engineers.

An example of private military enterprise was set in

the South, where Colonel Claude Lowther, the handsome, wealthy and eccentric owner of Herstmonceux Castle, Sussex, raised three battalions of "Lowther's Lambs" (Royal Sussex Regiment) at his own expense and was mortified for life when Kitchener refused to let him command them in France. The grave of their sheep mascot, Peter, in the castle grounds, is still tended by the gardeners of the Royal Greenwich Observatory, which now occupies the castle.

Recruiting staffs worked sixteen hours a day and slept on the floor under their desks. At the Central London Recruiting Office, Great Scotland Yard, on Saturday August 1, eight men enlisted in the Regular Army. The moment of crisis was not yet. There was apprehension but no feeling of grave emergency. On the following Tuesday, August 4, Bank Holiday intervening, the chief recruiting officer arrived to find "a seething mass of men waiting to be enrolled." The efforts of twenty policemen were needed to force a passage for him through the crowd. In Birmingham, traffic was held up by thousands of men waiting while extra affidavits were printed. From distant parts of the country came stories of men walking all night to the nearest recruiting stations, snatching sleep in ditches on the way.

There was no organised recruiting for the Territorials in 1914. By the end of the year, 90,000 men had joined the Force, unpersuaded. Many were prejudiced against "Kitchener's Mob." It was being moulded in the form of the Regular Army. They preferred the Territorials' amateur status which emphasised the individual rather than the mass.

The motives for joining were as many and various as those defined by Abraham Lincoln in the American Civil War: "Patriotism, ambition, courage, love of adventure, want of employment, convenience." For some it was a chance to solve intractable problems. "The war

27

offered a way out for all sorts of men with complicated lives, with debts that had been rather a worry, and with bills of folly that could not be paid at sight, and with skeletons in the cupboard."[1] Probably for a considerable part of the male population the war came, above all, as a relief from pointless labour, one of the major and possibly most dangerous discontents of twentieth century civilisation, which has produced the proliferating white-collar class of men engaged in essentially unmasculine jobs. For many, again, it was the answer to the work problem, aggravated in several trades and professions in the early months. The registered number of unemployed at the end of July 1914 was 90,000. By the end of August it had risen to 156,000 and in another month to 207,000, after which there was a progressive decline.

For other men, and they were numerous too, loathing war and seeing no honourable way of avoiding it, the hour was one of sacrificial decision. To them the logic of events was clear, whatever the pacifists said. The descent of the Germans upon Belgium was a threat to England. Only force could remove it. Heeding no advantage, asserting no virtue, claiming no righteousness, the August volunteers marched away, the vanguard of a generation doomed to die untimely.

3

The arrangements for housing, feeding, clothing and training the nation's new soldiers were overwhelmed by the rush to the recruiting offices. There was barracks accommodation in the British Isles for no more than 175,000 troops. That figure was exceeded in the first two weeks of the war, apart from the Reservists who were falling in at the rate of 45,000 a week. There was no

[1] Sir Philip Gibbs: *The Soul of War*, (1915).

room for the First Hundred Thousand or for the Canadian contingent, which was soon on its way over. Married quarters were abolished. Schools and other public buildings were commandeered. Thousands of men were billeted at a flat rate of 11¢ a day. Within two weeks of the start of the war, plans were passed for building the first hutment camps, which during the following months sprang up like wooden cities in desolate parts of the country. "One great bare moorland in the Midlands, uninhabited since the dawn of history, has now been covered with new roads, railways, pumping establishments, power stations and huts for some 40,000 individuals."

The Fortifications and Works Branch of the War Office built 300 new rifle ranges and doubled the pre-war number of 7,000 targets, not including miniature ranges. The normal length of ranges was cut down from 800 yards to 600, some to 400 yards, to facilitate the musketry practice of the new recruits. One of the new ranges had the record number of 232 targets. Commandants of the Royal Engineers had to deal with many protests from local residents about the siting of the ranges.

Overnight, the White City became a Territorial Army barracks, Alexandra Palace a reception centre for Belgian refugees, Olympia an enemy aliens' internment camp, the Crystal Palace a naval training centre. Territorials were drilling on the roof of Somerset House and in the courtyard of Burlington House, Piccadilly. Five hundred British and Indian Army officers on home leave had their return vouchers cancelled and were posted at once to impart the rudiments of drill and discipline to the first waves of recruits to reach the training camps. Ex-N.C.O.s of the Regular Army were recalled, some to be given commissions. The first of the 37,000 officers appointed "for the duration" were chosen from university men with O.T.C. experience.

Typical of them in temper, eclipsing most of them in performance, was Gerard R. L. Anderson, "Twiggy" to his family and friends, the scholar-athlete of Eton and Oxford of whom the consulting physician to the British Olympic Athletic Team that went to Stockholm in 1912 afterwards wrote: "Nature runs riot in her gifts on some occasions, and in an apparent desire to produce a very king of men, gives him beauty and health, grace, athletic ability and intellect."[1] Having attained an extraordinary influence over his Eton contemporaries, Anderson secured a First in Greats at Oxford and a Fellowship at All Souls. In athletics, "his hurdling was the nearest thing to human perfection. Surely he was the greatest hurdler of all time."[2] On the running track, where he scored many notable successes, he was as fleet as a greyhound, his effortlessness the result of much explicit investigation of the mechanical processes involved as well as of his natural ability. He was one of the first athletes to make use of the corrective facilities supplied by the camera. He would study photographs of himself in action and then go out to eradicate the faults that had been revealed.

Shortly before the war, he joined Cammell Laird at Birkenhead with another old Etonian, Alexander Boyd, subsequently managing-director of Metro-Cammell, Birmingham. It was intended that Anderson, too, should be trained for a high executive post. When war came, he applied at once for a university commision and went to France with the Cheshire Regiment. He was killed in November, 1914, leading a charge at Hooge. The news of his death, coming so soon, was a breath-taking omen of what the nation could expect if the war that was to end by Christmas went on longer.

[1] Major Adolphe Abrahams, M.D.
[2] Ibid.

The British Regular Army of 1914 was morally superior and probably not physically inferior to what it had been through the nineteenth century. The notion that it was composed of rascals led by gentlemen had not been valid since the Peninsular War in which, it was recorded, thirty coiners stepped from the ranks of a single regiment in response to a call for their sort of skill when a local French population refused to accept Spanish money. Recruits for the Army since the turn of the century had at least an elementary education, while civilian life quickened the wits of its Reservists. The British soldier still sang *Goodbye, Dolly Gray*, but he was not the chinless slouch of the anti-Boer War cartoonists or even the mirror of the Kipling image. He was more than a name in a roster or a regimental number. If he had taken the King's shilling because there were no other shillings to take, he was still a free man who had chosen his trade and made what he would of it.

Before 1914, only the Army's overseas formations were kept up to full strength. At home it was considerably below the establishment in fully trained men, its numbers maintained by young soldiers in training and new recruits. When the war came, both those categories were replaced by men of the Reserve, who supplied sixty per cent of the original Expeditionary Force. For many of them it was as great a wrench from accustomed ways and familiar scenes as joining the Army was for the men of the new divisions forming up at Aldershot, Salisbury Plain, Colchester, Crowborough, Abbots Langley, St. Albans and a score of other great training centres.

At Aldershot, the King inspected three new infantry divisions that included recruits from all classes. A member of *The Times* staff noted, not for publication in the newspaper, that "the third division presented a ludicrous spectacle, so motley was their array in the march-past. Few were fully equipped with uniforms, etc. Some were wearing old scarlet jackets with the kilt or with trousers of old uniforms, mingled with civilian attire, all in glaring contrast." Straw hats bobbed alongside cloth caps and bowlers. Frock-coated marchers strode beside scoutmasters in shorts. Rather more dress decorum met the monarch's appraising eye when, shortly afterwards, he walked along the lines of the Public Schools Corps, formed largely of young men with O.T.C. experience.

Khaki supplies had run out almost at once. Quantities of blue stuff obtained from stocks held by the General Post Office were made up into temporary uniforms. The men who wore them looked as if they were on parole from penal institutions. On wet days the dye in their forage caps ran in blue streaks down their faces. There was an embarrassing trouser button famine. Any recruit providing himself with a serviceable suit, an overcoat and sound boots, was entitled to claim a compensatory thirty-five cents. When Lord Denbigh, commanding the Honourable Artillery Company, met Lord Kitchener on the War Office stairs and told him that they had no rifles, no ammunition, no transport, Kitchener exclaimed: "Good God! And we call ourselves an *Empire!*"

A member of a battalion of 1,100 men, for which recruiting had stopped five weeks previously, wrote to a newspaper complaining that "we are wearing out our private clothing. None of us has a uniform yet. Six hours a day for five weeks with a rifle will spoil any jacket. I noticed today that the shoulders of the coats of all our men are covered with oil."

Training camps teemed with recruits drilling with

dummy rifles and lengths of lead piping, stirring their tea with pencils, wearing webbing belts over civilian jackets, using wooden rattles to simulate machine-gun fire on field exercises. At the Public Schools battalions' camp at Tidworth, three sons of Asquith, the Prime Minister, shared "in the new and queer sensation of eating hot mutton in one's fingers . . . or trying to learn the strangely elusive art of buttering bread with a fork."[1] At Dover Castle, the Territorial garrison had no knives, forks, spoons or plates. Hot joints from the cookhouse were served up on bare trestle tables. At the Tower of London, wartime volunteers slept on iron bedsteads without "biscuits," Army slang for barrack mattresses. Critics of the War Office supply situation blamed Free Trade for the shortages manifest on every side. "It enabled the Germans to build up stocks at our expense," and so on.

The lack of arms, uniforms, accommodation, training facilities, produced administrative dilemmas which the authorities tried to resolve by raising the height standard on September 11, 1914, as a means of checking the flow of men into the Army. It proved to be too effective, suggesting that the Government felt free to pick and choose, which in turn implied less urgency. Men who were preparing to join had second thoughts about their private commitments. By that miscalculation the War Office and their civilian advisers took the shine off the ardour of thousands of intending volunteers, nor was it fully restored by the rapidly applied expedient of reducing the height standard to 5ft 5ins a month later, and subsequently to 5ft 3ins.

"I wonder about the future," Charles Lister[2] wrote to a friend during those tempestuous days. "I fancy no

[1] Herbert Asquith: *Moments of Memory* (Hutchinson, 1937).
[2] Lieutenant the Hon. C. A. Lister, R.N.V.R., died of wounds, Gallipoli, August 28, 1915.

peace will be of a very lasting character . . . Europe an armed camp for years, broken up, dissolved in final ruin and revolution by those who have long suffered; it isn't a cheerful picture. But love seems for the moment to have fled the world."

CHAPTER THREE

First of the Fallen

1

ON SEPTEMBER 12, 1914, *The Graphic* printed the first set of pictures of officers reported killed or missing. The following week's issue contained a separate page of pictures of "Killed and Missing Scottish Officers," facing a page of pictures of "Killed and Missing British Officers," all but three or four of them Englishmen serving with English regiments. There had been protests from north of the Border. Apparently for some Scotchmen, "this blessed plot" had a sinister purport that Shakespeare never intended. Their touchiness was ascribed to the tensions of the hour.

"Nerves are still jangling," a reporter of *The Times* wrote on October 28. The English were having hallucinations, seeing the "hidden hand" in high places. They noted with envenomed suspicion that the *London Gazette* recorded changes of name from "Rosenheim" to "Rose," "Siengenberg" to "Curzon," "Schacht" to "Dent," "Festenstein" to "Fenton," "Schumacher" to "Maitland." A Scotch historian, J. M. Bulloch, proposed that "a new Gordon riot" should be raised if aliens persisted in adopting that famous clan name. Majestically immune from the popular clamour, a High Court judge awarded damages and costs to a naturalised British citizen of ex-enemy origin who had been libelled by imputation in an invasion serial story in the weekly paper *Answers.*

J. Lyons & Co. obtained an interim injunction against Liptons in respect of "speaking, writing or publishing words to the effect that J. Lyons & Co. is composed of Germans and that by purchasing their commodities the public is assisting the enemies of Great Britain." Mr. Justice Darling, delighting as always in his own wit, took the opportunity of suggesting, when announcing an amicable settlement of the case: "Perhaps the parties would care to take tea together." The nation was assured in a series of "splash" advertisements that "Bovril Has Always Been British," provoking the immediate and equally widely displayed rejoinder that "Oxo Is British." To those loud assertions of national identity was added a similar claim on behalf of Birds' "All British" Custard Powder.

Recoiling from the unseemly wartime scene, the scholarly romantic novelist, Maurice Hewlett, wrote that "it is all very hateful and makes one despair of mankind, surely the most inferior order of creation. Consider the trees! I take off my hat to them when I pass." A no less scholarly music critic, Ernest Newman of the *Sunday Times*, was distressed in print by the thought of "a Kreisler in arms against a Thibaud," both those virtuosi of the violin being on service with the opposing armies.

> *Hate by water and hate by land,*
> *Hate of the head and hate of the hand,*
> *Hate of the hammer and hate of the crown,*
> *Hate of seventy millions, choking down.*
> *We love as one, we hate as one,*
> *We have one foe, and only one,*
> *ENGLAND!*[1]

---

[1] Ernest Lissauer: *Jugend* (Munich), autumn 1914.

36

2

One of the first of England's amateur soldiers to fall was Riversdale Grenfell, of the Bucks Hussars, a yeomanry regiment. He may have heard the call to arms with feelings of relief, though he would have answered it no less promptly in other circumstances. The City finance house in which he was associated with one of his uncles rocked on the edge of a precipice. Liabilities had been incurred that, but for the war and the moratorium, might have been calamitous. "What good are you doing in the City?" his twin brother Francis, a Regular soldier, had written to him. "I have been thinking about you and I have come to the conclusion that you are wasted, hunting for money. In England people are very narrow-minded, and the ruling idea (especially in our family) is that one must be rich. I am beginning to think otherwise." He hoped that his brother would be guided by thoughts of serving the nation rather than filling his pocket.

"Rivy" Grenfell answered that he realised that "money is not everything," but it would enable him to prepare for the political career that was his ambition. "I shall gradually try to get to know fellows of the Hugh Cecil class.[1] I want them to see me as an earnest, hardworking chap, not a stupid stay-at-country-houses-go-to-balls sort of idiot." His political ambitions may have exceeded his ability to pursue them. The Grenfell twins were not conspicuously gifted, as their cousins, Julian and Billy Grenfell were. They shone their brightest at polo, at which their reputation fell only just short of international fame.

They were members of a large family of Cornish antecedents. With their lean swarthy faces and dark moustaches, they looked like Spanish hidalgos. Their

[1] Lord Hugh Cecil, later Lord Quickswood.

37

guardian was Field-Marshal Lord Grenfell, head of a line that produced admirals, generals and directors of the Bank of England. King Alfonso of Spain wrote them brotherly letters. As twins they were in complete accord and, to strangers, indistinguishable. When the war came and Francis was ordered away with his squadron of the 9th Lancers, Riversdale could not face the separation. With a Field-Marshal in the family, it was not difficult for him to be seconded to the Lancers as an intelligence officer. He joined his brother in France. They fought side by side at Mons. Every morning during the Retreat they retired to read together the 121st Psalm, *I will lift up mine eyes unto the hills*. After no more than a month of gallant service, "Rivy" was killed.

Francis was wounded shortly after the Retreat. An ambulance was called up. Before it arrived, he told a corporal: "I'm going back to the squadron. The doctors must make what they like of it." He was wounded again, helping to save the guns of the 119th Battery, Royal Field Artillery. Sent home to hospital, he was visited by the King, Lord Roberts, and Mrs. Asquith, wife of the Prime Minister. He had won the first Victoria Cross of the war. "What a muddle it all was!" he said when told of the award. His grief at the loss of his brother was made harder to bear by sympathisers inadvertently calling him by his brother's name, so alike had they been. John Buchan saw him "limping about London with a drawn face and haggard eyes, looking like a man searching for something that he could not find."

> *O heart and soul and careless played*
> *Our little band of brothers,*
> *And never recked a time would come*
> *To change our games for others.*[1]

[1] *To John* [Lord John Manners, Grenadier Guards, killed in action, September 1914] by the Hon. G. W. ("Billy") Grenfell, killed in action, July 1915.

There were no war correspondents to test, in the light of contemporary events, Lord Palmerston's judgment of sixty years before that the English as a nation were more adept than any other at mastering and applying knowledge of the military arts. The correspondents had been appointed. They were encouraged in Whitehall to fit themselves out with quasi-military uniforms and, not only that, to buy horses that would ensure their mobility in what was confidently expected to be a cavalry war.

Lord Kitchener's imperious will over-rode those arrangements. He would have nothing to do with the press, his objection a hangover from the South African years when Winston Churchill was an unruly war correspondent and Edgar Wallace, for the *Daily Mail,* "scooped" the peace terms at Vereeniging in 1902. One or two correspondents went to Paris and made contact with the French Army. The others languished at home, while their horses cropped the grass of Hyde Park. Conditions at the front, the ebb and flow of battles, the exploits of individual officers and men, were reported only in the impartial prose of the Press Bureau run by F. E. Smith (later Lord Birkenhead).

> *The Allies at the Germans lunged*
> *And won a fight at (name expunged);*
> *But French's Army was defeated*
> *Upon the field of (name deleted).*

American newspapermen reported the first months of the war with a large measure of freedom, not to say enterprise and, as neutrals, from both sides of the battle lines. Their dispatches were taken by the London newspapers, subject to scrutiny that frustrated and often infuriated Fleet Street. Otherwise, the most authentic information about what was happening "out there" came from men on leave and the wounded in hospital or hobbling about in the unromantic blue garb of official convalescence. Some "told the tale," exaggerating the loss of a handful of men into the destruction of regiments. It was also true that normally inarticulate men told their stories with a narrative accuracy and flow suggesting that the violence of their experiences had released secret springs of expression. No war correspondent could have bettered the description of incidents in the Retreat from Mons given in the personal account of Corporal B. J. Denore, of the Royal Berkshires:

"Again we were rearguard, but did little fighting. We marched instead, staggering about the road like a crowd of gipsies. Some of the fellows had puttees wrapped round their feet instead of boots; others had soft shoes they had picked up somewhere; others walked in their socks, with their feet all bleeding. My own boots would have disgraced a tramp, but I was too frightened to take them off, and look at my feet... One man (Ginger Gilmore) found a mouth-organ and, despite the fact that his feet were bound in blood-soaked rags, he staggered along at the head of the company playing tunes all day. Mostly he played *The Irish Emigrant*, which is a good marching tune. He reminded me of Captain Oates.

"It was the most terrible march I have ever done. Men were falling down like ninepins. They would fall flat on their faces on the road, while the rest of us staggered round them, as we couldn't lift our feet high enough to step over them, and, as for picking them up, that was impossible, as to bend meant to fall. About 9 a.m. we halted by a river and immediately two fellows threw themselves into it. Nobody, from sheer fatigue, was able to save them, although one sergeant made an attempt, and was nearly drowned himself. We marched till about 3 p.m.

40

—nothing else but just march, march, march . . . A sergeant irritated anyone who could hear him by continually shouting out, 'Stick it, lads. We're making history!' "[1]

4

After the rigours of the Retreat, the Army turned and fought at the Marne and the Aisne, surprising the German commanders who expected the French and British to fall back beyond the Seine. That possibility had to be considered by Joffre, the French Commander-in-Chief. The troops were fatigued to a degree at which they might not be capable of further calls on their powers of endurance. At that stage of the fighting fatigue was a greater liability than casualties, which were not so far heavy.

There was no doubt about the exhaustion of the troops. Sir John French, the British Commander-in-Chief, riding across the Marne on September 8, came up with the 5th Cavalry Brigade: Scots Greys, 12th Lancers, 20th Hussars. They had halted for rest behind wooded hills. Nearly every man lay fast asleep where he had dismounted. The Commander-in-Chief rode among them, his horse stepping over or walking round the recumbent figures. When the brigade commander, General Chetwode, asked if he should call the men to attention, Sir John French told him: "No, let them rest. I will say a few words for any who are not too done up to listen."

A curious and moving scene that composes in the mind as a great unpainted battlefield picture: the Commander-in-Chief addressing a sleeping regiment. A few of the men struggled to their feet when they realised his presence among them; others, leaning on their

[1] *Everyman at War* (Dent, 1930).

41

elbows, were only drowsily attentive to his words of cheer. He thanked them for what they had done, briefly outlined the situation, and affirmed his faith in the British Expeditionary Force. Many of the men stretched out before him were Reservists who only a few weeks earlier had been taking home a weekly wage from offices, factories and shops. They had admirably maintained the "march discipline" that was the pride of the Regular Army.

The battle of the Marne (September 6–10, 1914), often over-written in terms of the miraculous, liquidated the German hope of a short decisive war. General von Kluck, commanding the German 1st Army, was in pursuit of the French 5th Army under General Lanrezac. Both the French and British armies had re-crossed the River Marne early on September 3. Kluck expected to meet no real resistance after the ordeal of the Retreat, which left a great and productive region of France securely in German hands. It included coal and iron-ore resources of immense benefit to the enemy. Without them he might not have sustained the coming four years of static war in the West. The Kaiser was already scenting final triumph. "Only thirty miles from Paris!" he exulted in the hearing of a neutral diplomat whom he received in Berlin.

Almost it seemed as if there was an element of the supernatural in the sudden recovery of the French power to strike back. Jeanne d'Arc was a more substantial apparition than the Angels of Mons. With the ponderous sinuosity of a dragon, Kluck's army swerved to deliver a blow that would hurl French and British into the abyss of defeat. In doing so, it exposed itself to flank attacks of which effective though not the fullest advantage was taken by the Allies.

On September 9, the Germans had their first taste of the bitterness of retreat. Kluck's undoing was his adherence to the principles of Clausewitz, whose military doctrine was that a commander in the field must attack the enemy's strongest point. Thus at the Marne the legend of German invincibility was weakened, securing for the Allies more than a largely fortuitous military success. "It gave hope to the subject peoples of Central Europe," wrote Wickham Steed, foreign editor of *The Times*, a result that might not have been loudly cheered had it been made known to a British public then hardly aware of the existence of the Czechs and Slovaks, South Slavs, Transylvanian Rumanes, or Austrian Poles.

Politically influential, militarily unconsummated, the battle of the Marne also had an antiquarian interest in that it was one of the last actions in history fought with weapons that have long since been consigned to the museums. On September 7 a German patrol was chased out of the village of Moncel, near the Grand Morin, by a troop of the 9th Lancers. Two squadrons of German dragoons retaliated and were charged by the Lancers, who regained the village. The two sides had lined up, facing each other, before spurring their horses into the attack. The adjutant of the Lancers, Captain G. F. Reynolds, was severely wounded by a lance. Lieutenant Alfrey was killed "while extracting the lance from Captain Reynolds' shoulder."

British casualties were comparatively light but the battle drained away more energy from the fighting troops and made further inroads on reserves that were not readily expendable. It brought the day nearer when the citizen soldiers of the Territorial Force would be needed for purposes quite other than those for which they had originally engaged.

Three days later the guns roared out their prelude to the battle of the Aisne, a bloodier business that was exploited on the site for many years after by stereoscopic coin-machines in which battlefield excursionists were given ghastly glimpses in colour of the resulting carnage. The beautiful summer had ended. A north wind brought chilly rain followed by heavy autumn mists. On September 13, the Germans, suffering none of the disabilities that had worn down the Mons survivors, took up positions along a new line north of the River Aisne between Compiègne and Berry-au-Bec, north-west of Rheims. It was a scenically varied countryside to fight in: forests, chalk downs, wooded heights, coombes and spurs and little valleys in which children played as high-explosive shells, on range-finding missions, screamed overhead.

The battle lasted twelve days (September 13–25, 1914). In the British sector along the Chemin Des Dames, between the French 5th and 6th Armies, it raged fiercely up to the last twenty-four hours. The British soldier gained his first experience of "digging in" under intense artillery fire. The first secret weapon of the war, the new Krupp high-angle howitzer, appeared on the scene. It fired shells that sent up great billowing clouds of black smoke and scooped out craters twenty feet wide and ten feet deep. "Tommy", with his flair for nicknames, at once called them Black Marias.

For some years the experts of all the armies had agreed that siege warfare belonged to a past age. The new factor was the mobility ensured by the internal combustion engine. They recommended spending money on roads, railways, bridges, transport systems. Now the frustrating prospect arose of the war in the West becoming an interminable contest between two far-straddling giants facing each other from either side of a series of jagged man-made crevasses stretching from the sea to the Alps.

Sir John French's Operation Order No. 26, dated September 15, 1914, informed all concerned that "the Commander-in-Chief wishes the line now held by the Army to be strongly entrenched, and it is his intention to assume a general offensive at the first opportunity."

It was the first official indication of a change in the grand design of the war, in which up to then the armies had swayed back and forth in compliance with principles now suddenly outmoded. But the full meaning of the change was not then perceived. Those in the front line had little time for reflection. The guns of the German artillery were increasingly active. Their snipers and machine-guns were an equally unremitting menace. There was an impression up and down the front that the fighting might at any moment erupt into a full-scale battle presaging the end of the war.

5

Trench war was no new thing. It was part of the story of the American Civil War. Troops had entrenched in the Crimea and at Plevna in 1877–78; and again during the Russo-Japanese war of 1904. Studying that campaign, several military writers had forecast trench war as the logical outcome of a confrontation of the major Powers in Europe. Earlier by several years such a war had been imagined by a Polish banker, M. Bloch. None of the combatants in 1914 had made provision for it. The Germans never doubted that they would carry all before them. The French did not embody the idea in their military doctrine. The British Army practised "digging in" on manoeuvres but it had no fixed place in the training syllabus.

On the Aisne, where the ground was suitable for spade work, there was at first no connected trench system. Borrowing the idea of "funk holes" from the Boer War, the British dug a series of fire pits two feet wide, each holding about half a dozen men, none of whom would have agreed with Uncle Toby in Tristram Shandy that such places were "the noblest grave that a soldier could wish to lie down in." Some of the men on the Aisne were buried alive in them by shell explosions.

Their situation was made the more precarious by the nature of the enemy assault. On September 14, the Germans brought up their first consignment of engineer stores, originally assembled for use against the fortresses of Belgium. They included mortars, rifle-grenades and hand-grenades, searchlights, pistol flares and periscopes. To those new offensive means the British had no reply but their quickly improvised jampot bomb, almost as dangerous to themselves as to the enemy. The Royal Flying Corps, whose latest machines were equipped with wireless, helped to produce better target shooting by our artillery. Otherwise, for the time being the advantage was heavily on the side of the Germans, except in musketry.

In musketry the British infantryman was supreme. Sir John Moore's musketry school at Shorncliffe decisively affected events at Waterloo. The Kaiser's doom was sealed at the modern musketry school at Hythe. On more than one of those autumn days, especially at Mons and Le Cateau, "the might of the realm" rested on the ordinary rifleman, as Froissart recorded long ago of the English archers at Crecy who outshot the enemy cross-bowmen, driving them from the field. From 1909 onward, the British soldier was trained to increase his rate of fire to 15 aimed shots a minute. His proficiency as a marksman, steady and cool and first demonstrated at Fontenoy nearly two hundred years before, helped to halt the German drive into France in 1914. "The musketry of the British Expeditionary Force was such that its bursts of rapid fire were repeatedly mistaken for machine-gun or automatic rifle fire."—*Official History of the War, Military Operations: France and Belgium, 1914*, (Macmillan, 1927), quoting from German sources.

Facing those continuous mortar and grenade attacks

were young Special Reserve men of the type that was fast filling the ranks of Kitchener's new armies at home. Inexperienced fighters, they were called on at the Aisne to withstand a new kind of warfare. It is clear from the *Official History* that they acquitted themselves well. A sapper wrote to his people at home: "You would have thought they were at a football match. They were lying in the trenches with German shells flying all round, and they would make bets as to how many Germans they would get during the day. They laughed and joked all the time. A party of the King's Own went into battle shouting: 'Early doors this way! Early doors, ninepence!'"

Every day lent force to the view that the British Army reserves would be unlikely to last beyond Christmas. The old Army was fast running down in all but fighting spirit. Nothing, it seemed, could daunt men trained in that long and proud tradition. The morale of the survivors of those torn and battered divisions was indeed amazing. Replacing the wastage was becoming a most pressing problem. "The First Hundred Thousand" were not yet ready. The only immediate source of reinforcement (rather than replacement) were Territorials, of which some battalions were already in France, guarding lines of communication. They were the 1st Battn., London Scottish (14th London Regiment), the Oxfordshire Hussars, and Northumberland Yeomanry. They were about to be joined by the 5th Border Regiment, the 1st Battn., Artists' Rifles (28th London), and the H.A.C. Nineteen other Territorial battalions would follow by the year's end. The Northumberland Yeomanry, serving with seasoned troops of the 7th Division, were credited with being the first of England's citizen soldiers to meet the Germans in battle, that October.

CHAPTER FOUR

A Torrent of Young Life

1

DURING THE first week in October, sentries of the Sussex Territorial garrison at Dover Castle looked down from the battlements on columns of men of the Royal Naval Division converging slowly on the harbour, where cross-Channel steamers doing duty as troop carriers waited on a gently swelling tide. They were being embarked, after scanty training, for Dunkirk as part of the plan to relieve the German pressure on the city and port of Antwerp. The cheerful refrain of *Hullo, hullo! Who's your lady friend?* was borne up to the castle height on a freshening breeze.

The Royal Naval Division was the inaugural wartime project of Winston Churchill's tenure as First Lord of the Admiralty. The mobilisation of the Royal Fleet Reserve (ex-Royal Navy men), the Royal Naval Reserve (Merchant Service men), and the Royal Naval Volunteer Reserve (landsmen with some sea training), provided more men than the Admiralty needed. The residue was formed into two brigades commanded by officers of the Royal Navy and the Guards. The Royal Marine Light Infantry, an ancient corps, made a third brigade, commanded by a brigadier-general. To bring the numbers up to division strength, two thousand volunteers were recruited. A member of the Nelson battalion of the Division wrote that among them were "actors, book-

48

makers, remittance men, barristers, engineers, poets, journalists, musicians, men about town—all good of their kind."[1]

A closer view than was possible for the castle sentries would have shown that for want of equipment many of the Naval Division men carried ammunition clips in their pockets and had stuck their scabbarded bayonets in their short webbing gaiters. Some carried water-bottles in their hands, having no belts to which to fasten them.

The fading of the afterglow was a signal for the search-light stations to flick into action over town and harbour. As if under drill orders, their great glittering shafts towered vertically in the dusk like floodlit pillars of Thebes. In the gathering darkness the mood of the men below dramatically changed. The jaunty music hall chorus gave way to the consecrated chords of *Abide With Me*. Like giant batons conducting a deep-throated choir of volunteers who might not see the white cliffs again, the searchlights began to move back and forth across the heavens. No theatrically produced *Son et Lumière* display could have achieved the emotional intensity of those last minutes of the Royal Naval Division's departure from the shores of England.

2

Sub-Lieutenant R. C. Brooke was on Dover quay with that spontaneously solemn company, one of the bright particular spirits of a hybrid formation that enlisted recruits as sailors and trained them as soldiers. He transferred from the Anson battalion to the Hood battalion, "because there was no one I could possibly talk to." Douglas Jerrold saw him reading the *Poetry Review* in

[1] Douglas Jerrold: *Georgian Adventure*.

the billiard room of the Royal Naval Barracks, Portsmouth. "The most remarkable thing about Rupert Brooke in uniform was that he looked exactly like everybody else. His was, to me, a very rarefied charm." (Jerrold.)

To a public that did not read his poetry, or any other, Rupert Brooke was the hero-type volunteer who considered what his fate in war might be and went to meet it unafraid. No intellectual young man of his time won more posthumous esteem. His good looks were celebrated: "Stunning—it is the only appropriate adjective." (Leonard Woolf: *Beginning Again*). Jelly d'Aranyi, the internationally famous violinist, remembers as a young girl admiring his "long, graceful neck." His abundant golden brown hair was brushed into a broken arch over his good forehead. His skin was strikingly smooth, his complexion unusual, "with a tinge of sun-ripened fruit," said the Master of Magdalene, A. C. Benson. Another connoisseur of gilded youth, Henry James, saw him as "a creature on whom the gods had smiled their brightest." Yeats thought him "the most beautiful young man in England."

His voice hardly complemented the physical distinction, if Benson is allowed to be the arbiter. "It was far from beautiful, monotonous in tone, and somewhat hampered in his throat." Nor did he carry himself with godlike bearing. He had the grace but lacked the litheness of the classical hero and huddled in chairs as if to conceal it. Edward Thomas recalled that as he talked "he would thrust his head forward to look at you with his steady blue eyes," which in Benson's recollection were "small or deeply set." In conversation, he often drew his fingers through his hair from front to back. He liked to wear black flannel shirts with loose red or orange crêpe-de-chine ties. Having passed through a Shelleyan metaphysical phase that culminated in a nervòus collapse, he

50

endured more enjoyably a post-'nineties delirium in which his pink elephants were Pater, Wilde and Dowden.

Under the spell of the Webbs, he became a vegetarian and President of the Cambridge University Fabian Society (membership at the time: 6), prompted and no doubt preached at by his stentorian friend, Hugh Dalton. They sat up till many dawns discussing social problems, "for he wanted to get everything clear quickly." (Dalton). A May morning could make him "almost ill with excitement." He revelled in "the music of the birds and the delicious madness in the air." His senses were exquisitely attuned to natural phenomena, light and shade, scents, colours, echoes. In winter he bathed in the Cam. In summer he walked barefooted down dusty lanes. An American poet, Conrad Aiken, was introduced to him two years before the war and confirmed the memory of their meeting in the lines:

> *We talked of great things waiting to be done,*
> *Talking, as young men will, ambitiously.*
> *I smiled, then, seeing your open throat; soft tie;*
> *The golden, godlike head, your eyes' bold blue,*
> *Your burning seriousness . . .*[1]

In London, he attended the Thursday evening parties given by Naomi Royde-Smith, literary editor of the *Westminster Gazette*. She spoke of his "great social success" and of the "personal charm and glamour" that ensured it. In 1913, he was made a fellow of King's College, Cambridge. That year, Miss Royde-Smith (Mrs. Ernest Milton) commissioned him to write articles for the *Westminster Gazette* as a traveller in search of health in the United States, Canada, and the islands of the Pacific. He arrived in America, he said, "merely as a receptive organism." Complying with his newspaper

[1] *Atlantic Monthly,* 1915.

bargain, he "managed to grind out a few ramshackle articles," at twelve dollars apiece. The price did not strikingly endorse the remark of a friend of his at King's College, Cambridge, that "Rupert's public form is the youthful poet. The real foundation of his character is a hard business faculty." It was true that he had persuaded the newspaper management to pay his fares.

His articles, which were later introduced in book form by Henry James, showed him enjoying his travels the more when he could relate what he saw and experienced to an older cultural tradition. That was a missing element, defined in his account of passing through the Rockies. Wherever he went, he felt himself to be the newcomer in not simply the physical sense. "The land is virginal, the wind cleaner than elsewhere, and every lake new-born, and each day is the first day.' Even the flowers were "less conscious" than English flowers. "The breezes have nothing to remember and everything to promise. There walk, as yet, no ghosts of lovers in Canadian lanes." There was the source of the European's discontent. "It is possible, at a pinch, to do without gods. But one misses the dead."

He was asked, on his return, whether he would take an English teaching post at the university but gave no firm answer. In the course of his nervous illness he had apparently experienced some terror of the soul that scarred his imagination. It may have precluded him from viewing the future with the rosy optimism of his years. Staying with Middleton Murry and Katherine Mansfield, he told, "with a gay laugh, macabre and horrifying tales of old women in lonely houses being devoured by their own cats." (Murry). He discussed his recurring mental malaise with Benson, of Magdalene, himself often tortured by something akin to melancholia.

When the war came Brooke made no show of heroics. For him it was as imperative a summons to new ex-

52

perience as to proud service. Around him, others of his set were pleading conscientious scruples, some with success. He considered trying for a job as a war correspondent. "Base thoughts, those," he wrote, "when decent people are offering their lives for their country."

He and Ben Keeling joined the Inns of Court training battalion at Stone Buildings, Lincoln's Inn, before August was out. Keeling, from Winchester and Trinity College, Cambridge, who grew a beard to hide a freakish lack of chin, was remarkable enough to become, after his death in the trenches, the subject of a memoir by H. G. Wells. He wrote on August 24: "Rupert Brooke has dropped out. He wants a commission after all, and thinks he can get one through pushing in various quarters." Brooke was impatient for action. He believed wearing a Sam Brown belt would be a surer guarantee of seeing it. Through Marsh, who was Winston Churchill's private secretary, he was soon gazetted to the Royal Naval Division, training at Betteshanger Park, near Eastry, Kent. He was given a platoon of thirty men, mostly ex-merchant seamen.

3

During the wait for orders at Dunkirk, the Naval Division men were told that the journey to Antwerp would be made by train, that they were certain to be attacked, and that those who got through would probably die in the trenches. That was Brooke's version: he had a habit of over-communicating. He told Mrs. Arnold Toynbee in a letter that during the wait in the dark quayside shed he was "rather miserable" thinking of his old Rugby School companions "who are already wounded and missing or dead," and that he thought about the sons he might never have. He asked Mrs.

53

Toynbee to believe that he thought about it "over and over, quite furious."

Detraining near Antwerp, the Naval Division contingents went into the trenches alongside a Belgian division. A withdrawal was ordered after only a few hours. Brooke and his men marched twenty-five miles through scenes that they had read about in tales of war but never expected to see. "Unending lines of refugees, the old men mostly weeping, the women with hard drawn faces, the children playing or crying or sleeping." Railway stations blazed. Petrol from exploding tanks flooded meadows and roads with rivers of fire. Cattle and horses were roasted alive. Black smoke trailed its filth across the sky—"a Dantesque Hell, terrible," to Brooke. He thought it "one of the greatest crimes in history," and from that time on he was a dedicated believer in his country's cause. By October 9, he was back in London; in the evening of that day telling Winston Churchill at the Admiralty little that the First Lord did not already know. "It's all a terrible tragedy," he wrote. "And yet in its details, it's great fun. And—apart from the tragedy—I've never felt happier or better."

Another of his engagements was to dine at 10, Downing Street in the company of the Prime Minister and two of his sons, Arthur, ("Oc") a fellow officer of the Naval Division, and Herbert ("Beb") of the Royal Field Artillery. "Wearing his weathered tunic fresh from the line, he was a figure impossible to forget; he had a strange lyrical amusement glowing in his eyes, and his face was still lit up by the excitement of the action."[1]

As yet, he had comparatively little public reputation. He was hardly known for his *Poems* (1911), and even less for his critical studies of Donne and John Webster. Working on his war sonnets after the return from Antwerp, he referred to them as his "camp children."

[1] Herbert Asquith: *Moments of Memory*

He had undertaken that the Sonnets should appear in the fourth (and last) issue of *New Numbers*, a quarterly founded by Lascelles Abercrombie not long before the war in association with John Drinkwater and Wilfred Gibson. Brooke canvassed likely subscribers during that London leave. "Isn't it a scandal," he wrote to Drinkwater, "that Masefield doesn't take it in?"

4

At Oxford, "emptiness, silence, reigns everywhere," the President of Magdalen, Sir Herbert Warren, recorded in a letter. "The remnant of undergraduates, the invalid, the crippled, the neutrals, make absolutely no show at all." A Committee of Military Delegates sat in a shabby upper room in Alfred Street interviewing all those Oxford men who applied for commissions. "A torrent of young life surged through that little room, eager and even gay, light-hearted but not light-minded."[1] More than 2,000 candidates were interviewed in August and September and most of them received commissions. Short intensive training courses for commissions were held at several of the colleges. Instead of cycling undergraduates, marching cadets filled the streets. So far, 880 young men had gone from Christ Church, 780 from New College. Magdalen, a much smaller college, was third in the list with 670. Balliol had sent 550 and Trinity 510. "Every society in Oxford has given of its best in learning, in athletics, in social gifts, and all the varieties of Oxford men."[2]

The terrible bleakness had also settled on Cambridge like a pall. The *Manchester Guardian* reported that the university was "practically non-existent." Eighty per cent

[1] *Oxford University Roll of Service* (Clarendon Press, 1920).
[2] Ibid.

of its college rooms were vacant. University lodging-houses were deserted. At one of them, Causeway House, only two students finally remained, an Indian and a Burmese. The King Edward VIIth Professor of English Literature, Sir Arthur Quiller-Couch ("Q", the Cornish novelist), wearing loud-checked tweeds with long-stalked daffodils in his buttonhole, could be seen wandering in the town, looking superannuated. The young men who had listened with eager pleasure to his "familiar discourses" were away learning a jargon at variance with all that he had ever taught them. He could summon a memory of 1913:

"I see a cavalry troop of the Cambridge University O.T.C. clattering home over the bridge by Magdalene in a drizzle at the shut of the evening . . . calling to one another, as they wheeled by St. John's, as if all Cambridge belonged to them. They are gone. They have taken their cheerfulness out of Cambridge; and have left us to an empty university, to dull streets, the short days, the long nights."[1]

There were pious resolutions to return when Service leave permitted. Hearts failed at the thought of quadrangles haunted by the ghosts of the recent dead. "So many gone—so *many* that I can't feel it as I once did," an old Oxford tutor told Mrs. Humphrey Ward. "As blow after blow comes one seems to have lost the power," including the power to recall, he might have agreed, that such Oxford men as Michael Fane of *Sinister Street* ever existed. Before leaf fall, several colleges held memorial services. Those attending one of them at New College Chapel did not soon forget the sight of the white-haired Warden, "full of blameless years," kneeling on the bare stone floor to pray at the altar that "it may be granted to us to live lives such as those young men who have gone before us."

[1] *Studies in Literature* (Cambridge University Press).

56

Public school headmasters were signing applications for commissions every day. Many of the requests came from former pupils in every part of the Empire and Commonwealth. "We have hardly any boys left who are of an age to serve," a headmaster told the *Times Educational Supplement* as the new term began. In the first three months Cheltenham School had 59 old boys killed, Eton 65, Wellington 38, Charterhouse 21, Rugby 20, Harrow 21, Clifton 19, Haileybury 18. For the time being, Winchester preferred to withhold its Roll of Honour from the public domain.

5

"War is a boastful, beastly business; but if we don't plunge into it now we lower the whole pitch of posterity's life, leave them with only some dusty relics of racial honour." Walter Dixon Scott, who thus voiced his thoughts on joining the Army in 1914, was a small, eager-looking Liverpool bank clerk whose critical gifts were encouraged and refined by Professor Elton of Liverpool University. Scott saw in Henry James a "noble credulity." He wrote of Kipling's "swaggering virtuosity." Shaw, he said, had never outgrown his "premature philosophy." Max Beerbohm thought highly of that new talent. He wrote of Scott's "subtle and powerful brain," having no doubt that genius resided in it. Considerable promise undoubtedly did.

Never physically robust—"he was the last man one would have thought of as a soldier"[1]—Dixon Scott enlisted in the 3rd West Lancashire Brigade, Royal Field Artillery. He pondered his motives and moods as an Army recruit. "There do come moments when doubts descend on one dismally, when one's soldiering seems

[1] J. C. Squire, *The New Statesman,* November 13, 1915.

57

nothing but a contemptible vanity, indulged in largely to keep the respect of lookers-on." Agreeing that the love of adventure and the glamour of war as a supreme experience celebrated in the books and pictures of one's boyhood were stimulants of the martial impulse, he formulated his deepest feelings as an emotion for which the word "patriotism" was inadequate.

"One fights for the sake of happiness—for one's own happiness first of all, certain that did one not fight one would be miserable for ever—and then, in the second place, for the quiet solace and pride of those others, spiritual and mental sons of ours, if not actually physical —the men of our race who will depend for so much of their dignity upon the doings of the generation before." He believed that "to enter this material hell now" was to win a kind of heaven for those who came after. "There will be an ease and splendour in their attitude towards life which a peaceful hand now would destroy. It is for the sake of that spiritual ease and enrichment of life that we fling everything aside now to learn to deal death."[1] Death was dealt to him at Gallipoli in October, 1915. He was 34. C. E. Montague, of the *Manchester Guardian*, "grieving most really about Dixon Scott," wrote home from the front: "The extinction of all that boundless energy and eagerness of delight in our art and its subjects seems dreadful and foully wasteful."[2]

[1] Dixon Scott: *Men of Letters* (Hodder & Stoughton, 1916).
[2] Letter to Mrs. C. E. Montague, October 1915.

CHAPTER FIVE

Citizen Soldiers in Action

1

WHEN SIR JOHN SIMON, the professionally eminent and personally unpopular lawyer-politician, glibly hailed voluntary enlistment as "a real heritage of the English people," he was sharply answered by the Professor of History at King's College in the University of London. "It is not national service but the voluntary system that is un-English and un-historic. The Territorial Army dates from 1908, the Volunteers from 1859, the Regular Army itself only from 1645." A writer in the *Quarterly Review* considered that volunteering should have no part in the heritage of a proud imperial people: it was "a recent humiliation and disgrace." In other words, for every citizen it should be a privilege to defend his country.

Through long periods Englishmen were subject to shrieval summonses, commissions of array, mustering statues, militia ballots, and the press gangs. The volunteers of 1914 were in direct descent from "The 1859 Movement," described at the time as an uprising of "the most intelligent, active and enterprising of our people."

Tension with France had flared again after an attempt on the life of Napoleon III. The British Government was accused of harbouring the plotters. More disturbing than the angry suspicion was the discovery that the French were improving the fortifications at Cherbourg and building more war vessels. The bellicose enthusiasm of 100,000 Englishmen was roused. They formed volunteer units all over the country and designed their own uniforms, some with elaborately braided tunics and high-plumed shakos, evoking admiration at home and incredulity abroad. Tom Hood, in rhyme, and John Leech, in line, made fun of them. *Shoeblack to Volunteer: Now, Capting, clean yer boots and let yer 'ave a shot at me for a penny!*

Considerations of the vote precluded the Government from imposing the restraint urged by those who were worried about foreign repercussions. The crowning hour for the Volunteers came on March 7, 1860, when Queen Victoria, "wearing dahlia velvet, trimmed with point lace and bows to correspond," held a levee at St. James's Palace for 2,500 of their officers, giving to each her little marionette nod of approval as they were presented by the Lord Lieutenants.

From the lusty loins of "The 1859 Movement" sprang many of the battalions that figured in the Army reforms of 1881, when numbers for regiments were displaced by regional and county names, the basis of the Territorial Force brought into being by Haldane in 1908. It gave birth also to the National Rifle Association, which long shared with the Martello Towers of the south-east coast, and the widely distributed place-name of Telegraph Hill, the distinction of being the only permanent monument to a war scare in England. The exclusive skill nurtured by the National Rifle Association, which promoted the Queen's Prize at Bisley, had a profound effect on the national fortunes in 1914.

As for the Territorials, who received their first colours from King Edward VII at Windsor in 1909, they were by no means mere summer patriots. They had done what few Englishmen were willing to do in time of peace, forego their personal inclinations in order to serve the

60

nation. Their training, sketchy as it was, enabled them to detach themselves from the civilian context with efficiency and promptitude when the call came. That only 17,010 of them had signed the General Service Obligation, committing them to overseas duty if required, was as much an indication of the average Englishman's indifference to Continental affairs as of his pacific nature. The exceptions at that time were the Northumberland Yeomanry, the Dorset Fortress Company of the Royal Engineers, the 6th East Surreys and the 7th and 8th Middlesex.

When in the first week of the war L. S. Amery, M.P., praised the Territorials in a talk with Lord Kitchener, he was told: "I daresay we can make some use of them. What I must have now," Kitchener insisted, "is more soldiers," that was to say, presumably, more men of the stamp of those celebrated in the Kipling ballads whose bones whitened so many distant battlefields. The Territorials, it was true, were weak in musketry training, nor were they subject to the tight discipline of the Regulars. Their rifles were out of date; their artillery had seen service in the Boer War. Above all, though men like them had served in volunteer battalions that went to South Africa in 1901, they had no tradition of hard campaigning.

Lord Kitchener, it appeared, was labouring under a curious professional delusion. He could not divest his memory of the bad impression left on it by French Territorial troops in the war of 1870, when he was an observer with the French Army. He equated the indifferent conduct in battle of those French reservists with the inexperience of the British Territorial Force forty years later.

The Permanent Head of the Financial Department of the War Office, Sir Charles Harris, left it on record that in August 1914 Kitchener repeated his unwillingness to "take account of anything but Regular soldiers." Sir Charles suggested to him that the Territorials were "good half-wrought material" that would be ready for action long before the new armies could be brought to that state. "What Harris says is quite right," Sir John French intervened to say. "There are some Territorial battalions that I would like to take out with me next week, and many more that I shall be praying you to send me within a month or so." Kitchener answered French by repeating that he could "deal only with Regular troops." The Chichele Professor of Military History at Oxford University, Spenser Wilkinson, wrote in the *Morning Post*, September 15, 1914: "If the Government counts the Territorials after instead of before the new Regulars, it will be making two terrible mistakes—that of not appreciating its best men, and that of not understanding the value of time in war."

Lord Haldane, that man of wise prevision, subsequently made it clear that Kitchener pushed aside the existing satisfactory machinery for raising men in 1914–15 through the county associations and diverted the energies of an already overworked War Office department to the additional task of raising the entirely new armies that would bear his name. "The result was the confusion which arises from the sudden departure from settled principles."[1]

Sir Philip Gibbs, who, as a war correspondent, was with the armies in France from 1915 onward, said that "the Staff College was jealous of its own. Sandhurst and Woolwich were still the only schools of soldiering recognised as giving the 'right' tone to officers and gentlemen fit for high appointments."[2] Drawing on his experience as a wartime Guards officer, Lord Chandos (Oliver Lyttelton) remembered that "the professionalism of the

[1] Richard Burdon Haldane: *Autobiography* (1929).
[2] Sir Philip Gibbs: *Realities of War* (1920).

62

Army would not countenance an appointment unless it was held by 'one of us'."[1] Robert Graves said that the Regular battalions of his regiment, the Royal Welch Fusiliers, "never accepted the Territorials, dismissing them contemptuously as 'dog shooters'."

At a divisional conference of commanding officers in France, summoned to discuss the selection and training of officers for battalion commands, the only Territorial officer present jokingly remarked that there could not be any such officers in his regiment, as they were all Territorials. "No jest ever fell flatter," wrote Lieutenant-Colonel the Hon. Sir Sidney Peel, D.S.O., M.P., "for no one in the room regarded the remark as other than a perfectly natural statement of fact."[2] One of the few exceptions was Brigadier-General Noel Lee, killed in Gallipoli as the commander of the Manchester Brigade (T.F.). He was an old Etonian. The later Army careers of Generals Freyberg and Slim were rare examples of ascent from the lowest levels, like that of Field-Marshal Sir William Robertson before them.

The Territorials were a constitutional irritant under the skin of the military caste, an uncongenial reminder of the civil power to which the Army was ultimately responsible. Parliament's final authority was daily and historically demonstrated in the absence of sentries from its precincts. Many of London's important buildings were guarded by soldiers but not the House of Commons, even in time of war. It was a token of Parliament's independence of the military power ever since Colonel Pride's trespass in December 1648.

[1] *The Memoirs of Lord Chandos* (Bodley Head, 1962).
[2] *Army Quarterly*, 1920.

A Territorial subaltern was posted for temporary duty to an Army ordnance depot near Cambridge. The commandant was an old Indian Army major recalled from retirement in 1914. His face still retained the freckled tan of his thirty-seven years' service under tropic suns. His light khaki drill tunic was ablaze with ribbons. The subaltern made notes of his first encounter with that formidable survivor of an older order of regimental existence:

I gave him a strictly correct salute and my name and stated, in the routine manner, that I was reporting for duty under him. He grunted his indifference and went on with the writing that my entry had interrupted, leaving me to gaze in astonishment at the greasy top-knot into which what remained of his black hair was tied on his otherwise bald scalp. It appeared to be a relic of some Asiatic hairdressing custom belonging to his years abroad. Then the table shook under a blow from his sun-blotched fist and I was required to explain why I was standing there like a nincompoop. In the emergency, I resorted to the simple statement with which I had ushered myself into his presence.

"Second-Lieutenant P——, sir, reporting—"

"Reporting for what, sir? What are you *doin'* here?"

"I've been attached to this unit, sir."

"This *what*?" he shouted. "Unit, did I hear you say?" He rose threateningly from his office chair. "Unit be damned, sir, and you with it! I'll have you know that no such word is used here or anywhere else where *I* am in authority. Do you hear me?" The contempt in his voice withered the apology I struggled to offer. I managed to say, weakly: "I'm sorry sir."

"You New Army people don't know these things."

"I'm not New Army, sir," I hastened to inform him,

"I'm Territorial," a distinction it seemed important to make at a time when to a Regular Officer the new armies were the lowest form of military life.

"Good God!" he retorted, as if the unspeakable had been spoken; and then: "It's all the same to me, damn you." He resumed his writing, leaving me still standing at attention.

It was a fine warm day. The windows of the hutment office were shut tight. Wads of newspaper lined the sashes as further insurance against draughts. A coke fire gave off a filthy by-product smell. The major's fibrous neck was swathed in two obviously home-knitted khaki mufflers of exceptional length, so that their ends, thrown over his shoulders, trailed the floor on either side of his chair. Several times he sneezed, complaining to himself, rather than to me, about this "trickstering English climate, damn it." After each explosion he carefully folded his white silk handkerchief into a neat square and placed it in precise alignment with his desk blotter.

"And now, sir," he said with the air of one finally discharging a disgusting duty, "you should learn that in the British Army we use the term regiment, battalion, company, platoon, as the case may be—but never, *never*, the effeminate expression 'unit.' Understand?"

Having paused to receive my submission, he went on: "Not a week ago I heard one of you new people use that soft namby-pamby cat's-spit of a word *Tommy*. 'Sir,' I said to him, 'if you are not an only son with fifteen sisters and no testicles, then your people must have sent you to a gals' school by mistake.' It's sickenin', positively sickenin', all this slipshod, unsoldierly talk."

Apart from being re-educated in a number of Army practices, I had to endure the cleansing of my vocabulary of all expressions of a petticoatish origin (his phrase). I never referred a second time in his hearing to a taxi. "I assume you mean cab, sir, damn you."

"The British Army has fought many a defensive battle with success: Crecy, Agincourt, Albuera, Waterloo, Inkerman; and Ypres proved that the men of 1914, recruited haphazard by voluntary enlistment, were fully the equals of their forefathers in valour and determination. They were more than equals, not only of the flower of the youth of Germany in the volunteer units of the new Reserve corps, but also of the picked representatives of the German nation selected by the process of universal service."—*Official History of the War*.

At Ypres, October 15 – November 21, 1914, the Regular Army gained the highest honours of its long fighting record. Never were human valour and endurance more terribly tested in war. It was a battle of infantry in which the Germans sought a decision by overwhelming weight of numbers. In the hope of achieving it quickly they threw their reserves into the front line alongside their crack troops. Among the reserves was a battalion of the 16th Bavarian Infantry, composed mainly of volunteers from the Munich area, one of them Private A. Hitler. The Kaiser, whose dominion and power, though not his majesty, that slipshod recruit would eclipse in days to come, watched the battle. The German commanders were committed to a final all-out effort to take Ypres and seize the Channel ports. "Calais by the first of November!" was the Supreme War Lord's command.

For the British Army as the years of Empire had known it, the first battle of Ypres was the beginning of the end. Those three weeks of holding on against twice its strength in bayonets, of being ceaselessly battered by superior artillery power, depleted it of nearly everything but nerve. The losses were the worst of the war so far, 2,298 officers, 51,817 other ranks, a fearful foreshadowing of what was to come. Of the 12,000 officers and men of the 7th Division, 2,500 came out unscathed. One battalion of 1,100 men was cut down to 73, another of 1,350 to a few over 300. It was the virtual liquidation of the original British Expeditionary Force.

Ypres was the bloody font in which the first British citizen infantry to meet the enemy received their baptism. They were the London Scottish, formed by men of Scottish descent who joined the 1859 Movement as the London Scottish Rifle Volunteers. Their keen and efficient display won them official recognition the following year, and they were re-named the 15th Middlesex (London Scottish). Only one of their companies then wore the kilt. Later, the whole battalion adopted it. The battalion was finally dressed in a light heather-toned uniform known as "hodden grey," with royal blue facings on the tunics. In 1908, it was incorporated in the Territorial scheme as the 14th County of London Regiment (London Scottish). The battalion retained the grey uniform when the rest of the army adopted khaki.

"We had a bunch of fine fellows in the battalion, practically all college men, all Scots or of Scottish descent, and all over average height. With the exception of the Liverpool Scottish, formed about 1908, we were the only kilted regiment in the English Territorials."[1] When a brigade staff captain addressed the battalion in September 1914 with the announcement: "You are to have the greatest honour ever conferred on a Territorial battalion. You are to proceed to the front immediately," the London Scottish felt that the eyes of the whole British Army were on them, that they were custodians of the virtue of the Territorial Force.

The 1st Battn., London Scottish, 972 strong, left Southampton for France on the night of September 15,

[1] T. Baxter Milne, formerly of B. Company, London Scottish, in *The London Scottish Regimental Gazette*, October 1963.

67

1914, in the s.s. *Winifredian*. Survivors of the battalion today, numbering just over 100, call themselves "The Winifredians." The battalion was given a variety of duties during its first weeks in the battle zone, from guarding lines of communication to preventing an assault by furious Frenchwomen on German prisoners. F Company was chiefly occupied in providing firing parties with a piper for military funerals. "We bury twelve a day," a member of the company noted in his diary.

Calling in their scattered detachments, the London Scottish concentrated at Bethune. Each man carrying a full kit in his pack, plus his greatcoat, waterproof sheet, two blankets, emergency rations and two hundred and fifty rounds of small ammunition instead of the usual fifty, the battalion marched to St. Omer, where forty London General Omnibus Company buses, their destination boards and theatre bills still showing, were waiting to take them up to Ypres. Each bus had its own London driver. Some of the London Scots had ridden to their City offices in those buses less than three months before. Those who now rode up to Ypres on top of the buses were drenched by rain. "It was a strange procession, but a fine sight to see those buses, especially just outside Cassel where the road passed over a big hill, winding its way in 'S' curves. Looking back, we could see the whole column." One bus was ditched four times. "We all had to get out and push." (T. Baxter Milne). On the morning of October 30, the London Scots breakfasted in the famous Cloth Hall at Ypres.

4

October 31, 1914, was one of the highly consequential days of the war for England. In the glinting autumn sunlight the line of battle could be followed with the eye along the high ground of the Ypres salient to the north, over the Messines ridge to the east, and away to the south-east almost as far as Armentières, where shells bursting against a pale blue sky marked the right of the British line. It was held by seven divisions of infantry and three divisions of cavalry over a front of about thirty miles.

Soon after sunrise, a British airman landed his damaged machine and stepped from the flimsy cockpit looking white and shaken. "A near thing, was it?" he was asked. "No, it's not that," he answered, "—it's what's going on back there," indicating the enemy lines. "Three corps, I tell you, against our one!" He reported in detail what he had observed from above: roads and ridges swarming with troops in field grey, long columns of them, moving up into battle positions. "And we look so thin on the ground!" Between Gheluvelt and Messines, the enemy's superiority in all arms was later put at six to one. A German Army order issued on October 29 had proclaimed: "The breakthrough will be of decisive importance. We must and will therefore conquer." The intention was clear: to end the war by striking "the decisive blow against our most detested enemy."

The London Scottish were taken by bus from Ypres to St. Eloi as a reserve to Gough's cavalry in action on the Wytschaete-Messines ridge. After snatching some sleep, they were paraded at midnight to march into the line. A column of mounted troops clattered through St. Eloi in the darkness. When they were recognised as the Scots Greys, there were fraternal cheers for them from the London Scottish lined up on either side of the street. At daybreak, they took up a position in a small wood south-east of St. Eloi, where the men changed their under-clothes and socks, threw away their old things and dis-carded as much else of their kit as was feasible. "I suppose I reduced my pack and haversack by about

69

20 pounds in all." (Milne). They moved into the firing line at 10 a.m. in columns of half-companies extended at five paces. Each man was carrying a pack, a haversack, a water-bottle, greatcoat, an entrenching tool, a rifle, a bayonet, two hundred and fifty rounds of ammunition, and a pickaxe or a shovel. Thus encumbered, they advanced on Wytschaete, where shells were sending bricks and slates and tiles flying, and their own more lethal splinters.

They met shellfire of much heavier calibre as they fanned out towards the crest of the ridge, where the Dragoon Guards and the Gordon Highlanders were standing their ground against repeated enemy attacks. "How strong is the German army?" Private "Ginger" Bain, of the Gordons, asked Sergeant J. F. Bell of that regiment as they awaited a new onslaught. "About seven million," said the sergeant. "Well," said Private Bain from his rifle pit, "here come the bloody lot!"

The men in "hodden grey" had their first direct contact with the Germans that night. They had been told that they were to be used as support troops. Unexpectedly, they were thrust into the front line to fill a dangerous gap. Their steady rifle fire held off an attack that came at 9 p.m. At midnight, after heavy shelling, the Germans attacked again in the light of a full moon. They seemed to be approaching in a formless mass. Behind them, at intervals along the width of their advance, military bands were playing *Deutschland, Deutschland Uber Alles*. "The bands came right into the front line with the fighting troops. The one in front of us could not have been more than two hundred yards away."[1] The sound of cheering was heard above that extraordinary midnight music. "There appeared to be an endless stream of men, like a continuous procession, and it seemed to us as if we had been firing for hours.

[1] T. McColl Smith.

70

Some of our rifles jammed, others became too hot to hold, but again the attack failed and the enemy did not go through."[1]

Not all the London Scottish had done firing practice with the new short Lee-Enfield rifle. Some were handicapped by weak magazine springs and ammunition clips that were the wrong size, which meant single loading and a necessarily slower rate of fire. Still the line held. Two hours later the battalion faced a greater test. The Germans came on afresh, driving home their attack with ruthless energy. The battle fragmented into combats between small parties and often individuals, shadowy figures of the night jabbing at each other with gleaming bayonets, while streams of bullets sang their song of menace in the moonlight. "Every man was fighting his own little struggle for life. We did not notice the noise, we were too busy. On the whole line, there was irregular fighting backwards and forwards. None of us knew what was going on anywhere except in our own immediate vicinity. Bayonets were freely used, and I think we were shouting and cheering just as loudly as the Germans."[2] The battalion medical officer, an ophthalmic surgeon, Captain Angus McNab, was bayoneted while attending to a wounded man. A little more than three months previously he had been treating patients in Harley Street. "I stepped on the face of one German in order to stick my bayonet into another. I could not get the bayonet out quickly enough, and so fired a round of ammunition in order that the recoil would pull the bayonet out. Life seemed too full of Germans. I know that I nearly fell over when the bayonet came out."[3] The London Scottish lost 34 per cent of their effective strength in the action. "Rarely, if ever, have second line

[1] T. Baxter Milne.
[2] Ibid.
[3] Ibid.

71

troops sustained unshaken so high a percentage of casualties," General Allenby wrote, reporting to the Commander-in-Chief. He referred to the "magnificent behaviour" of the battalion. "In discipline and efficiency they have been up to the standard of the best Regular troops."

Two weeks later, when First Ypres was nearing its climax, the colonel commanding the battalion wrote to tell Haig that "the men are thoroughly broken," after five successive nights of sleepless vigilance in the firing line. "It is not that they are not brave, because I think they have proved their steadiness under fire, but being highly educated they are more highly strung." Sir John French told them that they had given "a glorious lead and example to all Territorial Corps fighting in France." They were relieved by Hertfordshire Territorials, who also were cited by the Commander-in-Chief in one of his early dispatches.

He inspected the London Scottish when they came out of the line. "How they had suffered was only too pathetically apparent," he subsequently wrote.[1] "When these Territorials returned for a term of well-earned rest, with the excitement and danger behind them, a severe reaction came upon them. The heavy losses amongst their friends and comrades bowed them down with grief; for they necessarily lacked as yet the professional training and stoicism of men whose real business is war."

Their reserve battalion, composed of 460 clerks, 364 men with professional qualifications, 226 business men, 100 students, 10 apprentices and 1 member of Parliament, sent a detachment to the Lord Mayor's Show that November. They received the loudest cheers of the day as the deputies of the first Territorial infantry battalion to meet the enemy.

[1] Field-Marshal Sir John French; *1914*.

72

The dismounted Oxfordshire Yeomanry (Queen's Own Oxfordshire Hussars), who had moved up into the Messines fighting with the London Scottish, took over a sector between the 9th Lancers and the 4th Hussars, both Regular regiments. For four days they endured a savage enemy bombardment in which sleep was impossible for any man. Major-General De Lisle, commanding the 1st Cavalry Division, went to see them as they were being relieved. When he told them that he rated their conduct equal to that of any of his fully trained troops, the yeomen of Oxfordshire stiffened with pride and bore away their dead.

5

"An endless reproach to mankind," a young German cavalry officer in the XXVI Reserve Corps, Rudolf Binding, wrote in his diary on October 17, 1914. "When one sees the wasting, burning villages and towns . . . dead or half-starved animals, cattle bellowing in the sugar-beet fields, and the corpses, corpses, corpses, streams of wounded—then everything becomes senseless, a lunacy, a horrible bad joke of peoples and their history." His notes continued:

"I have just read that the splendid von S. has been killed. You know my friendship for him, his house, his pleasant wife, who was so fond of her horses. He was a friend to many, and helpful to so many too. It is very hard to keep one's end up against all this." The German Army, he wrote, had Ypres as its objective. "These young fellows we have, only just trained, are too helpless, particularly when the officers have been killed. Our light infantry battalion, almost all Marburgh students, the best troops we have as regards musketry, have suffered terribly. In the next division, just such young souls,

73

the intellectual flower of Germany, went singing into
an attack on Langemarck, just as vain and just as
costly."[1]

6

On November 5, 1914, a small group of newly joined
men of a Territorial battalion stationed at the Tower of
London mutely watched a spy go to his execution in
that place of appalling precedents. The doomed man was
a long-nosed senior lieutenant of the German naval reserve, Carl Hans Lody, whose trial at the Middlesex
Guildhall had ended in the death sentence two days
before. Troops of the Brigade of Guards were escorting
him to the miniature rifle range, where he was about to
be shot. The chaplain of the Tower, intoning from the
Prayer Book, was last in the small procession, which
moved rigidly as if it had been set going by clockwork
behind the scenes. The pulse of London could be heard
beating beyond the timeless walls. Tower ravens sat
among the plane tree branches like a discharged jury.
A Thames tug hooted with innocent intent. During the
night, Lody had written to his people in Germany: "My
dear ones—I have trusted in God, and He has decided
that my hour has come, and I must start on the journey
through the dark valley like so many of my comrades
in this terrible war of nations . . . I have had just judges,
and I shall die as an officer, not as a spy. Farewell. God
bless you." He disdained the eye bandage. The officer in
charge of the firing party shook him by the hand. "You
are a brave man," he told Lody. Then the volley rang
out.

Though the grim processional scene was not *memento
mori* in the classical context, it was a no less ruthless

[1] *A Fatalist At War*, trs. Ian Morrow (Allen & Unwin, 1929).

74

shock to those young volunteers from the Weald, the Arcadian part of Sussex. One of them noted the stricken looks of his fellows without being in a position to record his own. That night he could not sleep. He saw himself as the victim of a greater betrayal than was possible to any spy. He was not alone. It was the end of happy endings in life as in art. The halcyon days were over for all of his generation.

"Nasty rumour of the trenches," an N.C.O. of the Honourable Artillery Company wrote in his diary at the end of November. "Not really funk, but an uncomfortable feeling of something unpleasant to come, something one has never experienced before."

If it was not a *cri de coeur*, it echoed the impassioned surprise of a generation thrown off balance, as if they felt the earth spinning under their feet. Young men who had never thought of war except as a fantasy of boyhood, who had certainly never imagined it as a threat to personal life and happiness, now peremptorily faced the battle and murder and sudden death from which they had prayed for deliverance in the Litany every Sunday.

One of the volunteer battalions of an English county regiment was being moved up into the battle zone by train from Le Havre, a journey of nineteen hours in cattle trucks. At St. Omer, the train rumbled to a brief halt. There was a rattle of sliding doors as men sought relief from the fetid air and gloom of the trucks. A solitary Regular Army artilleryman lounged on the opposite platform, hands deep in his breeches pockets, a cigarette sticking out of a sardonic smile. Scanning the tiers of faces at every door along the train, he removed the cigarette to inquire: "Are you down-'earted?" The otherwise deserted station rang with the echoing assurance: "No-o-o-o!" The artilleryman turned away, calling over his shoulder: "Then you bloody soon will be!"

75

Little did I dream, England, that you bore me,
  Under the Cotswold Hills beside the water
    meadows,
To do you dreadful service, here, beyond your
    borders
  And your enfolding seas.[1]

---

[1] From *Strange Service* by Private Ivor Gurney, The Gloucestershire Regiment.

CHAPTER SIX

Bad News from Debrett

1

MANY SONS and heirs had fallen, bearers of names
woven into the fading tapestry of the English past:
Cavendish, Wyndham, Grenfell, Manners, Stonor,
Cholmondeley, Archer Clive, Cecil, Cottrell-Dormer,
Lumley, Mercer-Nairne, Coke, Pleydell-Bouverie, Duff,
Annesley, Morgan-Grenville, Legge-Bourke, Baillie,
Carington, Bingham, Hughes-Onslow, Wellesley, Kinnaird, Barrington-Kennett, Legard, Antrobus, de Crespigny, Weld-Forester, Stucley, Kerr, Hamilton, Fraser,
Balfour, Payne-Gallwey, Ogilvy, Bruce, Lambton. In a
few months, 6 peers, 16 baronets, 6 knights, 164 companions of orders of chivalry, 95 sons of peers, 82 sons
of baronets, 84 sons of knights, were listed among the
dead.

The Northeys of Box, Wiltshire; the Cathcarts of
Mowbray House, Ripon; the Walkers of Beverley Hall,
East Riding; the Loder-Symonds of Hinton Manor,
Berkshire; the Berties of the Vale of the White Horse;
the Chaworth-Musters of Sherwood Forest; the Van
Necks of Lily Hill, Bracknell; the Foljambes of Osber-
ton; the Leys of Epperstone; the Hawleys of Leybourne;
the Dudley-Smiths of Strensham Court, Worcester-
shire; the Jenkinsons of Eastwood Park, Wiltshire; the
Moncktons of Stretton Hall, Staffordshire; the
Marsham-Townshends of Frognal, Kent; the Owens of

Little Grimsby Hall, Lincolnshire: all had lost sons.

Lord Penrhyn lost his eldest son and two step-brothers, Sir George Dashwood, Bart, lost two sons; Sir Henry Clarke, Bart., two sons; Sir Archibald Lucas-Tooth, Bart., two brothers; the Snead-Coxes of Broxwood, Herefordshire, two sons; Sir James Hayes-Sadler, Governor of the Windward Islands, two sons. The Lyons family of North Berwick lost three sons, all under thirty years of age. Two sons of Robert Erskine Pollock, K.C. were killed; two brothers and a step-brother of Lord de Freyne.

Families were terminated in the male line after hundreds of years. Those who died in the first months were nearly all young officers of the Regular Army who had responded to an hereditary tradition of service or had answered some other call of the blood. Through the century their families had helped to subsidise the nation's defences by the money allowances paid to sons following an ill-rewarded and latterly unpopular career. Some had held their commissions only a few months and were as new to war as the volunteers crowding into the recruiting offices.

These young men represented the old chivalry of England in more than the heraldic sense. Moulded in the gentleman image that time has since misted over, subservient to the good form that mean spirits still joke about, they were confident in their role of standard-bearers of a code entitling them to be called, in Mark Antony's words, "all honourable men." Proud-lipped, elegantly mannered, incomparably brave, they provided leadership of the tenaciously self-sacrificing kind that was the highest virtue in war. It succeeded on the foundation of a close and considerate relationship with those whom they led; and never was it more valiantly displayed than in the fateful last four months of 1914.

The American ambassador in Paris, Myron Herrick,

saw three British soldiers in a remote French hamlet, wounded, bedraggled and hungry. He offered them a lift to Paris, promising to look after them until they could rejoin their regiment. They thanked him and declined. Their officer, killed in the heavy fighting of a day or two before, was buried close by. "We hate to leave him alone in a foreign land." They were waiting for their regimental transport to fetch them.

"He died a soldier's death, leading his platoon in the firing line against the Germans." Lieutenant Percy Lyulph Wyndham's batman, Durrell, was writing to a relative of that dead young officer of the 3rd Battn., Coldstream Guards. "He was like a father to his men, and I have seen him in the night, after a long and weary march during the retirement from Mons when he was tired out himself, rubbing ointment on his men's blistered feet." Percy Wyndham, "one of the most loved of all his generation,"[1] was one of three members of his family to fall early in the war.

In loving memory of my master, Lieutenant Maclean Proctor-Dilworth, killed somewhere in France at 1 p.m. November 20th, 1914.

No mother or father saw him die,
No sister or brother to say goodbye.
No friends or relations to grasp his hand,
But they hope to meet in the better land.

R.I.P.—His servant, Private E. V. Kennedy, 1st Battn., Sherwood Foresters.

—from the Personal Column of the *Morning Post.*

Though it might not be true of all those "golden lads" that, by Burke's definition of chivalry, they had the enthusiasm of the strong for the rights of the weak, their dreams were not necessarily polo-centred. Not all were caste-ridden or impatient of ideas. Exempt from affecta-

[1] *Pages from a Family Journal,* edited by Lord Desborough (1916).

tions, impressing by having no need to impress, the best among them carried themselves as if they existed to prove that the gentleman is a type and not a class.

Some, like Julian Grenfell,[1] 1st Royal Dragoons, rejoiced in the "noble sport" view of war held by the men who fought the ancestral battles of Crecy and Agincourt. Having written that he longed to be able to say that he liked war, "but it is beastly," he confessed in the same letter (published anonymously in *The Times* of November 4, 1914): "I *adore* war. I have never been so well or so happy . . . The fighting excitement vitalizes everything, every sight and word and action."

Love of country was still a valid and admissible emotion. It was just as much the animating spirit of those young professional soldiers as of the volunteering amateurs. Not all who were trained to the soldier's life accepted Julian Grenfell's proud assertion that "*he is dead who will not fight, and who dies fighting has increase.*" Another officer of the Regular Army wrote to his wife on November 3, 1914: "It is VILE that all my time should be devoted to killing Germans whom I don't in the least want to kill. We are really only fighting because we are all so ignorant and stupid."[2]

In the first four months British losses on land numbered not many short of 100,000 in killed, wounded and missing, approximately the strength of the British forces engaged at the battle of Mons. Naval casualties for the same period were about 4,000. The destruction of the battleships *Aboukir, Cressy* and *Hogue*, in which many cadets were serving, and a little later of the *Good Hope* and the *Monmouth*, added the names of many splendid

[1] Captain the Hon. Julian Henry Francis Grenfell, D.S.O., eldest son of Lord and Lady Desborough; Eton and Balliol; died of wounds, France, May 26, 1915.

[2] Brigadier-General Philip Howele, C.M.G., 4th Hussars; Lancing and Sandhurst; killed in action, France, October 7, 1916; aged 38.

young men to the toll of the brave. They were mourned by a people deeply attached to the Service that produced the legendary young heroes of the Marryat stories. Always a favourite British naval character, Peter Simple in 1914 was no longer the boy "high upon the giddy mast." He was more at home in a 15-inch gun turret.

2

"We had suffered fearful casualties and the proportion in officers was higher than in any other rank." Sir John French, who knew as well as anyone that an army is strong not through numbers but through leadership, said that he was positively at his wits' end (his own words) to know where he could find officer replacements. It was not yet obvious that an important immediate source was being dammed by the unwillingness of battalion commanders to part with the best qualified men in their ranks. Such men helped to raise the level of smartness and efficiency in a battalion. Take them away and the colonel had less cause for pride in his command.

The Artists' Rifles (28th London Regiment) was formed in 1860 by Chelsea painters, art students and engravers, with the future Lord Leighton and Sir John Millais in the original muster of 119. In 1914, the Artists enlisted musicians, actors, architects, and others on a principal of election rather than recruitment. On their way up to the front in November 1914, they were intercepted by an order from the Commander-in-Chief, halting them at Bailleul. After an informal inspection, he asked that fifty of their N.C.O.s and privates should be selected for immediate commissions. Those chosen were posted to Regular battalions as "probationary officers," serving forty-eight hour periods in the firing line. The Artists became the first officers' training school with the

Army in France. From their ranks went many of the officers who subsequently led the new armies into battle on the Somme and after. Nineteen hundred members of the battalion were given commissions in the first fifteen months. They served in every regular regiment of infantry and in four of the five regiments of Foot Guards.

Another fount of leadership was the Honourable Artillery Company, the oldest regiment in the British Army, consisting, in 1914, of two batteries of horse artillery and a half-battalion of infantry. In the first week of the war they went into training at Belhus Park, Aveley, Essex, where the regiment was stationed at the time of the Spanish Armada. It turned out so smartly during the Napoleonic invasion scare of 1803 that its Wednesday evening parades in Finsbury Fields attracted sightseers from Mayfair, who came "to promenade to the music of the band and the roar of cannon."

The H.A.C. still recruited its strength on a time-honoured formula of personal "vetting" by its Court of Assistants. Those who were accepted paid an entrance fee of two guineas and were entitled to call themselves Members of the Company. The regiment was composed of university and public school men with O.T.C. experience, ex-members of the Colonial Police forces, and others with previous military training and in particular with "a sound knowledge of drill." Included in the muster in August 1914 were 31 bank clerks, 6 medical students, 8 engineers, 3 farmers, 4 undergraduates, 3 authors, 1 journalist, 3 solicitors, 1 company secretary, 1 fine art dealer, 1 detective sergeant, 1 stained glass artist, 3 architects, 2 brewers, 1 antique dealer, 2 civil servants and 4 men of independent means.

Mobilised for war service and lacking transport, the H.A.C. commandeered two Pickford furniture vans, a delivery van bearing the name of Gorringe's department store, a milk van, and a London borough watercart.

With that motley train they marched to their coast defence duties in Norfolk. When the time came for them to go to France, in November 1914, they found that a laughable rumour had preceded them: it inspired a drawing in *Punch*. "We know *your* lot," men of the 4th Middlesex called to them as the H.A.C. took over relief duty in the trenches at Ypres. "You're volunteers and you've paid six dollars each to get out here. You must be bloody well mad!"

The Honourable Artillery Company, the Artists, and other volunteer battalions like them, stamped their quality on the wartime environment in a way that no others did quite so thoroughly. The crested signboards at their training camps were works of art. The fences and gates were those of a well-tended demesne. The paths were cindered and rolled with extravagant care, the grass verges cut as close as manorial lawns. The assembled talents in those battalions, achieving standards of camp maintenance and embellishment far above those of the Regular Army which despised them, gave an almost poignant effect of permanence to an inevitably transient scene.

The Officers' Training Corps, formed under Haldane's direction in 1907 out of the old universities' volunteer corps and the public schools' cadet corps, supplied at once a large number of young men trained to a point at which they were capable of taking over the duties of platoon commanders. Many were already training with the Public Schools Corps. Oxford University O.T.C. sent 2,500, Cambridge 2,300. The northern universities supplied 3,000. Within fifteen months more than 20,000 O.T.C. members were commissioned. The Inns of Court O.T.C., which trained young barristers and law students, and other men with acceptable qualifications, contributed 1,800 new officers in 1914–15. Many more came from the Dominions and Colonies, men with special capacities for leadership not to be acquired at the military academies.

Typical of the overseas volunteers was Alexander Lorimer Miller, son of a Berwick-on-Tweed auctioneer and estate agent, who shortly before the war had sailed out of Glasgow in a French barque bound for New Caledonia. In search of adventure, he joined a German-led party supposedly prospecting for oil; in fact, they were under secret orders to find a submarine base in the islands. A snake bite laid him low. He woke one morning on an island in the Loyalty group, stranded. The rest of the party had sailed. His only belongings were his dungarees, four English pennies, and the revolver that he had hidden under his pillow. Islanders brandishing spears made him understand that the Germans had left to "fight in a big battle."

Miller appealed for help to the king of the island, who, in return for his having taught the local children to sing *All Things Bright and Beautiful* from the English hymnal, arranged for him to be sailed by cutter to Noumea. There he met another Englishman, a baronet's son, who had deserted ship to enlist. He told Miller: "We are at war with Germany and I haven't a penny to get home with." Miller recovered a suitcase that he had left with a dentist in Noumea. It was sold to provide the cost of two steerage passages to Sydney. The two men slept a night in a park and enlisted the following day. Miller's training was recurrently interrupted by illness attributed to after-effects of his snake bite. He finally recovered, was commissioned in the 10th Battn., Australian Imperial Force and, after a period as Town Major in Cairo, went to the Western Front, where he was killed; aged 25.

The numerous battalions of Kitchener's Army formed under the "Pals" scheme were largely officered by young men from the ranks recommended for commissions by the local recruiting authorities and chairmen of Territorial Associations. By no means all the candidates had the social or educational standing ordinarily demanded. Many were brighter-than-average types with what was then known as a good address, that is, an approved appearance and manner. Never before had leadership been sought at such levels of society or by such empirical methods.

Ardent intellects saw in those young officers promoted from the lower middle-class the vanguard of a great democratic advance in England after the war. The outcome was almost comically different from that expectation. The "temporary gentlemen," mixing with their social superiors in the mess, developed a class consciousness that confirmed rather than diminished the old social patterns.

Sir John French's worry about officer losses was shared by the military tailors, who scanned the casualty lists with daily concern for unpaid bills. Many young officers were killed before the official kit allowance had been credited to their accounts at Cox's or other Army banking agents. Rates of officers' pay continued to be fixed on the assumption of private income. A second-lieutenent received $1.05 a day, a lieutenant $1.19, a captain $1.75.

3

An American Civil War treatise, *The Soldier in Battle,* anticipating Chapter V of the second edition of Darwin's *Descent of Man* (1874), argued that the voluntary system of recruitment "ground up the choicest seed corn of the nation, the young, the patriotic, the intelligent, the generous, the brave, wasting the best moral, social and political elements of the republic, and leaving the cowards, shirkers, egoists and money-makers to stay at home and propagate their kind." Of the world conflicts that came after, another observer wrote: "Science may tell us that in the struggle for life it is the fittest who survive, but we who have lived through two great wars have seen with our eyes that it is the bravest, the noblest and the best who perish."[1]

The last United Kingdom census showed that out of the population of 45,297,114, 22,017,000 were males, of whom 5,408,000 were between the ages of 20 and 35. With the age limit put at 17–45, it meant a reserve of over 4,000,000 men.

In 1914, between August and December, 1,186,337 men enlisted in the new Regular Army ("Kitchener's") and the Territorial Force. Supporters of the voluntary system considered it amply justified by that result. Perhaps we too should see it as a vindication of their faith in the system, remembering that indifference is an English characteristic and apathy too often the state of a people long habituated to peace and easy-going. What could be said with more certitude was that most of the recruits of 1914–15 were of the nation's best quality, morally, intellectually, and physically. Many of them, in larger proportion than those who joined after 1915, were men who, like Cromwell's Ironsides, knew what they were fighting for and loved what they knew.

There was hardly a family that did not have a direct link with one or more of the 69 regiments of the Army, including the 10 Scotch, 8 Irish and 3 Welsh regiments. It was essentially an army of Englishmen, serving in 48 regiments, with their numerous satellite battalions, from the counties and shires. Later in the war, they were prominent as replacements in some Scotch and Irish regiments. Lieutenant O'Leary, V.C. said at a recruiting rally in 1915 that in his battalion of the Connaught

[1] Duff Cooper: *Old Men Forget* (Hart-Davis, 1954).

Rangers Englishmen made up nearly three quarters of the strength.

In some villages only the grandfathers were left. At Wroxall, Isle of Wight, 70 men had gone from its population of 460. At Cosgrove, Buckinghamshire, all its 35 eligible men were in uniform. From 61 houses in Chapel Street, Altrincham, Cheshire, 82 men had enlisted. Hever, Kent, sent 74 men from its population of 366; Buckland, Berkshire, 79 out of 302.

Forty per cent of the men of the North Riding had gone from the dales and fells, many of them to join the Princess of Wales' Own Yorkshire Regiment, the "Green Howards," whose second battalion, 1,000 strong, arrived in Belgium on October 6 and came out of action after the first battle of Ypres with 250. Lieutenant William Orde-Powlett, of Wensley Hall, was killed early in the fighting. Captain Hugh Clervaux Chaytor did not survive to return to Spennithorne Hall; and the death in action of the Hon. Hugh Dawnay, youngest son of Lord Downe, was a loss to more than the North Riding.

A senior of the war generation, in his late 'thirties, Hugh Dawnay was a soldier who thought beyond his profession, to which he was none the less sincerely devoted. One of his friends who was at the great anniversary service at St. Paul's Cathedral in August 1915 wrote of having had "a sudden vision in my imagination of Dawnay striding down the choir, in full armour, like St. Michael—with his head thrown back, and that extraordinary expression of *resolution* which he always seemed to me to possess more than anyone I have ever seen. His wide-apart eyes had more of the spirit of truth in them than almost any—also an intolerance of falsehood—or rather perhaps a disbelief in its existence." The author of *Ordeal by Battle*[1] said that "he was one of that race of men whose recumbent figures are seen

[1] F. S. Oliver.

87

in our old churches and cathedrals, with hands clasping crusaders' swords against their breasts, their hounds crouching at their feet."

He left the headquarters staff to command the 2nd Life Guards. On November 6, 1914, he headed an attack on some enemy-held farmhouses at Zillebeke. A corporal of the regiment told how "the men leapt after him—he was always in the forefront and was the first to reach the farmhouses. We took two of them but at the second Major Dawnay met his death. When we realised that he was killed some of us wept. If you knew how we loved that man, you would understand."

Men from the vales of the West Riding filled the ranks of the West Yorkshire Regiment with those from the lower ranges of the shire where the changing cloud-scapes rolled above the smoke of Sheffield, Leeds and Huddersfield. Before the war, Leeds had been indifferent and often hostile to its Territorials. There was even resentment of the Boy Scouts. "It was partly genuine pacifism," wrote Captain Frank L. Watson, who served in a local battalion—"that is, opposition to war in any circumstances, partly an ancient prejudice connecting soldiers with immorality and drink, and partly a strong objection felt by Trade Union leaders to their young members coming under the personal influence of the 'boss class' to which they conceived the officers to belong." Those attitudes vanished in the first week or so of the war. "We could have filled the battalion twice over with likely fellows. Our headquarters were besieged by them."[1]

From the East Riding towns and villages north of Beverley men marched into battle with the Hallamshire Rifles, the Hull Rifles, and the Yorkshire Light Infantry. Their officers had been architects, solicitors and business men. The same pattern of local affinities was repeated

[1] *Everyman at War*

88

throughout the volunteer battalions of the regiments that drew their strength from the provinces. When, as happened in 1915, the War Office ordered that Territorial battalions under 400 strong should amalgamate, there arose what Sir John French reported as "a serious state of affairs." In two battalions there was "something like a mutiny. Very strong representations against it have been received from C.O.s of standing and capacity. It is entirely due to lack of drafts for Territorial troops. The order is rescinded and Kitchener has been informed of a somewhat dangerous situation."[1]

4

Rupert Brooke to John Drinkwater:

> Royal Naval Division,
> Blandford.
> *January* 16–25, 1915.

My dear John—It was ignoble of me not to answer. But one becomes ignoble at this game. Or, at least, brutish. This mind becomes, not unpleasantly, submerged. The days go by. I plough through the mud: march: drill: eat and sleep: and do not question more. There was some affair at Antwerp, I remember . . . It was rather exhilarating, and rather terrible . . .

Still, it is the only life for me, just now. The training is a bloody bore. But on service one has a great feeling of fellowship, and a fine thrill, like nothing else in the world. And I'd not be able to exist, for torment, if I weren't doing it. Not a bad place and time to die, Belgium 1915? . . .

The world'll be tame enough *after* the war: for those that see it. I had hopes that England would get on her

[1] Sir John French, diary, June 22, 1915.

legs again, achieve youth and merriment, and slough the things I loathe—capitalism and feminism and hermaphroditism and the rest. But on mature consideration, pursued over muddy miles of Dorset, I think there'll not be much change. What there is, for the better, though. Certain sleepers have awoken in the heart.

Come and die. It'll be great fun. And there's great health in the preparation. The theatre's no place now. If you stay there you'll not be able to start afresh with us all when we come back . . .

But first, or anyhow, borrow a car, pick up Wilfred [Gibson] and Lascelles [Abercrombie] one Saturday, and come to Dorset; and on Saturday afternoon, or Sunday, or both, walk over the Roman downs with me, and drink greatly, and talk once more, and bury *New Numbers* with a *Resurgam*. I *may* have only four more weeks in England.

Love to you both,

RUPERT

5

In the first weeks of 1915, the casualty lists began to index the change in the status of the Army from an exclusively recruited profession to a great national force. The names of wartime volunteers, men who heard a call that could not be denied, appeared with those of officers and other ranks of the diminished Regular Army. From that time forward the nation, and not simply a class, would become acquainted with grief. "The dyers," Wells's Mr. Britling noted, "had a great time turning coloured garments into black."

Leslie Coulson, of Reuters news staff in London, suffered much ill health before the war. Disregarding the chance of its recurrence, he enlisted in the Royal Fusiliers in 1914. His parents wanted him to join an officers' training battalion. "No," he said, "I'll take my place in the ranks." St. John Adcock, editor of *The Bookman*, who knew him from boyhood, wrote that "to him it was the plain path of duty. He was high-minded, conscientious, self-critical." He left England with his battalion at the end of the year.

"He was not naturally a combatant. He was gentle, affectionate and, like all sympathetic natures, he shrank from inflicting pain." He was one of the countless men in uniform who detested war as thoroughly as any of the intellectual objectors who declaimed before the tribunals against the wickedness of war and the system of false beliefs that led to it. The sincerity of some could not be doubted. Yet was it ever finally so impressive as the compassion and the sacrifice of such as Sergeant Leslie Coulson, who deliberately chose to share the sufferings of his fellow men? Recovering from fever in Gallipoli, he presently went with the Royal Fusiliers to the Western Front. He never returned.

> *God knows—my dear—I did not want*
> *To rise and leave you so,*
> *But the dead men's hands were beckoning*
> *And I knew that I must go.*
>
> *The dead men's eyes were watching, lass,*
> *Their lips were asking too;*
> *We faced it out and paid the price—*
> *Are we betrayed by you?*[1]

Luke Coleridge, of Ottery St. Mary, left Oxford in the autumn of 1914 to join the Coldstream Guards. They said of him at Balliol that "he was lively and good-tempered and had friends everywhere, and nobody

[1] *To Sylvia:* Ewart Alan Mackintosh, Seaforth Highlanders; killed in action, November 21, 1917.

minded his occasional troubles with the College and even more august authorities."[1] He aspired to a Foreign Office career and was studying modern languages. After only two weeks in the front line, at La Bassée, he was killed early in 1915. A young artist, F. F. Crisp, of Warboys, Huntingdonshire, who won the Gold Medal of the Royal Academy and was one of the most original pupils of its School, was killed on January 5, 1915. That same day, Anson Lloyd Silvester, an Oxford honours man and an athlete "of splendid physique" was killed, aged 26. Every day the news had its threnodic undertones, which in many more homes swelled into chords of mourning, as if, as the Athenian said, spring had gone from the year.

J. R. B. Weeding, son of the Clerk to the Surrey County Council and himself a member of its staff at Kingston-on-Thames, was killed near Ypres on January 11, aged 32. R. W. R. Gramshaw, son of the rector of Fittleworth, Sussex, died of wounds on January 21, aged 34. Gareth Hamilton-Fletcher, of Sherbourne, was captain of his house at Eton and played twice at Lords. He wrote to his mother when he was 15: "Why are we deceived into thinking that Germany really means well to us? What fools we are! God grant that I may be old enough to fight for my country when the time comes." He was killed at La Bassée on January 25, 1915, aged 21. Harold Vernon Hutt, of Wallington, Surrey, had gained first place with distinctions in his final civil engineering examination and was intending to specialise in tube railway construction. He joined the Artists' Rifles in August 1914 and was killed in action on January 27, 1915.

Many who by superior education or professional attainments could have had commissions chose the anonymity and the drudgery of life in the ranks, where

[1] *Balliol War Memorial Book.*

their self-surrender and quiet resolution were part of the nation's hidden strength. Maurice Gurney Jameson, son of the vicar of St. Peter's, Eastbourne, studying agriculture in Oxfordshire, enlisted in the Honourable Artillery Company on August 5, 1914; killed 1915, aged 28. W. F. Dalrymple-Sewell, son of an Indian Army colonel and grandson of a general, joined the Seaforth Highlanders as a private soldier; killed 1915, aged 18. T. Andrew Pace, lance-corporal, London Rifle Brigade, was a barrister of 4, Essex Court, Middle Temple; killed 1915. Basil Heathcote Clark, assistant scoutmaster, 91st North London Troop, left his desk in the offices of the London Electricity Corporation, Cockspur Street, S.W., on August 5, 1914, to join the Queen's Westminsters; killed 1915, aged 19. John Leslie Elmslie, of Bidston Road, Birkenhead, was at Leys School, Cambridge, its best swimmer and captain of the first football eleven. He at once joined the H.A.C. In France, "he always undertook the daring jobs," and his company commander saw in him "a potential V.C." He was killed in 1915.

"It is to preserve the future, not the past, that most of those I know are fighting and have fought." A. W. R. Don, a medical student who joined The Black Watch, was writing to his parents in January, 1915. "It is at a time like this, when the whole future is so uncertain, a glorious comfort to know that the new outlook on life and humanity, which characterises the rising generation, will readily be voiced by those who remain all the more ardently and passionately because of those that this war has and will render silent. *Here indeed is death becoming creative* . . . In those who survive, the ardour will be quickened and deepened. They will be responsible no longer to themselves alone but to the memory of their friends as well."[1] Behind the rarely voiced idealism, the

[1] See page 255.

strong sense of moral obligation, was a faithfulness that in the many would be a more powerful determinant of victory than the genius of the few.

6

On Wednesday, March 10, 1915, Mr. Asquith, the Prime Minister, noted at the end of the day: "We held our War Council this morning, which was attended for the first time by Lansdowne and Bonar Law. They did not contribute very much. I thought that Grey did best, and after him A. J. B. [Balfour]." From *The Times* it was learnt that "Mrs. Lloyd George, who has had a severe cold, is now able to leave her room." The Countess of Clanwilliam left for Dromore, the Earl of Derby for Knowsley. "Mrs. McMicking arrived at 46, Draycott Place, S.W." Lord Kesteven, "who was reported last week to be progressing slowly, is not so well." Lord Clonbreck "celebrates his 81st birthday today."

That day, the General Officer commanding the London District, Major-General Sir Francis Lloyd, a corseted soldier who appeared to enjoy showing himself to the public in full dress on a prancing horse, issued an order forbidding officers in uniform "to visit any dancing or night club in the metropolis." Commending the order, a *Times* leading article hinted at a "sinister organization of gambling and blackmail" that governed the management of clubs exploiting the officer class of patron.

"Mother anxiously needs $14 to buy Army Revolver for son at the front; clergyman's reference. Box U558, *The Times*." Women named Irene, Constance, and Kathleen were asked to subscribe to a fund for the purchase of beds for an emergency hospital in France. A war hospital in London solicited the gift of a washing-

94

machine. An appeal was made for "old bagpipes for H.M.S. *Natal* on active service," another for the "City of London Truss Society for the Relief of the Ruptured Poor." An "experienced nurse for four children, $80–$85 a year, Protestant," was required at 8, Chaucer Road, Bedford. There were vacancies for a cook-general and a house-parlourmaid, $60–$65 a year, at 104, Drayton Gardens, South Kensington.

Newspapers reported the appearance at Bow Street police court of George Smith, of Richard Road, Shepherds Bush, remanded on a charge of causing a false entry to be made in a marriage register. It was the prelude to a case famous in forensic history, "The Brides in the Bath" murder trial. *The Times* printed lines by an anonymous poet who may not have been aware of what was pending in Flanders.

> *Risen in righteousness,*
> *Tried in hard training;*
> *Patient your souls possess,*
> *Winter is waning.*

> *Then for the day that's due,*
> *Fired as are few men,*
> *Forward the first of you,*
> *New troops and true men!*

While England was at breakfast that morning manmade violence reached a crescendo of power beyond anything of the kind known before to mortal senses.

CHAPTER SEVEN

The Battle of Neuve Chapelle

1

TIME'S WINGED chariot has borne away fifty years since the Battle of Neuve Chapelle, in West Flanders. The date, March 10, 1915, is not in the school books. It has no place in the calendar of history with Hastings, Waterloo or the Crimea. Impervious to the obliterative violence of the Somme and Passchendaele battles, the noise of Neuve Chapelle still echoes in many memories.

Strongly defended by the Germans in the fighting of October 1914, the village of Neuve Chapelle formed a salient from which they enfiladed the British positions all through the winter. Apart from nullifying that disagreeable liability, capture of the village and of Aubers Ridge two miles to the north-east would weaken the enemy hold on Lille, key-point of a busy and productive industrial region of France. The Germans had built a maze of earthworks in front of the village and were disposed to consider them impregnable. For that reason, and because they did not think that the British were capable of offensive action, they held the sector with only a thin line of troops.

Approving his staff's plans for the attack on March 10, Sir John French was probably guided by two ideas: (a) the need to prove to sceptics of the French Army that the British Expeditionary Force had decisive striking power and (b) to make a demonstration stressing the importance of the Western Front at a time when public attention seemed likely to be diverted to the Dardanelles.

The heaviest concentration of artillery ever known was to be the chief feature of the operation. Air reconnaissance and photography were to be combined for the first time. Another new concept was preliminary low-level bombing of selected sites, the railway junctions at Courtrai, Menin and Douai. Supply dumps of rations and engineering stores were to be laid right up to the fighting lines. They were maintained by wooden tramways. Models of the terrain were laid out in back areas, where details of the attack were explained to officers about to take part in it. A miniature bombardment tested the effect of shell fire on trench defences. Dummy breastworks were built in other sectors, and minor assaults launched, to mislead the enemy. Signals and communications were organised to a new pitch of efficiency. It was all supposed to embody the "scientific outlook" of the younger generals.

The order to the artillery was to smash the German front line. Then, with range increased, a curtain of fire four hundred yards deep was to check the advance of enemy reinforcements, while the infantry of Haig's 1st Army and Smith-Dorrien's 2nd Army went in with the bayonet to wipe out the salient. It was another example of the new military thinking, "the first time that an artillery barrier or 'barrage' had been put down to isolate enemy forces holding the objective of an infantry assault."—*Official History*. Above all, there was a moral objective: to disprove finally the legend of German invincibility.

The attack which we are about to undertake is of the first importance to the Allied cause. The Army and the Nation are watching the results, and Sir John

97

French is confident that every individual in the IVth Corps will do his duty and inflict a crushing defeat on the German VIIth Corps which is opposed to us.

(Signed) H. RAWLINSON,
Lieut.-General,
Commanding IVth Corps.

March 9, 1915

There was no calm as before Thermopylae. The rival camps, at points no more than two hundred yards apart, did not bawl at each other as before Agincourt. Orders were spoken and passed down the lines, not shouted. Transport wheels creaked discreetly in the slushy lanes of Estaires, Laventie, Richebourg St. Vaast. The beat of marching boots was muffled by banks and hedges for miles around; men from English shires, London streets, Scottish glens, swinging in columns of four through dark and dead villages: Middlesex, Sherwood Foresters, Berkshires, Worcestershires, West Yorkshires, Leicestershires, Lincolnshires, Staffordshires, Devonshires; and Seaforths, Gordons, Camerons. Accents were the identity badges of those marchers through the night, which shrouded the silver cross of the Rifle Brigade, the red hackle of The Black Watch, the star-and-bugle of the Scottish Rifles, the Sussex plume. Men of the Lahore and Meerut divisions marched with them: Scinde Rifles, Bhopals, Baluchis, Sikhs, Garwhalis, Gurkhas. There was a feeling of an Homeric host moving through the darkness towards a crux of history.

> *Each leader gave his men the word,*
> *Each warrior deep in silence heard;*
> *So mute they marched, thou couldst not ken*
> *They were a mass of marching men . . .*

How it all comes back, that prodigious mission of surprise, that apprehension of incidents mysteriously shaping into events! The chill of that dawn is still felt

in the heart if not in the bones. The high tower of
Bethune rises again like an apparition out of the mist
drifting over a countryside that was never fair to look
upon.

2

At 7.30 a.m., as precisely as if a switch had been
thrown in some cosmic power house, the sky was filled
with thunderbolts and sheeted flame. It was awe-
inspiring, like a tornado, a convulsion of nature. A landscape reeled under the impact of shells fired from three
hundred and fifty guns. The field artillery, firing as fast
as it could be reloaded, blazed and cracked from a wide
arc of sites at targets up to 2,000 yards. The heavies
belched and boomed from emplacements 5,000 yards
behind them. The thunderous unison rent the heavens.
In thirty-five minutes more shells were fired than in
eighteen months of the South African war, as many as
could be made in seventeen days at the current rate of
production in the munition factories at home.

Regular troops in the British front line, waiting with
their scaling ladders for the whistled signals that would
send them over the top, had been issued with cotton
wool ear plugs. Territorial infantrymen, lying in support
in the fields and orchards of Hazebrouck, Locon, Vielle
Chapelle and Lacoutre, found little protection in their
knitted Balaclavas. They pressed the palms of their
hands to throbbing eardrums. One of them remembers
his astonishment at seeing that the orange corona of
bursting shells was quite as lurid as in the *Illustrated
London News* pictures of the Boer War.

The bombardment of Neuve Chapelle was not only
part of a new military formula embodying theories never
before tested on such a scale. It was a new human ex-

99

perience. Survivors of the exhausted old Army were as amazed as the youngest Reservist. "It was an awful sensation," a private of the Cameronians wrote home. "Deafening—I don't know where the artillery got all those guns." For the Territorials, who had never known

Death whining down from heaven,
Death roaring from the ground,
Death stinking in the nostril,
Death shrill in every sound,

Neuve Chapelle was a traumatic event.

The three-days' battle fills eighty-two pages of the *Official History of the War: France and Belgium, 1915,* where it is put on record as "the first planned British offensive." It disappointed hopes that Aubers Ridge would be wrested from the German grip and the way laid open for the advance on Lille of Allenby's cavalry, whose thousands of horses were coralled in a valley within sound of the fearful cannonade. The bombardment that was to have demolished all before it, and make a resumption of open warfare possible, failed of its purpose. Barbed wire remained uncut, holding up assault troops, who suffered heavily in consequence. A great weight of shells had fallen on trench lines no longer occupied by the enemy owing to winter waterlogging.

Staff work was defective, aerial reconnaissance hampered by low hanging cloud, ammunition supplies inadequate. A communications failure, largely caused by our own gunnery, led to congestion in the support trenches. "The whole machine clogged and stopped," Brigadier-General John Charteris, of Haig's 1st Army staff, wrote in his diary.

A British infantry subaltern noted as they waited to move in: "The crowd of troops is altogether too great. There is little shelter from the ceaseless stream of bullets. Some of our men have to crouch where they are in the open. A strapping fellow topples forward groaning into the trench, his hands clasped to his forehead from which blood pours. Another rolls quietly over on his side—stone dead. The lad next to me, virile and strong a moment ago, now lies feebly moaning, shot through the body. Two or three others, variously wounded, sit half-conscious with their backs against the parapet." Some of the men were spattered with the blood of German bodies thrown up by the heavier shell explosions. The upper half of a German officer, his cap still on his head, fell in the middle of one of the waiting groups.

3

So, Aubers Ridge was not taken. The way was not opened for Allenby's cavalry to advance upon Lille. Only a few hundred yards of ground were gained along a two-mile front, though the awkward salient was rubbed out. The military thinkers considered Neuve Chapelle an indication of the lines on which the battles of the new warfare would be fought. "It demonstrated that a break-in was possible under certain conditions."—*Official History*. It was also held as proof that a surprise offensive could be achieved, a kind of success that was not re-peated, however, until the great tank assault of two and a half years later.

Presumably it satisfied the Commander-in-Chief's desire to impress his allies, the French. "Neuve Chapelle has made the French think highly of our Army," Charteris wrote. The leader of the French military mission attached to British General Headquarters, General Huguet, had no doubt that the battle "influenced sub-sequent operations to an important degree, in fact be-yond the lessons it actually taught." The verdict of another authority was that "it provided the army with a kind of preliminary grammar of offensive trench-war which, though enormously expanded, was never in its principles superseded."[1]

What the war historians have inadequately noted is that it brought more volunteer troops than ever before into the penumbra of battle, that it was in effect the proving ground of the Territorials. They were represented in Sir John French's battle order by ten battalions from English and Scottish regiments and some field companies of the Royal Engineers. Of those Territorial battalions, the 4th Seaforth Highlanders, the 3rd London and the 13th London ("The Kensingtons"), were sent in to take over positions vacated by Regular assault troops advancing after the bombardment. "The Kensingtons," in whose ranks were many men from the London department stores, Harrods, Barkers, Derry & Toms and Selfridges, were ordered to support the advance into the village of Neuve Chapelle. They were held up in the churchyard, its contents horridly exposed to the light of day. All round, the grass was stained yellow by lyddite fumes, which discoloured alike the faces of the living and the newly dead. "Utterly impossible," their commanding officer wrote in his report, scribbled as they waited. "Our casualties are terrible. Awful sights to be seen," among them German bodies sprawled in every posture save that of easeful death, some with unexploded grenades in their hands.

Late in the night of the first day of the battle, between desultory bursts of rifle fire, a German voice was heard calling out over the narrow No-man's-land: "Let's get this bloody war over and done with!" A shout went up from the indomitable Londoners in their forward trench: "All right, Jerry—we'll run you out of it soon enough!" They laughed again when a portly German

[1] C. R. M. F. Cruttwell: *A History of the War, 1914-18* (Clarendon Press, 1934).

appeared with his hands held so uncomfortably high in surrender that he could hardly speak. "Mercy!" he gasped, purple in the face. "I am married—I am married!" One of the Londoners retorted: "Your missus won't thank us for sending *you* 'ome, mate!"

Another Territorial battalion, the 3rd London (Royal Fusiliers) delivered what an eye witness described as "a splendid charge" at a German strongpoint between Neuve Chapelle and Biez Wood. They raced across the pitted earth, skipping over the dead as they went, their bayonets flashing wickedly in the sunlight. Regular troops, watching them go into action, cheered them as they passed. At the same time, Territorials of the Cameronians, the Scottish Rifles as they preferred to be called, launched an attack in the Rue Tilleloy and, finding the wire still intact, tore at it with bare hands, twisting and tugging at it and getting shot down as they did so, their uniforms cut to shreds. The men of one of their support companies broke down in pity at the sight of their dead comrades clustered about the wire that had been their doom. The battalion lost all but one of its officers and numbered no more than a hundred and fifty men after the fighting.

With the publication of Sir John French's dispatch on the battle, the Territorials came into their own as a fighting force. Neuve Chapelle was the last of the old Army's battles and the Territorials were proud to have shared its splendours and miseries with men who had fought from Mons to the Marne and the Aisne and at First Ypres and who were already legendary as the Old Contemptibles. The Army of which they were the last effectives had run its valiant course through history. Now it was little more than a muster of ghosts. In March 1915 only one hundred and fifty of its original officers were serving in the line. Others were helping to train the new Regular Army, but most were dead.

There was fitness in the decree of fate that the old Army should fade out at the onset of the great trench war. It had gained its renown and honours in the field. To its successors it bequeathed a splendid tradition, what was considered the best rifle in the fighting armies, its unrivalled 18-pounder gun, and its unconquerable spirit. Its partnership with the Territorials at Neuve Chapelle had satisfied the generals that, in spite of mistakes, the new "scientific approach" pointed the way to future successes on the grand scale. Before the battle no one could say with confidence that an entrenched position could be carried with less loss to the attackers than to the attacked. It was now believed that given an unlimited shells supply, artillery power could be counted on to do all that was necessary to ensure a break-through.

For the volunteers who in the months to come would stream into the trenches from every part of the British world it was a dire assumption.

4

In the Neuve Chapelle casualty list of 583 officers and 12,309 N.C.O.s and men were many more August volunteers than before. Among the killed were S. G. Paterson, son of the Professor of Divinity, Edinburgh University, aged 30; T. S. Lukis, Demonstrator in Physiology, St. Bartholomew's Hospital, London, a devoted part-time worker at Toynbee Hall, aged 29; George Llewellyn Davies, who with his brothers was adopted by Sir James Barrie on the death of their mother, formerly Sylvia Du Maurier, aged 21; William Sprott Montgomery, of Bromborough, a well-known footballer serving with the Seaforths, aged 34; William Louis Tate, Cheltenham and Corpus Christi, honours in Classical Moderations and Literae Humaniores, aged

24; Arthur Lonsdale, son of a rector of Fontmell Magna, Dorset, scholar of Eton and Radley, aged 24; Harold Gostwych May, a young master of his old school, Sherborne, of whom it was said: "His was eminently a case in which offering his services was a deliberate act of devotion to his country;" A. Hood Wilson, captain of Merchiston School, Edinburgh, Cambridge honours in science and a Rugby blue, aged 23; C. S. Hedderwick, Royal Scots, son of the editor of the *Glasgow Citizen*; Bernard Berrill, born in Australia, educated at Beaumont School, Windsor, and Balliol College, Oxford, where it was forecast that he would become one of its outstanding figures, aged 20; J. K. S. Moxley, Oxford classicist and college oarsman, aged 21; Angus V. Makant, who played cricket for Harrow against Eton and, after leaving Cambridge to join his father at Gilnow Bleachworks, Bolton, qualified as full-back of Bolton Wanderers' reserve team, aged 27. The silence that fell on Neuve Chapelle after the great bombardment fell also on homes all over England in that second week of March, 1915.

One of those whose lives were "sunlit afternoons, having no tomorrow," was Anthony Wilding, who is remembered as an heroic figure for more than his strenuous freelance war service. He had won the All-England Lawn Tennis Championship at Wimbledon in 1910. His tremendous victory in 1913 over the reigning American champion, M. E. M'Loughlin, raised him to the pinnacle of tennis eminence and fame—"the greatest player of lawn tennis we have ever seen or ever shall see."[1]

Tony Wilding was New Zealand born and Cambridge educated, his university years mainly passed in pursuit of perfection at the game in which he ultimately excelled. He had little of the ballet dancer grace of many of the best tennis players. He was sturdily built, not very supple but with lightning reflexes that made him

[1] E. B. Osborn: *The New Elizabethans* (1919).

105

supreme on the Centre Court. Like Scott of the Antarctic, he set himself a programme of rigorous discipline aimed not, as in Scott's case, at conquering original weakness but at achieving the highest possible pitch of physical well-being. His body was described by one of his contemporaries as "a mechanism of power and precision that was never allowed to become slack for a moment or lose its bright vigour through any form of self-indulgence. Within and without he was as clean and bright as a new pin. And he also had a certain bright mysterious quality which caused him to be liked at first sight by all sorts and conditions of men and women."

He projected his obsession with the efficient working of the human machine into motor engineering. He rode a motor-cycle from London to Constantinople at a time when the internal combustion engine was far from being the refined and reliable mechanism that it afterwards became. No man of his generation was more adventurously ready to face the impending technological challenges.

When the war started he was the Continental representative of a motor tire company. He joined the Royal Marines and, receiving a commission, was attached to the Naval Air Wing under the redoubtable Commander Charles Rumney Samson. He and Samson made a series of unreported sorties in armoured cars behind the German lines in Belgium. Samson had his own brand of toughness. He marvelled at Wilding's hardihood in sleeping outdoors on some of the coldest nights of that first war winter.

Working with armoured cars, Wilding developed aptitudes that might have cast him for a role in civilian life far removed from the tennis courts. His inventiveness of mind led to his being given command of a small independent battery of 3-pounder guns for which he had devised a special mobile mounting. At Neuve Chapelle, he was asked to undertake the liquidation of enemy sniping posts and while he was thus engaged he was struck down by shellfire. He was 31.

The sorrow of his friends and admirers was great. Tributes flowed in from all parts of the world. The sentiment of many of them endorsed the words of Lieutenant-Commander (later Sir) Warden Chilcott, M.P.: "I always felt that Tony Wilding was an example to his fellow men in everything."

5

Four years before the war, Edward Horner, son of Sir John and Lady Horner, of Mells, Somerset, entered the Temple Chambers of F. E. Smith, not yet ennobled as Lord Birkenhead. Edward Horner, the law pupil, was 26, six-feet-four in height, broad-shouldered and muscular, with a superbly shaped head and neck, a picture of radiant masculine beauty: the description is Birkenhead's.

To the exceptional physical attributes was added an intellect not readily harnessed to the steady concentration required of the serious student. But his master believed that he would have succeeded at the Bar. "Quick, polished, handsome and intelligent, he brought to its competition a rare and rich accumulation of gifts." At Eton, he is recalled by Lord Chandos with "Patrick Shaw-Stewart, Charles Lister, Ronnie Knox, Julian and Billy Grenfell, shining figures in a golden age of young men, and all killed except Ronnie Knox in the holocaust . . . I still remember the effortless scholarship and brilliance of this galaxy."[1]

Lady Cynthia Asquith wrote of Edward Horner's "singular radiance and almost Greek good looks." His

[1] *The Memoirs of Lord Chandos.*

107

mother had been Burne-Jones's ideal of beauty. Lady Diana Cooper says that those who knew him found him irresistible. She has also recalled that "he had a lot of real melancholy woven into his *joie de vivre*. He could not bear to be humdrum."[1] He wrote a letter timed to arrive on the morning of Lady Cynthia Asquith's wedding: "For the last time, I am asking you to marry me."

He held a junior commission in his county yeomanry. Impatient for action, he secured a transfer to a Regular regiment, the 18th Hussars, but had to wait longer than he had hoped before reaching the front. He was shot in the stomach at Neuve Chapelle, lost a kidney, and lay between life and death. His fine constitution saw him through a long ordeal. Offers of staff posts were made to him, one direct from the Commander-in-Chief. The Hussars had suffered heavily. He knew that he was needed. He returned to the fighting line. Helping to beat back a German bayonet charge at Noyelles, during the fighting at Cambrai later in the war, he was wounded again: "hit in the same place as before," his squadron commander told Lady Horner. A few hours earlier, Edward had written to her : "I suppose it was reaction after leave, but on arrival here I felt cross, and they would all draw attention to it, asking why and so forth, which always makes one worse. Today things have changed, and everyone seems attractive again . . . and I feel the connection between my love for my companions and my love for you. Bless you all." It was his last letter. He died of his second wound.

"It was overwhelmingly dreadful," Lady Diana Cooper wrote of his death. Lord Birkenhead was profoundly moved. "There passed a gay, sunny and adorable nature, the love of which made life sweeter and will keep it permanently sweeter for many. With him perished the last hope of direct male succession in an

[1] In *The Rainbow Comes and Goes* (Rupert Hart-Davis, 1959).

ancient and honourable English house." The Horners
had been at Mells for four hundred years.

> *Doomed to know not Winter, only Spring, a being*
>   *Trod the flowery April blithely for a while,*
> *Took his fill of music, joy of thought and seeing,*
>   *Came and stayed and went, nor ever ceased to*
>   *smile.*[1]

[1] R. L. Stevenson.

CHAPTER EIGHT

The Secretary of State Regrets ...

1

YOUNG MEN who, a short while before, had been part
of the morning swarm over London Bridge, or wearers
of other kinds of "livery of the laborious week," were
squatting in hastily thrown-up advance trenches that
gave little protection from bullets and none from shells.
Ten men of a Territorial battalion, none with more than
six months' soldiering experience, were holding such a
post on Palm Sunday, 1915, near Festubert. They were
three hundred and fifty yards in front of the British
line and forty yards from the enemy.

Civilians so recently, they felt starkly vulnerable as
they crouched in that dangerous forward place. To them,
as to the majority of their fellows in khaki, the Germans
were a race of fanatical warriors, out for glory and conquest. That behind the all too solid-looking ramparts
opposite there lurked men as inexperienced and as in-
cipiently frightened as themselves was a likelihood that
they would have rejected with expectorating scorn. They
would have jeered at assurances that the German Army
included many volunteer battalions like their own.

That ingrained prejudice of the chemist's assistant,
the two farmhands, the estate agent's junior clerk, the
musician, the beach photographer, the village school
teacher, the street trader, the groom and the insurance
agent, was confirmed when the enemy sent up a kite with

English wording inscribed on its face. Within minutes, the trick claimed two victims, shot through the head by marksmen with telescopic sights when the luckless ones peered above the low parapet to scan the message. Later that morning, when a grey sky had lightened with a promise of spring sunshine, a bullet penetrated the thin sandbag cover and struck the school teacher in the stomach. One of the survivors wrote in his diary the following day:

"There was no way of getting him back to the c.c.s. [casualty clearing station] in daylight. We had to let him lie on the earth and die, with a rolled greatcoat for his pillow. At first he rejoiced at having got a 'blighty' one. Gradually, as the light of morning grew fainter to his sight, he seemed to know that he would not see his home again. Before the end, his blasphemies rang out on the morning air. It is evidently very hard to die to the song of the lark."

Their training, after the febrile and sometimes funny improvisations of the first weeks, had been crude and corrupting; in learning to kill by bayonet, for example, the ghastly exercise in which they were expected to show a fiend's delight. Innocence had been torn from them like the habiliments of shame. Many of them had never heard of "VD". Every evening the gates and railings of the London barracks where they had first been stationed were besieged by girls of school age offering themselves to young men who blushed as they went out "on pass" through the screeching throng.

"Out there" those young apprentices to war saw the last victims of Field Punishment No. 1, the old Army version of the eighteenth-century village stocks. The offender was sentenced to "attachment to a fixed object," usually the wheel of a gun limber. With legs and arms outsplayed, he was exposed to the common gaze and every kind of weather for periods up to two hours daily, according to the nature of his "crime." The German Army had already abolished that barbaric form of punishment, though General Ludendorff thought it fatal to good discipline to do so. The British Army maintained it until 1923.

Untried spirits found it harder still to endure the early morning recital on parade of the names of men sentenced to death for desertion or cowardice in the face of the enemy. Standing to attention in a cold and steely silence as the adjutant performed that duty filled most hearts with hatred for a system so brutally disposed towards the victims of unprecedented stress. "Help me, God! Where are you? Give me a chance—I've never had a chance!" The screams of the young sapper who was being dragged to the place of execution haunt the pages of the autobiography of Sir H. Morris-Jones, who served as medical officer at the front with a battalion of Kitchener's Army.

2

The sound of the Flanders guns, "roaring their readiness for revenge," set pheasants clucking in the primrose woods of Kent and East Sussex that spring. The propinquity with awesome events was heightened by the afternoon "leave train," which arrived regularly at Victoria Station, London, bringing home men with the mud of the trenches hardly dry on their boots and puttees. They might have been battlefield commuters; a reminder that there was fighting and dying within less than a day's journey of the capital city of the Empire. Every day there were touching re-unions with mothers, wives, sweethearts, children, and family dogs. The eyes of many of the men were harassed by more than fatigue. They looked about them desperately, as if every minute was in pawn to fate.

Thrice weekly the one o'clock "war train" left the same terminus with men going back to the Front. The farewell of Hector and Andromache, "smiling through her tears," was daily re-enacted without his plume and not always with her infant. Perhaps it was the newspaper pictures of those routine arrivals and departures of men at war that prompted a young woman to write to her Guardsman brother in France: "You must be terribly tired when you get back to your barracks after the fighting."

The Sportsmen's Battalion of the Royal Fusiliers advertised for recruits, aged 19 to 35, "upper and middle-class only." There was an entrance fee of nine dollars. "Apply: E. Cunliffe Owen, Hotel Cecil, Strand, London." The 3rd Battn., (Old Boys') Central London Regiment (Volunteers), at Lord's Cricket Ground, N.W. (Tel.: Paddington 613), invited candidates for their officers' training course, fee $9.00. "Over 350 members have obtained commissions."

"The Adams Trenchoscope: The New Practical Trench Periscope, recommended by Captain V. C. Crespigny," was on sale at 24, Charing Cross Road, London, price $1.50, post free. At 26, Charing Cross Road, a fund was opened for the purchase of periscopes for non-commissioned officers at the front, sponsored by the glamorous Gaby Delys, then appearing at the Alhambra, close by. Anxious aunts were given an alternative opportunity of vicarious participation in front line activities by subscribing to a fund for the purchase of extra wire cutters. Its promoter, the Rev. T. H. Falkiner ("late Capt., Connaught Rangers"), 85, Gore Road, Victoria Park, S.E. considered the British Army regulation issue of 48 per thousand men insufficient, quoting in his advertisements sombre information about the results in

113

battle of uncut wire. Charity appeals rose like incense on the air. Good works multiplied as never before. $15,400,000 was collected for the National Relief Fund, $4,200,000 for the Red Cross, $2,800,000 for Belgian refugees. There was a Serbian Relief Fund, a Russian Relief Fund, a Polish Relief Fund, and a Turkish Relief Fund, on the ground that the Turks deserved sympathy for being misled into fighting alongside the Germans.

Wounded officers counted themselves favoured by fortune when they were admitted to the small exclusive hospital at 17, Grosvenor Crescent, S.W. conducted by Miss Agnes Keyser, celebrated in Army medical and nursing circles as "Sister Agnes." Her lack of professional qualifications was no bar to her success as an unofficial matron. As a friend of King Edward VIIth, she was a co-founder of the hospital for officers that still bears his name. The king dined with her at Grosvenor Gardens two nights before his death in 1910.

A woman of small stature, formidable energy, and commanding will, Sister Agnes wore her whiter-than-white matron's wimple with an air of invisible precedence. "Thank you, sire, for your most gracious thought," she was saying on the telephone as the present writer, then an infantry subaltern, was shown into her room. "That was the King," [George V], she said with satisfaction in her voice as she put down the receiver. "He is giving me a key to the garden at Buckingham Palace." An anaesthetist who worked at her hospital in the war has a kindred recollection. Speaking to him about King Edward's patronage of her work, she drew back the sleeve of her nurse's blouse to show him the Government cipher tattooed on her forearm. "Property of His Majesty!" she said with a twinkling eye.

An outcry against "war babies," implying sexual irresponsibility among home-based troops, was refuted by a formal committee of inquiry. It was followed by a powerfully sponsored crusade against drink. "Misdirected effort," objected G. K. Chesterton. "All that has been proved is that the working classes are drinking as usual; that is, far more than the middle classes and less than the upper classes." It was the middle classes that queued at the wine merchants and off-licences for the suddenly limited whisky supplies, at 49¢ per bottle, in 1915. A wit of *London Opinion* nicknamed them The Decanterbury Pilgrims.

3

It was said of the brothers Fletcher, Walter and Reginald, sons of Charles Fletcher, history tutor at Magdalen College, Oxford, that "each thought the other the greatest man he knew." Walter, the elder (more usually called by his second name, George), was thickset and bucolic in appearance, with stiff upstanding fair hair, his brother a young Viking, fair-haired and pink and lithe. Both were scholars of Eton and Balliol. George, nicknamed "Hoj", was "humorously truculent" in manner and is remembered for his "gorgeous laugh." His brother, who had much of Homer and Aeschylus by heart, stays in the memory of those who knew him for his "unique charm that made him welcome in every College room." He had been active in the gunnery section of the O.T.C. at Oxford and graduated naturally to the Royal Field Artillery in the first week of the war. He was killed while serving with the 8th Howitzer Brigade at Gheluvelt on October 31, 1914.

George, that brother cast in a different mould which disguised his scholarship, his discerning taste, his deep religious sensibility, but not his abounding pleasure in being alive, was a Conservative patriot who gloried in

115

war and a soldier's death. He had rowed for his school and college and was an accomplished mountaineer. While he was at Oxford, he wrote so many letters to Viola Tree, daughter of the famous actor-manager of His Majesty's Theatre, that there was what she describes as "a fuss—his parents were bewildered as to who or what I was."

In 1910–11 he was in Germany, learning the language, teaching English, and acquiring a lasting respect for the German people which he never concealed in peace or war. That their history was not enriched by conquistadores, Pilgrim Fathers, Polar explorers, sportsmen or humorists of renown, was of no moment to him. Returning home, he became a master at Shrewsbury under Dr. Alington. The wish of his life was granted when he went back to Eton to teach: "a likely future Headmaster."[1] His short time there was "infinitely happy," he said.

In August 1914, he went to France as an interpreter with the British Expeditionary Force. After the battle of the Aisne, he joined the 2nd Battalion of the Royal Welch Fusiliers at the invitation of its colonel. "His men adored him. His bravery was unbounded." Going on his trench rounds as a company officer, he usually carried on his shoulder a stray cat that had attached itself to him. Where the lines were close, he exchanged "friendly banter" with the enemy in their own tongue. One night he crawled out alone across No-man's-land and retrieved a captured French flag which the Germans were flaunting from a tree in their lines. It was sent to Eton, a treasured trophy of impetuous courage. "He ought to have been given a court-martial and a V.C." On March 20, 1915, he was supervising the building of a breastwork when a single shot rang out and he fell, mortally wounded by a sniper's bullet. He never doubted

[1] L. E. Jones: *An Edwardian Youth* (Macmillan, 1956).

that he would meet his death as a soldier. His fellow officers said that "he faced it with perfect coolness."

4

Killed March 24, 1915, George Heremon Wyndham, of Clouds, near Salisbury; joined the Army from Cambridge; aged 22: "He gave promise of being a great man." Killed March 27, Arnold Seymour-Jones, chief chemist, Brunner, Mond, Ltd. Killed April 8, Cecil Macmillan Dyer, grandson of Alexander Macmillan, publisher; volunteered in August and was at the front, seeing much hard fighting, before Christmas 1914: "I've never felt fitter in my life. I'm quite enjoying things;" aged 21. Killed April 13, Charles Aubrey Vintcent, of Cape Province, South Africa, Cambridge Rugby blue; aged 22. Killed April 14, Bruce Douglas, eldest son of Lord Sholto Douglas; aged 18. Killed April 15, Michael Fitzroy, son of Captain the Hon. C. A. Fitzroy, M.P., himself wounded in the autumn fighting. Killed April 18, F. J. Chubb, scholar of King's College, Cambridge; aged 21. Killed April 18, Bernard Craig Job, son of the vicar of Lower Gornal; enlisted in the Liverpool Scottish, August 6, 1914; aged 27. Killed April 18, Hugh Grenville Malet, Harrow and Cambridge, law student; aged 23. Killed April 21, Dudley Summerhayes, solicitor's articled clerk, Wimbledon; aged 26. Killed April 21, Wilfred Allen Davis, Stonyhurst and Jesus College, Oxford; rowed in the College eight; aged 21.

Busy with their space-saving nonpareil and minion type, the newspaper compositors set up the ever-lengthening "Killed in Action" columns. The tenebrous chords of Chopin and Mendelssohn surged and throbbed in cathedrals, minsters and school chapels. Tenor bells tolled in little lost churches for Hardy's peasants.

117

Requiems were sung for squires' sons, whose swords were laid on altar steps. For the last time in the annals of several great families, mourning hatchments ("corrupt. of Achievement,"—*Concise Oxford Dictionary*), were hung over front doors. Half-mast flags flew from castle turrets. Blinds were drawn in unnumbered little houses. On Sundays, more village girls walked home from church alone.

More, many more, mothers were wearing black. Mr. Balfour's approval of a suggestion that white armbands were preferable as mourning symbols was not widely shared. Letters of condolence were being written and acknowledged on the extravagantly black-bordered notepaper for which Queen Alexandra, writing of her "poor broken heart" to the people at the death of Edward VII five years before, had set the vogue. Some families had the harrowing experience of receiving letters returned from the front with KILLED scrawled across the envelope. The War Office was asked to discourage that heartless practice. Telegraph boys speeding by on their red bicycles were messengers of doom: *The Secretary of State regrets to inform you* . . .

Sobbing French mothers and wives watched the burial of British soldiers behind the lines. C. E. Montague, the middle-aged volunteer from the *Manchester Guardian* office, saw a Frenchwoman "who had come with some white flowers to put on the grave of, I should think, her son. While she was arranging them on the grave there came into the cemetery one of the usual little processions—an English sergeant leading, then the chaplin, then a dead soldier on a stretcher, sewed up in a blanket, with a Union Jack over him, and half a dozen privates walking behind." The Frenchwoman picked up half her flowers and walked behind the funeral party. As the chaplain began to read from the Prayer Book, she fell to her knees and remained so, praying, until the

118

service was finished. "She then came forward, evidently overcoming her shyness with an effort, and dropped the flowers on the man in the grave, and then went away, weeping."[1] British officers in 1914 were punctilious in saluting the heavily veiled women of France.

The imminence of death inspired articles on spiritualism in the soberly reflective pages of the *Quarterly Review* and the *Nineteenth Century*. The Fine Art Society arranged an exhibition of "Designs for War Memorials and Rolls of Honour." Every Sunday, Heaven was refurbished in sermons that made it seem as vividly desirable as it was to the early Christians. Grief abounded and was daily renewed from the fathomless depths of human folly. "As I stepped on English soil at Dover, I felt as though I had entered Westminster Abbey." A Serbian writer, Lazare Kossovac, was describing his visit to wartime England. "All this land is an abbey."

---

[1] *C. E. Montague*, by Oliver Elton (Chatto & Windus 1929).

CHAPTER NINE

The Leave That Has No Ending

1

AS DEAN INGE went up into the pulpit of St. Paul's to preach the sermon at morning service on Easter Sunday, 1915, a man in the congregation shouted a passionate protest against the war. In the language of newspaper reporting, "he was persuaded to leave."

The Dean's voice, never a commanding instrument, was muffled by a cold, making it still less capable of stirring the cathedral echoes or the hearts of men. He had just read, he said, "a beautiful little poem, a sonnet by a young poet who will, I venture to think, take rank with our greatest poets." He spoke the lines, *If I should die, think only this of me: That there's some corner of a foreign field, That is for ever England.*

"Fine and elevated patriotism," the Dean declared, "free from hate, bitterness and fear, has never had a nobler expression, though it fell somewhat short of Isaiah's vision and still more of the Christian hope." *The Times* reported the sermon and quoted the sonnet. From that day forward the name of Rupert Brooke was known in circles wider than those of friendship and the schools.

By then, he was in the Middle East with the Royal Naval Division, bound for Gallipoli. "I have never been quite so happy, I think," he wrote to Violet Asquith (Lady Violet Bonham-Carter). "I suddenly realise that

120

the ambition of my life has been—since I was two—to go on a military expedition against Constantinople." Two brigades went into camp near the golf course at Port Said and it was there that the Commander-in-Chief of the Gallipoli Expedition, Sir Ian Hamilton, offered Brooke a staff post, "not as a fire insurance . . . but as enabling me to keep an eye on one of the most distinguished of the Georgians." Sir Ian's diary note continued:

"Young Brooke replied, as a *preux chevalier* would naturally reply—he realised the privileges he was foregoing but he felt bound to do the landing shoulder-to-shoulder with his comrades. He looked extraordinarily handsome, quite a knightly presence." Brooke comforted his mother in his next letter, telling her that he might consider the offer "when the present job's over," the landing of the Expeditionary Force.

Sunstroke and dysentery knocked him out for several days, first at Port Said, where he was medically ordered to bed at the Casino Palace Hotel, then on board ship bound for the Aegean. Patrick Shaw-Stewart, the Eton and Oxford scholar, was a fellow victim. Both grew apostolic brown beards and recovered sufficiently to take their place in the dining saloon with Arthur Asquith, Charles Lister, F. S. ("Cleg") Kelly, an Australian musician with a fine record as an Oxford and Henley oarsman, "Johnny" Dodge, an eager-hearted young American who had volunteered for service in England's cause, and Denis Browne, another musician, who was in Brooke's circle at Cambridge. Because their conversation was spattered with allusions in Greek, the mess waiters gave their table the name of the Latin Club.

Aeneas of Stympholes, "The Tactician," wrote in 350 B.C. that "when people, leaving their country behind them as a base, are faced by dangers and difficulties beyond their own shores, even if a reverse shall fall by

121

land or sea, yet the survivors have still remaining for them their native land and state, so that they cannot all be destroyed." That assurance was made to seem still more antique to the scholars in uniform in May 1915 when news came of the first air raids on England in that month. In those classical surroundings the Homeric mood lost its grip on them. They turned with relief to Plato, Xenophon and Virgil, hoping perhaps to discover messages from the dead to the living.

A more recent past was fatefully at work on Rupert Brooke's constitution. In Tahiti, two years before, he had caught coral poisoning while swimming. The infection had not been finally expelled through the boils and other skin eruptions that laid him low during his stay. Now, on another island, it was activated afresh in his lowered state after the sunstroke and dysentery.

Still feeling unwell, he took part in a field exercise carried out on twin-peaked Skyros, where as a boy Achilles, whose name survives in Ahkili, a bay on the eastern shore of the island, played on the sands.

> *He scanned the lonely cliffs and valleys wild*
> *Hearing the seagulls call to one another*
> *While far below the great Aegean smiled ...*

Many traces of the old Hellenism remained; for Brooke, a place of enchantment, where shepherds sat alone on the rocky slopes and breathed air fragrant with mint and wild thyme. On the day of the exercise, he lunched in an olive grove with Lieutenant Eric Gamage, of Hood Battalion, who remembered that "Brooke seemed a bit depressed and quite suddenly said: 'What a lovely spot to be buried in!'" His thoughts may have strayed to the legend of Theseus's burial there after fleeing from Athens. That night he went to bed exhausted.

There have been confusing accounts of the subsequent course of his illness. It seems to be agreed that it developed into acute septicaemia. He fell into a coma and was carried to a French hospital ship lying off Skyros. Kelly, his fellow officer and friend, wrote in his journal: "I have had a foreboding that he is one of those, like Keats, Shelley and Schubert, who are not suffered to deliver their full message." He died on St. George's Day, 1915; and it was a monk of the island monastery of St. George who consecrated the ground in which he was buried.

The grave was dug by men of his platoon in a lonely valley running down to the sea. His friends Arthur Asquith, Denis Browne, "Cleg" Kelly, and Bernard Freyberg saluted as his body was lowered into the stony earth. Patrick Shaw-Stewart was in charge of the firing-party whose triple volley summoned time's oldest echoes from the rocks. Pieces of the island's rose-and-yellow veined marble were then heaped over the grave. Rupert Brooke did not lie there alone. Near by was the subsequently exhumed grave of a Roman woman with her unguent jars.

"Rupert Brooke is dead . . . The rest is silence," Sir Ian Hamilton wrote in his diary and went on to ruminate there: "Death on the eve of battle . . . death grins at my elbow. I cannot get him out of my thoughts. He is fed up with the old and sick—only the flower of the flock will serve him now . . . the first-born in intelligence must die."

Edward Marsh wrote to Violet Asquith on May 26 that "dear old Winston, at dinner last night, had suddenly broken out that nothing grieved him, or went on grieving him, so much as Rupert's death, and went on to abuse me quite angrily, as he has done several times, for not bringing them together sooner." Churchill's personal obituary contribution, printed in *The Times*, carried the young poet's name far beyond the range of the sounding-board of St. Paul's pulpit. Telegraphing his wish to be represented, if possible, at the funeral, Churchill had added: *We shall not see his like again.*

123

Churchill had looked Rupert Brooke in the eye and felt the grip of his hand. His tribute was not to a laurelled adolescent. He was mourning a vividly memorable young man whose sonneteering patriotism, so distasteful to "the sick hearts that honour will not move" in two world wars, flaunted the mood of an hour but was subservient to the sovereign quality of his being and heroic purpose.

His brief life shone with more than poetry. He had the impalpable thing called presence, rare at any age and extremely so in youth. It endowed him with a kind of royalty that made his entry into a room an event rather than an incident. All heads turned. Those who knew him best never doubted that it was in him to transcend the emotional immaturity by which he continues perversely to be judged; some believed that he would have reached the eminence in public affairs predicted for him by a far from worshipful admirer. Walter de la Mare said that he was "a vigorous, healthy creature who, if he did not live long enough to see life whole, confronted it with a good steady and disconcerting stare. With him," de la Mare also said, "there was that happy shining impression that he might have come—that very moment —from another planet," one of those visitors to our world who help to redeem the desperate mediocrity of the human scene.

> *He who sang of dawn and evening, English glades*
> *   and light of Greece,*
> *Changed his dreaming into sleeping, left his sword*
> *   to rest in peace.*
> *Left his visions of the springtime, Holy Grail and*
> *   Golden Fleece,*
> *Took the leave that has no ending, till the waves of*
> *   Lemnos cease.*[1]

[1] *R. B.* by Aubrey Herbert.

On April 15, members of the Press Gallery in the House of Commons saw that a slip of paper was being passed along the benches below. M.P.s, scanning it, threw back their heads in dismay. Some showed no feeling beyond a tightening of the lips. The message told of the death in France two days before of Lieutenant W. G. C. Gladstone, M.P., grandson of the Grand Old Man and heir of Hawarden. Lord Bryce's comment on hearing the news was that "of all the infinitely sad things in this war, none is sadder than the passing of such as he."

Will Gladstone, aged 30, the Liberal member for Kilmarnock Burghs, had something of the frame and looks of W. E. Gladstone in youth. Not only on his good showing at the Oxford Union, much was expected of him as a public figure. It was confidently thought that the Gladstonian mantle would fall on him. The effect of that high supposition on some members of the House was curious. They were so apprehensive of his success that when he rose to speak they left the Chamber. In general, he acquitted himself well for his years, at his ease and without mannerisms.

Like other Liberals, he was opposed to the declaration of war on Germany. According to Robert Graves, "his Hawarden tenantry, much ashamed, threatened to duck him in the pond."[1] As his health was far from robust, the threat may have been an idle one if it was made at all. There is perhaps naturally no mention of it in the memoir written by Viscount Gladstone, who makes it clear that when Belgian sovereignty was violated his nephew realised that the time for protest had passed.

Echoes of an old speech of his grandfather's stiffened Will Gladstone's resolution. At Edinburgh, in 1880, the

[1] *Goodbye to All That,* 1929.

elder Gladstone said that if Belgian neutrality had been infringed during the war of 1870 he would have supported action by Great Britain. That was enough for his grandson in 1914. The General Officer Commanding, Western Command, offered him a staff post. Will Gladstone replied that his "dread and dislike of military service was intense," that he had "no natural appetite for it," and that he had "never done a minute's military service." For that reason, he was not prepared to accept responsibility for others "without knowing the ropes well from the beginning." He therefore proposed to serve as a private soldier. When it was impressed upon him that as Lord Lieutenant of his county his position would be a difficult one, he agreed to take a commission as a second-lieutenant in the 3rd Battalion, Royal Welch Fusiliers.

The Right Hon. C. F. G. Masterman, a sometime Liberal Cabinet Minister, said that Will Gladstone was "no soldier and the particular military instincts were quite deficient in him. In a curious way, it was just because of the absence of the impulse that he felt he had to go." He seems to have had a conviction from the beginning that, giving his service, he was giving his life, "that there never was any question of his returning home with honour and glory." He arranged his affairs at Hawarden as if it had been a foregone conclusion and wrote to his widowed mother after his last home leave: "I hope you have settled down now and are resigned to my departure. Really you will be wrong if you regret my going, for I am very glad and proud to have got to the Front. It is not the length of existence that counts, but what is achieved during that existence, however short."

His height made him conspicuous in the firing line. "I did not like to be seen crouching," he wrote, "as the men might think I was funking it." On April 13, he was hit in the forehead by a sniper's bullet and lay unconscious in an exposed position. Hearing that he was still breathing, the battalion medical officer, Captain William Kelsey Fry,[1] most gallantly went out with a corporal and fetched him in on a stretcher in full view of the enemy lines. Gladstone was beyond help.

There were murmurings of surprise when his body was brought home to England for burial in the "Gladstone Temple of Peace" at Hawarden. "Do the Gladstones think they are royalty?" No doubt the intention was to honour the dead young officer as Lord Lieutenant of Flintshire. *The Times* printed valedictory lines which donnish readers promptly turned into Latin and Greek, their respective versions appearing in the next few days.

> *From Generation to Generation*
> *One gave long years with heart and brain*
> *One, youth's fiery blow*
> *For Freedom: whence the greater gain*
> *Only the high gods know.*

3

The voluntary impulse was beginning to weaken. A recruiting drive launched in April 1915 met startling apathy. A rally in Guildhall Yard, London, made "a negligible impression," for all the fervour of a military band, resounding rhetoric from the platform, and ceremonial flag-waving when "our gallant Allies" were mentioned. At a meeting on Tower Hill, 2 recruits came forward, a result so disappointing to the chief speaker that he threw up his hands and cried in dismay: "It's a sorry outlook for us all!"

A convenient turn of argument just then was: "The

---

[1] Later Sir William Kelsey Fry, M.C., well-known as an associate of Sir Harold Gillies, the eminent plastic surgeon.

127

French are doing all right. And how about the Russian steamroller?" The excessive praise lavished on the Dominion contingents, while the exploits of the English county regiments were almost entirely ignored, also tended to create the feeling that the Empire could supply all the reinforcements that would be needed. Besides, the Royal Navy was still there, the invincible shield in excuse as in reality. In the meantime, our voluntary system had helped to bring about the strategic conditions that were to keep us pinned down for four years between the Yser and the Alps. "The triumph of your voluntary system is a German triumph: it is the ruin of Belgium and the devastation of France."[1]

Conscription was the bitter topic. Conservatives believed it to be inevitable and necessary. Liberals insisted that it was neither, the more radical members of the Party still regarding soldiers with the austerely distrustful attitude of the Protestant Alliance to the Jesuits. Trades unionists contended that conscription was the negation of democracy and a potential instrument of dictatorship.

In the last preserve of the romantic view of war, the public schools, where the course of battles was diligently followed on wall maps marked by flags, and where almost every boy put his name down for a commission at 18, there was eager longing to be "in the skirmish."

Is this to live?—to cower and stand aside,
While others fight and perish day by day?

young Francis St. Vincent Morris, son of Canon Morris of Ashbourne, Derbyshire, asked himself that year. He was 18 and at Brighton College. The streets of that watering place were full of reminders of the sacrifices of others, wounded Indians, for example, from the Royal Pavilion,

[1] Quoted from *Ordeal by Battle* by F. S. Oliver (Macmillan, 1915).

above: French peasants at the grave of a Seaforth Highlander, September 28, 1914

below: Remnants of a London Scottish company returning from Messines Ridge, October 31, 1914

above: Public school boys arriving in camp, Autumn, 1914

below: An Eton charade, 1906: (*extreme left*) Patrick Shaw-Stewart, (*centre, at desk*) Edward Horner, (*wearing jacket*) Julian Grenfell, (*extreme right*) Charles Lister

G. R. L. ('Twiggy') Anderson, Olympic athlete, killed in action, November, 1914

above : Middlesex Hussars training in Richmond Park, February, 1915

below : Men of the 9th London Regiment (Queen Victoria's Rifles) training on Hampstead Heath, 1915

(*Radio Times Hulton Picture Library*)

above: Returning from the Front, Victoria Station, London, 1916

below: Charing Cross Hospital, London, 1915

(*Imperial War Museum*)

Anthony Wilding, tennis champion, killed at Neuve Chapelle, March, 1915

(*Imperial War Museum*)

bove: The 'Kensingtons' (13th London Regiment) training at Saffron Walden, 1915

elow: Honourable Artillery Company's dug-out at The Ramparts, Ypres, May, 1915

(*Imperial War Museum*)

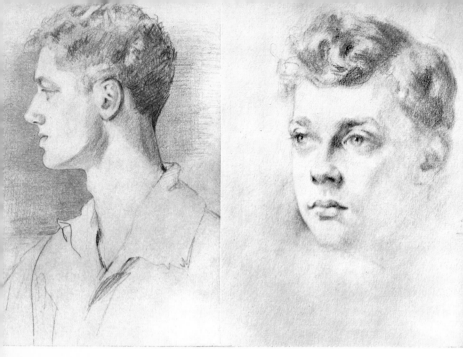

Julian Grenfell   Billy Grenfell

Edward Wyndham Tennant   'Sister Agnes'
from a portrait by Sargent)

Leslie Coulson

Rupert Brooke

John William Streets

Robert W. Sterling

above : Before going into action on the Somme: 17th Battn., King's Liverpool Regiment
July, 1916

below : Lancashire Fusiliers fixing bayonets before the assault on Beaumont Hamel,
July, 1916

(*Langfier*)

W. N. Hodgson

Charles Hamilton Sorley

Francis St. Vincent Morris

Richard Dennys

Wykeham)

W. B. R. Rhodes-Moorhouse

Harold Chapin

Eric Waterlow

Albert Ball

and bandaged officers from their hospital at Kemp Town, close by.

> . . . *I will go forth; I hold no more aloof;*
> *And I will give all that I have to give,*
> *And leave the refuge of my father's roof.*
> *Then, if I live, no man shall say, think I,*
> *"He lives, because he did not dare to die!"*[1]

He was gazetted a second-lieutenant of the Sherwood Foresters. Restless at being kept in England while training, he secured a transfer to the Royal Flying Corps and, daring to die, crashed in a blizzard over Vimy Ridge.

The oath was still being gabbled in recruiting offices: *I . . . will be faithful and bear true Allegiance to His Majesty King George the Fifth, His Heirs, and Successors . . . So help me God.* The fountain-pens of the certifying officers no longer raced across the enrolment forms as in the frantic August days. At Great Scotland Yard, there was a drop in enlistments for the infantry at 14¢ a day and a rise in those for motor transport and tunnelling at 84¢ a day. Numbers of men taken into those categories were soon found to have no aptitude for either.

A new appeal by Lord Kitchener for 300,000 more men produced a far from striking response. His lack of organising genius was held to be in some degree answerable. Since the great success of his original appeal in August 1914 he had made a series of confusing decisions, some of which were put on record by L. S. Amery, M.P., then Director of Civilian Recruiting for Southern Command.

---

[1] *Poems* by Francis St. Vincent Morris, R.F.C., (Blackwell).

Another retarding influence was the news of the first German gas attack. The nauseous pale yellow mist that drifted over the Allied lines near Ypres at sunset on April 22, 1915, had effects that reached far beyond its barely predictable course. A Territorial of Queen Victoria's Rifles wrote an account of an event that sent a shudder of horror through the civilised world.

The Q.V.R.s, a London battalion, had just come out of the fighting for Hill 60. Utterly weary, they were resting in a meadow near the Poperinghe-Ypres road. Many of the men dropped their kits and fell instantly asleep. "Suddenly down the road from the Yser Canal came a galloping team of horses, the riders goading on their mounts in a frenzied way; then another and another, till the road became a seething mass with a pall of dust over all. Plainly something terrible was happening. What was it?"

Officers, including some of the Staff, were astounded. While more horses and shouting men filled the road, "over the fields streamed mobs of infantry, the dusky warriors of French Africa; away went their rifles, equipment, even their tunics that they might run faster. One man came stumbling through our lines. An officer of ours held him up with levelled revolver. 'What's the matter, you bloody lot of cowards?' says he. The Zouave was frothing at the mouth, his eyes started from their sockets, and he fell writhing at the officer's feet."[1] On the northerly breeze was borne a sickly odour that was followed by throat irritation and smarting eyes. Men going home on leave had dreadful tales to tell of the slow asphyxiation of their comrades.

"There was no difficulty in finding them," wrote an officer who visited a field hospital the next day. "The

[1] Anthony M. Hossack in *Everyman in War* (Dent, 1930).

noise of the poor devils trying to get their breath was sufficient direction. Twenty of the worst cases were on mattresses, all more or less in a sitting posture, propped against the walls. Faces, arms, hands, were a shiny grey-black. With mouths open and lead-glazed eyes, they were all swaying backwards and forwards trying to get breath, struggling, struggling for life. There was nothing that could be done except to give them salt and water emetics. The gas fills up the lungs and bronchial tubes with froth, which finally suffocates the victim. It is like slow drowning, taking sometimes two days."

No one who saw (as the present writer did) those first victims, many of them the finest specimens of young Canadian manhood from Winnipeg, can ever forget it. Hiroshima was distant in time. The two events, great and small, are linked by the intensity of their revelation of human heartlessness.

Reacting from the new horror facing their men, thousands of London women besieged the Royal Army Clothing Department in Pimlico with offers of help in making respirators. Many brought cotton, needles and scissors, ready to begin work at once. Within a week of the news from Ypres three hundred thousand home-made respirators were on their way to the Front. Chemists' shops ran out of cotton wool and another immediate result was a butter muslin famine.

Discords at home were as insidious in their effect on recruiting as bad news from elsewhere. An unscrupulous campaign was launched by groups opposed to inoculation. It impeded drafting at several depots. At one of them, a hundred men who had finally been persuaded to receive anti-typhoid injections stampeded in fright when the first in the line fainted at the jab of the needle. It was mischievously put about that civilian doctors advised inoculation because they earned fees by it. Minor grievances among the troops were wilfully magnified into sources of alarm and criticism.

Some Labour leaders, despising patriotism, quoted Ruskin's definition of it as "an absurd prejudice founded on an extended selfishness," unaware perhaps that he also credited war with bringing out fine moral qualities. Others, like J. H. Thomas, of the National Union of Railwaymen, Stephen Walsh, who spoke for the miners and was later Secretary of State for War in a Labour Government, and James Sexton, the dockers' leader, banged the drum for "ultimate victory." Liberal opinion, vehement about the war and its consequences, halted the resolution of many who were disposed to come forward. Conservatives, who had bled copiously as a class, still as a class tended to justify Goldsmith's sneer at their eighteenth-century arrogance as "lords of human kind." Men in hospital blue could still "grouse" with Siegfried Sassoon's soldier: *Two bleeding years I fought in France for Squire; I suffered anguish that he's never guessed.*[1]

5

Flanders mud had given way to dust. The goatskin jackets that stank of primeval sweat had been discarded. Shell holes that gleamed as lifelessly as cracked mirrors all through the winter were now lined green as if by tender design. Celandines sprinkled old parapets with gold. The nightingale was a recurring theme of wonder in letters home, whence came news for the amateur ornithologists of the trenches that there was a great accession of the plover flocks of England, thought to be a result of the battlefield commotion.

Private Maxwell Green, killed that spring while serving with the H.A.C., wrote to the *Selborne Magazine*: "It is curious how little the sound and turmoil of

[1] *Memorial Tablet* (Great War, 1918).

this great struggle has impressed itself upon the animal and bird life of Flanders. One might have imagined that the daily sound of shells plunging and bursting into the woods would drive the natural inhabitants to forsake their ancestral haunts. The hares can still be seen feeding in the fields. The blackbirds merely cease their chatter during a bombardment, then, as if in becoming thankfulness, the danger over, they burst anew into song. The call of the little owl is still heard at night."

Long silences often lay over the earthworks that cut jigsaw patterns in unmeasured square miles of landscape. Trenches, dugouts, fire pits, forward posts, were full of beleaguered men. Yet for hours at a time there was no obvious sign of life in the whole vast front line complex. Cuckoos calling from trees as bare as rotting gallows mocked the scene.

CHAPTER TEN

"Almost Every Man Was Crying"

1

WHAT WAS being lost in human worth had not been writ so large before. A Rhodes Scholar, Alan Wallace, serving as a sergeant of the New Zealand Engineers, aged 26; Thomas William Callinan, modern languages master at Merchant Taylor's School, well-known in London Rugby football, aged 32; William Black Noble, director of the Cairn Steamship Line, aged 25; T. L. Bainbridge, electrical engineer at Swan, Hunter's, the Tyneside shipbuilders, aged 32; W. D. Powell Jarvis, of Toronto, a well-known Canadian yachtsman, aged 23; Allen Barclay, of Sydenham, geologist and mining engineer, aged 27; Hugh Kemp, a cousin of Sir John French, serving as a private in the Canadian Army; John Pound, an assistant master at Shrewsbury School, aged 27; J. T. Monkhouse, managing director of the Llangynog Stone Quarries, Montgomeryshire, aged 30: all fell while the cuckoo called and the blackbird sang. It was a lovely spring.

Private Frank Brignall, a former Brighton Grammar School boy who was farming in Canada and had joined the 11th (British Columbia) Regiment, Canadian Expeditionary Force, wrote from France on April 18, 1915: "A most anxious and trying day . . . A boom from the enemy cannon, a rushing shriek that you feel must be coming at you personally, a fountain of mud (and in some cases sandbags) rises high, and then listening intently one hears the long drawn out wail, almost like a human scream of terror, made by the screw-cap of the shell as it flies off and hurtles through the air. It has fallen in the trenches of our No. 2 Company and we wonder, has anyone been hurt? The question is soon answered, for word is passed down our line quickly from mouth to mouth, 'Stretcher bearers at the double.' "

Six days after, they came for him at the double, too late.

"I've been longing for some link with the normal universe detached from the storm," Robert Sterling, of Ashton Gardens, Glasgow, wrote that day. He went on to tell how he found "just such a link" while in the trenches south-east of Ypres, where the German lines were eighty yards away. "Between the trenches lay pitiful heaps of dead friends and foes." The only standing trees were riven of branches, twigs, leaves, "little more than stumps." After a turn of heavy shelling by the enemy, "there fell a few minutes' silence; and, still crouching expectantly in the trench, I saw a pair of thrushes building a nest in a 'bare ruin'd choir' of a tree, only about five yards behind our line. At the same time, a lark began to sing in the sky above the German trenches." It seemed to him "almost incredible." Thinking of the nest-builders, "they seem to repeat in some degree the very essence of the Normal and Unchangeable Universe carrying on unhindered and careless amid the corpses and the bullets and the madness."[1]

Aged 21, Sterling was a classical scholar and Newdigate Prize winner (*The Burial of Sophocles*) who often forsook the study for the football field and the river without impairing his reputation as "something of a visionary." He went to Pembroke College, from Sedburgh, whose laureate he was, taking with him a scholar's mental poise, sound physical health, and a flair

[1] *Letters of Fallen Englishmen* (Gollancz, 1930).

135

for friendship. "He could convey a rare warmth of welcome in one exclamatory word. In his mouth the use of a Christian name at some surprise meeting was a thing not lightly forgotten."

Hearing of the death in action of one of his dearest friends, he wrote lines that his own death in the trenches on April 23, 1915, made more deeply poignant:

> *O brother, I have sung no dirge for thee:*
> *Nor for all time to come*
> *Can song reveal my grief's infinity:*
> *The menace of thy silence makes me dumb.*

Also on April 23, Charles Darwin's grandson, Erasmus, was killed, aged 34. He was a Darwin in a new field of activity. Having taken second place in the English Tripos at Cambridge, he joined a Middlesbrough engineering firm, where he made a lasting impression on his colleagues. They remembered him for his "good judgment and exacting standards of performance: he liked to do things, and to see them done, as well as they could be done." He had "strong views about the human side of industry and a sincere sympathy with the men on the shop floor."

He was given a commission in a local battalion of the Yorkshire Regiment. When it was ordered to France early in 1915, he was offered a post in munitions, "one that would have suited his capacities." He had come to like the men he was serving with and chose not to be parted from them. Instead, he went to his death on the Western front. It was written of him memorially that "he is only one of many of whom it may be said that they would have done much; but whatever he might have achieved he could never have left a more honourable memory."

The death on April 27 of William Barnard Rhodes-Moorhouse, aged 27, Royal Flying Corps, had the impact of a national loss. The public knew him as a daring aviator, a leading light of the Royal Aero Club, the first to cross the Channel with two passengers, flying a fragile Breguet biplane, one of the heroes of the round-England Aerial Derby in which he came in third. His friends and associates admired him for other things, the charm of his disposition which made him attractive to all kinds of people, and the force of his character which eclipsed his small figure and light-toned voice. His "frequent quizzical smile" is still remembered.

His war exploit was one of the most gallant in the whole long drawn-out campaign. He was ordered to drop bombs on the railway junction at Courtrai. "They perhaps did more definite service than any bombs let fall during the war . . . They had the effect of a great strategical move,"[1] stopping the advance of 40,000 Germans. He hit the objective from a low level which made him "the target of hundreds of rifles, machine-guns, and anti-aircraft guns."[2] He was dangerously wounded and might have saved his life by landing in enemy territory. Knowing that his information was vital, he made the forty-minutes return flight to base, where he had literally to be cut out of the blood-soaked cockpit of his machine. As they bore him away to die, he made a grim jest at the horrifying nature of his wound. He was awarded a posthumous V.C.

2

The Lancet of April 26 considered the possible effect of the war on England's declining birthrate. Conceding that "it cannot be estimated," the medical journal suggested that "the maintenance of the supply of human

[1] Sir William Beach Thomas.
[2] "Eyewitness" (General Swinton).

beings needed for the re-establishment of the nation's prosperity is likely to be a source of anxiety to this and coming generations."

The Chief Medical Officer of Health of the Board of Education reported that "the terrible burden of destruction caused by the war" made child nurture "more urgent than ever." Already, education authorities in England employed 1,271 doctors and 1,237 nurses for child welfare purposes. They made grants for Schools for Mothers and for day nurseries and crèches. The Provision of Meals Act 1914 was another indication of social legislation on the march.

Pamphlets, leaflets, tracts, came in a continuous flow from organisations promoting maternity and child welfare. "Is the war, with its slaughter of so many potential fathers, rousing Great Britain to the need for a torrent of babies?" the *New Statesman* asked.

Those who pondered the racial aspect of the war had even more cause to be anxious when the losses of Second Ypres (April 22–May 31) were revealed. In those five weeks the slaughter rose to a new pitch of horror, in which England's citizen soldiers suffered heavily. For the first time, they were present in battle as a complete division, the Northumberland, only a few days out from the training camps in England. Queen Victoria's Rifles, King's Liverpools, and North Somerset, Leicestershire and Essex Yeomanry were all in the thick of it. "If you see the L.R.B.s [London Rifle Brigade]," a brigadier said to a war correspondent, "tell them that we want them back. We look on them as Regulars now."

Sir John French wondered "if the eyes of the country will ever be opened to what these Territorials of ours have done." They had been called on to do what was normally expected only of experienced soldiers, to hold the front line while fresh troops were being made ready. The Commander-in-Chief reminded the country: "They were quite different from professional soldiers . . . who, on being confronted with the enemy, fulfil the great ambition of their lives. Equally distinct were the Territorials from what has been called the New Army, whose officers and men had ample time to prepare themselves for what they were required to do."

It was a time of calamity for the officers who had replaced those of the old Regular Army. Many were commemorated on the front page of *The Times*: on May 4, the names of 39 officers killed in action or died of wounds appeared there; on May 6, 20 names; May 8, 37 names; May 13, 20 names; May 14, 62 names; May 17, 50 names; May 18, 53 names; May 24, 29 names; May 26, 35 names. "And some there be which have no memorial," except the small print of the official casualty lists. The total officer losses for the period was 2,150, in "other ranks," 57,125.

May 9, which saw the futile attack on Aubers Ridge with 11,000 casualties and not a yard of ground to show for them, was a day of reckoning for the politicians. Blamed for the shells shortage, the results of which Sir John French saw for himself as he watched the attack from the tower of Laventie church, the Asquith administration fell and the first Coalition Government took its place, under the same leadership.

At Gallipoli, three thousand miles away, there was a fearful smell of death after the slaughter of May 18–19, when the Turks charged the Australian and New Zealand positions and were cut down in such numbers that their dead were piled like cordwood in a clearing. An Australian eye-witness wrote that "no sound came from the dreadful space, but here and there some wounded or dying man, silently lying without help or hope of it under the sun which glared from a cloudless sky, turned painfully from one side to the other, or slowly raised an arm towards heaven."

139

Telegrams went to the next-of-kin of Kenneth Rose Dennys, Royal Munster Fusiliers, a young actor who appeared in Maeterlinck's *Blue Bird* and who had been private secretary to Monsignor R. H. Benson; Lucas King, King's Royal Rifle Corps, one of Lord Northcliffe's nephews; Leonard Stein, aged 24, of "The Kensingtons" (13th London Regiment), son of the minister of the East London Synagogue, and active in the social work of Toynbee Hall; Brian Melland, Royal Naval Division, a nephew of the Prime Minister; Alastair Hunter Macfarlane, 20, younger son of Lord Ormidale, 9th Royal Scots, "a most lovable personality, whose gentle courtesy and admirable good nature endeared him to many at school, in college, and in his battalion;" Roy Fazan, Royal Sussex Regiment (Cinque Ports Battalion), medical student, aged 25; Charles Robert Herbert George Martin, Demonstrator in Zoology, Glasgow University, "a scientist with a European reputation," aged 33; John Harrison Sellars, trainee engineer of Newcastle-upon-Tyne, a grandson of the sculptor of the Albert Memorial frieze, aged 18; Sidney Hellyar, East Yorkshire Regiment, engineer, aged 25, of whom a sergeant of his battalion wrote: "A shell burst right in the middle of our company, killing four outright and wounding eight, including Mr. Hellyar, who had an arm blown off, his other arm broken in two places, and several other wounds. He would not let us touch him until all the others had been attended to."

"We are using the same methods as at Neuve Chapelle," General Charteris wrote in his staff diary just before the Aubers Ridge attack. "Heavy bombardment for an hour, then an assault by infantry." Territorials of the Northumberland Fusiliers and the Royal Sussex were cut down almost as soon as they were over the top. The Sussex battalion commander, Colonel Langham, a Hastings solicitor, wept at the fate of his men and his list of recommendations for decorations was said to have named practically every officer, most of the N.C.O.s and "every other private." Those invalided home after the attack did not hide their bitterness at the ineffectual preliminary bombardment, which left much of the enemy wire untouched. Too many of their friends had been left hanging in it, like flies in a web. With no more than 22 machine-guns, 15 German companies had successfully fought off an attack by 3 British brigades.

Princess Patricia's Canadian Light Infantry lost 317 officers and men. "The Buffs" (East Kent Regiment) were shattered. The York and Lancasters lost their commanding officer, 13 other officers, and 411 N.C.O.s and men; the 2nd East Yorkshires, 14 officers and 369 men; 2nd Duke of Cornwall's Light Infantry, 200 of all ranks; 5th King's Own, nearly 300. All but 70 of the officers and troopers of the Leicestershire Yeomanry were killed or missing. The Northamptonshires lost 17 officers and 543 other ranks; the 2nd Sussex, 14 officers and 537 other ranks. Only 20 men of two companies of the Middlesex remained. Great gaps were torn in the ranks of the Devons, the Seaforths, the Royal Welch Fusiliers, the King's Shropshire Light Infantry, the Hampshires, and the King's Own Scottish Borderers.

A voice from the Border was heard in the lamentation: "Since Flodden Field there has been no such tithing of our young men."[1] The Borderers lost an exceptional leader in Robert Gibson, Fellow and Tutor of Balliol, aged 29. Having begun to do "interesting work in philosophy," he flung aside his gown in August 1914 and within two months was in action on the Western Front. He fought through the autumn battles and was seen in hand-to-hand encounters in Ploegsteert Wood, using his revolver and home-made bombs.

His death at Hill 60 in May 1915 was recorded as

[1] Miss Agnes Falconer writing to *Country Life*, August 14, 1915.

"an irreparable loss to the College teaching staff." He was respected and remembered for his penetrating intellectual honesty. A friend of his wrote: "I never knew a man before whom one felt so mentally and morally naked—a wholesome experience, no doubt, but it meant that, while we all admired him, only some knew him well enough to realise that his heart was as warm as his brain was ruthless, and so learned to love as they admired." His "white-hot sincerity," his "contempt for shams," were imprinted deeply on the minds of those who knew him. "To spend a day or two with him was to have no illusions about oneself."

3

In the foggy light of dawn one day that month a lieutenant of the 4th Berkshires (Territorials) stood on the roof of a dug-out, inspecting repairs that had been done during the night. A stray shot was heard. It was thought to have glanced off the barbed wire in front of the trench. The young officer staggered and fell, hit in the right side below the armpit. Taken down into the dugout, he was seen to be dead. "Ronnie" Poulton would never hear the roar of the crowd at Twickenham again. He would not fulfil the promise of his career ·as the innovator of a new era in industrial harmony.

He is still remembered in the Rugby football world as "an immortal of the game, one of the greatest three-quarters of all time, perhaps the very greatest." Sir Rex Benson, who played Rugby at Oxford with him, says that Poulton's power of acceleration on the field was phenomenal: "he appeared to be equipped with an extra sense that enabled him to know precisely what was going to happen one move ahead and to act with complete assurance in readiness for it." His pre-eminence in the game gave him the standing of a leader of English sportsmanship.

The son of Professor E. B. Poulton, Sc.D., F.R.S., he went up to Oxford with an exhibition in natural science and entered the newly established engineering school as the prelude to a working life with the well-known firm of Huntley & Palmers, the Reading biscuit manufacturers, whose chairman was his uncle, G. W. Palmer. At the university, he was thought "a bit pi" (Sir Rex Benson). The sound of College crockery crashing down the stairs as part of the escapades of members of the Annandale Society gave him no pleasure. He organised a revolt against a system that required the College to defray the cost of such delinquencies. He is recalled by a Balliol contemporary as "a Conservative of the Christian and Reformist kind."[1] He was a devoted patron of the Balliol Boys' Club at St. Ebbes, Oxford.

He appears in the pages of a privately printed memoir of Keith Rae,[2] one of his closest collaborators in the work of the Boys' Club, as "strikingly handsome, with a smile that could disarm anybody. Ronald loved everyone, and everyone loved him. The transparent honesty of his life meant that he had no secrets of which he was ashamed, and this made him delightfully easy to know. His intellect ranged over a wide field, and his sparkling vivacity gave point to everything that he said." Although the paragon among men is always exposed to the world's hostility, we need not question the sincerity of his friends.

Leaving Oxford, Poulton entered on his business career with purpose and zest, determined to make the human side of factory life his particular study. He started social and athletic clubs for the workers at Reading. Other welfare schemes were evolving in his mind when, at his

[1] Ivor Brown: *The Way Of My World* (Collins, 1954).
[2] Keith Rae: *A Memoir of Oxford and Marlborough* (1926).

143

uncle's wish, he went to Manchester to take a year's course at the Municipal School of Technology. It was to qualify him for a seat on Huntley & Palmers' board. While he was in Manchester, his uncle died. Ronnie Poulton was named in his will as the heir to a considerable estate. There was a proviso that he should assume the additional surname of Palmer.

He stayed to finish the technology course; then went back to Reading with plans of betterment that would have brought the welfare of the workers constantly to the fore in boardroom discussions. As the new managing head of the business, he hoped to accomplish a revolution in industrial relations. His friend, the Rev. E. C. Crosse, thought it "unquestionable that the world would have witnessed the amazing spectacle of a gigantic business run on definitely Christian lines." That such shining idealism could be fulfilled in the profit-making *milieu* was more debatable then than now, when we are sadly wiser.

Poulton returned to Reading in the summer of 1914 and was on holiday in the first days of August. He volunteered at once, forsaking all, like the rich young man of the Gospel. "Of all vocations, the soldier's had least attraction for him; he thought war a bitter anachronism." He was at the front only five weeks before the chance bullet struck him down, aged 26. Many of the men of his battalion came from Reading and knew his worth. A brother officer wrote on the day of his death: "When I went round the company as they stood to, at dawn, almost every man was crying."

4

Francis Grenfell, who had never ceased to mourn his twin brother Riversdale, was mortally wounded on

May 25, 1915, having returned to the front after six months in hospital recovering from his earlier wound. "Tell them I died happy, loving them all," he said as his life ebbed away in the dust. Around him stood spectral figures, all that remained of his squadron of the 9th Lancers. Their faces were hideous yellow masks, the result of mustard gas that had rolled over them in a cloud at dawn. He bequeathed his V.C., the first of the 633 awarded during the war, to his regiment, "because the honour of winning it was entirely due to their splendid discipline."

That week, a war correspondent, Valentine Williams, who afterwards joined the Guards and fought with them in France, saw remnants of a volunteer battalion of the London Rifle Brigade come out of the trenches. "A tatterdemalion lot, in ragged uniforms, with the tense expressions of men who have looked death in the face," he wrote in his despatch. General Charteris, at Haig's headquarters, recorded in his diary: "A feather in their cap, for some Regulars, who are more tired and stale, tried to take these trenches and failed last week. It is very encouraging, for it is units like these 'Terriers' that will form the bulk of our army next year." (May 25, 1915.)

145

CHAPTER ELEVEN

A Professor's Proud Remembrance

1

AT HOME, there were widening lesions in the connective tissue of tradition, social habits, convention. Not a little of the modesty, real or affected, in sex relations was disappearing. Englishwomen still wore long skirts and were still reluctant to show an ankle. Paris, no longer cowering under the threat of occupation, decreed that "skirts will be wider but will not trail the ground." Short coats in colours contrasting with those of skirts were being worn. The fashionable figure was "perfectly flat front and back with full hip pleats."

Female emancipation was near. War was bringing it more surely than self-sacrifice on the race course or forcible feeding in prison. One of the overlooked portents was that some of the English Red Cross nurses who went to Antwerp six months previously had worn trousers instead of skirts. The arrival of the sex "in munitions" was about to make that innovation less startling, just as factory life would change women's hair styles from the "bun" to the "bob," the latter being a safety precaution first and a fashion afterwards.

Men coming home on leave in the spring of 1915 were among the first to see women driving delivery vans in London streets, acting as ticket inspectors at Paddington station, taking menservants' places at that loftily exclusive masculine preserve, the Athenaeum Club, Pall

Mall. A few girls were employed as typists in City banks. Selfridges of Oxford Street engaged a woman commissionaire, much photographed. A policewoman was enrolled for duty with the Brighton force.

Dumfries overwhelmed by hosiery orders; Northampton working overtime on boot production; the mills of Yorkshire pouring out rivers of khaki cloth, all meant new opportunities for women in the labour market. Domestic service was soon to become a major casualty of the war among social institutions. Signs of it were to be seen in the lengthening newspaper columns of "wanted" advertisements under the headings of "Governesses, Companions & Lady Nurses," "Lady Housekeepers, Housekeepers & Cooks," "Parlourmaids & House Parlourmaids," "House, Kitchen & Scullery Maids," "Between Maids, Generals & Laundry Maids." Vacancies were fast outrunning the supply, particularly in the towns, where basement servitude was joyfully renounced after the long years of Dickensian drudgery.

In May, 1915, a London newspaper lamented the passing of the parlourmaid. "Many families are compelled to wait on themselves at mealtimes." Soon, for want of help butlers would be reduced to cleaning the silver. The decline of the stately homes into 35-cent peepshows was about to be accelerated. By the end of May over 65,000 women had registered for war work. The full implication of the announcement was that a large reserve of the nation's energies would be released for war purposes. Was it one of the subtler decrees of nature that the liberation of women coincided with that time of widespread mourning for their men?

The swirling currents of change were affecting military styles, long in thrall to rigid rules of taste. The new race of officers were taking the cane stiffeners out of their Service caps, producing a *négligé* effect that was a source of apoplectic wrath among their seniors.

147

Shirts, ties, puttees, were worn in contrasting tones, from dark green to pale coffee. The subalterns stuffed white handkerchiefs, instead of khaki ones, in their left sleeves, and invented an immortal phrase to meet rebuke: *Life is very difficult.*

Officers of the Regular Army invariably put off their uniforms when on leave, an assertion of good form, of civil rights possibly, of welcome relief, anyhow, from the trappings of authority. The new officers flaunted uniform on all occasions, deriving from it a public prestige exhilaratingly new in their experience. Again, the officers of an older tradition, receiving promotion, let a decent interval pass before displaying the insignia of their new rank. The raw young officers of Kitchener's later battalions had no such reticences. Their extra "pips" were sewn on to their tunics with the eagerness of Boy Scouts collecting badges of merit.

2

Professor Gilbert Murray wrote elegiacally of "a wonderful band of scholars" who went from New College, Oxford, "young men quite exceptional in intellectual powers. They were the sort of men," he said, "who could never be suspected of evading a duty or of voting for their own interest rather than the common good."

He had a particular regard for Arthur Heath, who entered New College with an Open Classical Scholarship from the Grocers' Company School, "which has educated many thoughtful men." (Murray). Heath gained some of the great university prizes. "I remember him waiting in my study," Professor Murray wrote, "a slender, delicately-made freshman, very good-looking, dark, with regular features and great luminous eyes; rather silent and entirely gentle and unassuming." It

148

seemed to Murray that Heath lived "an intense inner life of watching and thinking; making up his mind on a multitude of subjects, reflectively quiet." He had not had as much teaching in Latin and Greek as the young men coming up from the great public schools, "a fact which just prevented him from getting the two blue-ribbons of scholarship, the Hertford and the Ireland. But he came second for both," and in due course gained a Craven Scholarship, a First Class in Moderations, and a First Class in Greats, following which successes he was elected a Fellow of New College.

After a year of Continental travel and study, he returned to Oxford as a Greats tutor. Gilbert Murray found him "pining for a field of work with more life in it and a clearer prospect of effectiveness." Heath reacted strongly from the ties of teaching those "who had already been well schooled." Like some other good Oxford minds of his day, he was attracted by the aims of the Workers' Educational Association, founded in 1902 to extend university facilities into areas of society that otherwise could have no access to them. He was on the point of making a decision about his future when war came. His home being at Bromley, he joined the Royal West Kent Regiment, spending his last evening in college "playing his beloved German music on the piano." (Murray).

He wrote from the front to another Fellow of his College: "I do certainly think that the French and English are fighting for what I should call toleration and decency in international relations, and England at any rate is carrying on her traditional opposition to any Power that tries to dominate the Continent. But what is the good of treating the Germans as aliens to a civilisation for which they have provided half the science and more than half the music?" To his mother he wrote:

"I would like to hope that my love of music might be for those who love and survive me more than a memory of something past, a power that can enhance for them the beauty of music itself. Or, again, we love the South Down country. Now I would hate to think that, if I died, the 'associations' would make these hills 'too painful' for you, as people sometimes say. I would like to think the opposite, that the joy I had in the Downs might not merely be remembered by you as a fact in the past, but rather be, as it were, transfused into you and give a new quality of happiness to your holidays there . . . Will you at least try, if I am killed, not to let things I have loved cause you pain, but rather to get increased enjoyment from the Sussex Downs, or from J. singing folk songs, because I have such joy in them, and in that way the joy I have found can continue to live." He further besought his mother:

"Again, do not have all this solemn funeral music, Dead Marches, and so on, played over me as if to proclaim that all has now come to an end, and nothing better remains to those who loved one than a dignified sorrow. I would rather have the Dutch Easter Carol, where the music gives you the idea of life and joy springing up continually. Please forgive me if I have worried you by all this talk. If we loved one another less I could not have written this, and, just because we love one another, I cannot bear to think that, if I died, I should only give you trouble and sorrow."[1]

He wrote to Gilbert Murray: "These are days when men should be born without mothers." He was often troubled by doubt whether his courage and endurance would be equal to the strain of trench life. Gilbert Murray said that "he was like the Brave Man in Aristotle who knows that danger is dangerous, and fears it, but goes through with it because he knows that he ought." In the fighting at Loos later that year the 6th Royal West Kents were ordered to forestall what

[1] *Letters of A. G. Heath* (Blackwell, 1917).

150

appeared to be an imminent German attack in front of Vermelles. The men were worn out by an incessant bombardment and for them the assignment was a difficult one. As they went forward, Heath was shot through the neck. "Don't bother about me," he told some of the men of his platoon who gathered round him. He died almost at once. He was 28.

> Far off we hear your music echoing yet;
> And we forget
> That you are silent for us, save in dreams . . .[1]

3

An unprecedented break occurred in the five-hundred-years-old connection between Winchester College and Oxford University. No Wykehamist went up to Oxford at the beginning of the new academic year. Of the 549 Old Wykehamists who left Winchester during the previous six years, 531 were serving in 1915 in His Majesty's Forces or had served until they fell.

Winchester had its lithic reminders of earlier sacrifices in its Crimean Porch and its South African Gate. The imagination of one of its doomed sons encompassed a more imposing vision. Douglas Gillespie, of the Argyll and Sutherland Highlanders, wrote from the trenches to Dr. Rendall, the Headmaster, proposing a Sacred Way for the pilgrims of peace in the years to come.

"In May the fruit blossom was beautiful where our trenches ran through an orchard, and we used to go back at night to a ruined village and plunder the gardens in order to make our own. So we have rose trees, too, and pansies and lily of the valley, but not in this unquiet corner where I am at present; for here the Germans are

---

[1] *To A. G. H.*, by J. G. Mann.

151

almost on three sides of us, and the dead have been buried just where they fell. There are graves scattered up and down, some with crosses and names upon them, some nameless and unmarked—as I think my brother's grave must be, for they have been fighting round the village where he was killed.

"I wish that when the peace comes our Government might combine with the French Government to make one long avenue between the lines from the Vosges to the sea, or, if that is too much, from La Bassée to Ypres. The ground is so pitted and scarred and torn with shells and tangled with wire that it will take years to bring it back to use again; but I would make a fine broad road in the No-Man's-Land between the lines, with paths for pilgrims on foot, and plant trees for shade, and fruit trees, so that the soil should not be altogether waste. Some of the shattered farms might be left as evidence, and the regiments might put up their records beside the trenches which they held all through the winter. Then I would like to send every man, woman and child in Western Europe on pilgrimage along that Via Sacra, so that they might think and learn what war means from the silent witnesses on either side. A sentimental idea, perhaps, but we might make it the most beautiful road in all the world."[1]

Gillespie, from Linlithgow, was one of the band of scholars of Gilbert Murray's proud remembrance. He was Ireland Scholar of his year and carried much else before him at Oxford, as he had at Winchester. One of his intimates there was Cyril Asquith, who wrote that "he had all I value most—kindness, intelligence, sympathy, taste, humour, wisdom, vitality, and a certain moral elevation." That is a sum of excellence endorsed by more than a loyal friend, who never doubted that

[1] *Letters from Flanders,* by A. D. Gillespie (John Murray).

152

"the State lost in him just the type of servant it can least afford to sacrifice."

He was reading for the Bar, intending to make international law his special study. He was at first refused a commission because of defective eyesight and he enlisted as a private in one of the new battalions of the Seaforth Highlanders. The heavy losses among junior officers led to his being offered a commission towards the end of 1914. Within two months he was a platoon commander in France. "I was always proud to be your son," he had written to his mother, "but you have made me prouder than ever. My greatest help will always be to think of you at home, for whatever comes I shall be ready for it ... When a man is fighting for his country in a war like this the news is always good if his spirit does not fail, and that I hope will never happen to your son."

Writing home in May, he told how the previous night in the trenches he had heard the nightingale. "There was something infinitely sweet and sad about it, as if the countryside were singing gently to itself, in the midst of all our noise and confusion and muddy work; so that you felt that the nightingale's song was the only real thing which would remain when all the rest was long past and forgotten." He thought of "all the men who had been killed in battle—Hector and Achilles and all the heroes of long ago, who were once so strong and active, and are now so quiet. Gradually the night wore on, until the day began to break, and I could see clearly the daisies and buttercups in the long grass about my feet. Then I gathered my platoon together, and marched back past the silent farms to our billets."

Nine days before his death in action that year he wrote in a last letter: "I met young Quiller-Couch, who used to be at Winchester with me, and twenty yards farther on there was another link with the literary world, the grave of Marion Crawford, the novelist's son, a lieu-

153

tenant in the Irish Guards. Today I see from a paragraph that G. L. Cheesman has been killed at the Dardanelles, a very great loss to New College and to me. He was a most loyal and honest friend and gave everyone who knew him something of his passion for learning, and hatred of repeating other people's ideas at second-hand. He was a really fine historian and, by the irony of fate, he had a great respect for Germans and German scholarship. But, like many scholars, he had an intense admiration for men of action, especially for the Romans and the Roman Army, which was his great subject. I know he entered on this expedition to the Dardanelles with double zest, because he was fighting on historic ground, to win back the Roman capital from the Turk. Now he lies like a scholar and a soldier beside the Hellespont; but for me he will always haunt those rooms at New College where I have talked with him so often far into the night. He wrote to me from his troopship on the way out, saying how different we shall all be when we meet there again. It's true, but I'm afraid the half of us will not be there at all."[1]

Cheesman's last letter to Gilbert Murray was in defence of the Turks against some prevalent misconception. Remembering him, Murray also recalled in that penumbra of regret three other New College men who gave their lives that year: Leslie Hunter, R. C. Woodhead and Philip Brown. "All left an impression of extraordinary and yet unconscious high-mindedness. No grossness or graspingness ever found a foothold among them, no germ of that hate which rejoices to believe evil and to involve good things with bad." Leslie Hunter, on the day before he was killed, spoke to a friend of his presentiment that he was soon to die. He lay for a while in a meadow behind the lines "singing a favourite German song." Woodhead, waiting to advance under

[1] *Letters from Flanders.*

154

machine-gun fire and knowing that the first to rise would be a certain victim, chose carefully the moment and rose first among his men, and fell to rise no more. The only words that Philip Brown spoke after he was mortally wounded were of thought and praise for his batman.

And here for dear dead brothers we are weeping,
Mourning the withered rose of chivalry,
Yet, their work done, the dead are sleeping, sleeping
Unconscious of the long lean years to be.[1]

4

Sweethearts, wives and sisters were being taken to see Laurette Taylor in *Peg o' My Heart* at the Globe Theatre; Potash & Perlmutter at the Queen's; *Raffles* (with Gerald du Maurier) at Wyndham's; *The Man Who Stayed At Home* (with Dennis Eadie) at the Royalty. Some theatres advertised "Evening dress is optional but not fashionable." At His Majesty's, Sir Herbert Beerbohm Tree was playing Mr. Micawber in *David Copperfield*. At The Haymarket, the cast of *The Flag Lieutenant* included Allen Aynesworth, Ellis Jeffreys and Godfrey Tearle.

Elsie Janis, Arthur Playfair, Gwendoline Brogden, Nelson Keys and Basil Hallam were the stars of *The Passing Show of 1915* at the Palace Theatre. At the Alhambra, Madame Rejane, who had won fame in *The Lady of the Camellias*, was in a programme with Violet Vanbrugh, Arthur Bourchier, Malcolm Scott, Florence Smithson, Will Evans and G. H. Elliott, "The Chocolate Coloured Coon." Maskelyne & Devant's mysteries were at St. George's Hall. "Clarice Mayne & That" were at the Palladium with Sam Mayo and the Two Bobs. Harry

[1] The *Wykehamist*, July 31, 1917.

Tate was in *Business As Usual* at the Hippodrome. There were as yet no cinema circuits. Some of the West End theatres, including the Theatre Royal, Drury Lane, were being equipped to show the great silent epics coming from Hollywood: *Intolerance, The Birth of a Nation* and *Broken Blossoms*.

For want of more useful employment, John Buchan, the romantic novelist and war historian (later Lord Tweedsmuir) was lecturing on the war at the Bechstein Hall (now the Wigmore Hall). "Mr. Herbert G. Ponting's Thrilling Story and Complete Moving Picture Record, *With Captain Scott in the Antarctic*," was being presented twice daily at the Philharmonic Hall. The snows had closed over the lost explorers in their tent only three years before. Captain Oates's soldierly self-sacrifice was being hallowed by that of the generation that had been most moved and inspired by it.

Avant garde art, exhibited at the Goupil Galleries, included new works by Wyndham Lewis and Edward Wadsworth, "whose pictures," *The Times* art critic wrote, "are not so much pictures as theories illustrated in paint." Another of the group, the angriest young man of his day, C. R. W. Nevinson, showed a battle study, *Return to the Trenches*, which suggested, said the critic, that "he himself has begun to return from the wilderness of abstractions."

Varnishing day at the Royal Academy that year was notable for "the complete absence of young painters with flowing hair, eccentric neckties and velvet jackets. The atmosphere of the studios was missing."—*The Times*. The artists seen at Burlington House that day were "bronzed of face, alert in bearing and garbed in khaki." Some of them drilled in the courtyard as members of a volunteer battalion called the United Arts which trained a succession of officers for the new armies.

War subjects were foremost among the attractions

156

"on the line" when the Academy opened to the public: "Ypres Cathedral After the Bombardment," "Homeless: The Refugees of War," "Coldstream Guards at Landrecies; 25th August, 1914." "The Bombardment of the Hartlepools; December 16th, 1914," and "The *Lion* in the North Sea Fight; January 25th, 1915." The note of truth, so conscientiously striven for by the painters of those works, proved elusive. No easels had been set up on the battlefield or on the decks of warships.

Lady Butler, whose celebrated battlepiece, "The Roll Call," was first exhibited as far back as 1874, was showing her latest work, "The Cuirassiers' Last Reveille," at the Leicester Galleries. An historical footnote to military glory was supplied that month by the death of the widow of Lord Cardigan, of Balaclava fame.

Anti-German riots, provoked by the sinking of the *Lusitania*, disgraced a vaunted English virtue. At Gravesend, soldiers with fixed bayonets were sent to disperse a mob of dock workers who were wrecking and looting the premises of German shopkeepers, many long naturalised. The entire stock of a furniture shop was pitched into the river. A protesting citizen was thrown through a plate-glass window and seriously injured. Dachshund owners were stared at suspiciously and their pets kicked in the streets. *The Graphic* published seven new lists of alien names that had been changed for English ones.

To the editor of *The Times*:

Sir—There are 40,000 Germans at liberty in England —free to plot and spy. German prisoners on the *Aurania*, moored off Netley Hospital in the Solent, are kept so little in order that recently, when a large fleet of transports carrying our brave soldiers passed by, the Germans booed and hooted and yelled at them! If this sort of thing is punished by death in Germany, why is it not punished by death here? How much longer are our rulers going to delay justice? An eye for an eye, a tooth for a tooth, is the old law of Moses.

Yours very truly,

LUCY BYRON

Byron Cottage,
Hampstead Heath.

It was remarkable (and many censors in the field confirmed it) how little of that kind of resentment was shown in the letters written by serving soldiers. A minister of religion noted in 1915: 'I have on my table letters from almost every camp in England, from Scotland, from Egypt and the front. I search in vain for one bitter or angry word against Germany."

Hate, preached from pulpits and inflamed by newspapers, was not in the English soldier's code. For him, it lay at the bottom of a deeper well than truth. Like General Lee, in the American Civil War, he did not wish his enemies dead. He wished that "they were all at home attending to their business and leaving us to attend to ours." The editor of *Punch*, Sir Owen Seaman, having declared his feelings against "the Huns," wrote the lines:

> *But where you have met your equals,*
> *Gun for gun and man for man,*
> *We have noticed other sequels,*
> *It was always you that ran.*

He was rebuked by A. G. Gardiner, editor of the *Daily News*, who pointed out that the War Office had just issued a dispatch which praised the devotion of a German officer who, "remaining alone at his battery, served a field-gun single-handed, until killed. The great bravery of this officer aroused the admiration of all ranks."

158

CHAPTER TWELVE

Hotspur's Flame of Life

1

JULIAN GRENFELL died of wounds, May 26, 1915, a day of deep shadow for those who had known him and, because of the glamour of his name, for many who had not. In his last conscious hours he spoke in a weak voice with "overpowering longing" his favourite lines from Hippolytus: *O for a deep and dewy spring, With runlets cool to draw and drink, And a great meadow blossoming, Long-grassed, and poplars in a ring, to rest me by the brink . . .*

His soldier's life was but one side of "one of the most complete Englishmen ever to come from Oxford," scholar, artist, poet, sportsman. His *Into Battle* was acclaimed as "the one incorruptible and incomparable poem which the war has yet given us in any language." (*Morning Post*). During the week of April 1915 in which he wrote it, he knocked out two professional boxers in contests behind the lines in France. One of his women friends, Viola Tree, said that his boxing had given him the look of a faulty Greek statue, "with bits chipped off its face."

He had something of Hotspur's flame of life, an Elizabethan in spirit and style whose silver spoon was designed and chased for supping with the sublime company at the Mermaid. Born to privilege, he remained true to his estate, a debonair steward of the values of *noblesse oblige*. Yet he had his own views about how life should be lived, as Raymond Asquith said, knowing him not intimately but admiringly, "His thoughts seemed always to be a genuine part of himself because they were his and not another's" Again, it was Raymond Asquith who wrote: "There was something primitive in Julian, a simplicity, force, and directness which were almost savage, but tempered with a natural courtesy and grace which gave him the finest manners and a smile which was indescribably charming and intimate. The union in him of strength and grace, of fierceness and sweetness, was a thing which we can record but only he could express."[1] Grenfell wrote to his mother from Oxford when he was 21:

"Character is *the* thing that you can make and mould for yourself; it is the result of continuous working upon the faculties which one starts with. The faculties may be chance, but character is the exact opposite of chance, every single thing you do influences it, it is the net result of what you have been doing by choice since you were born. I think that 'dedication, devotion and service' *are* very near to the roots of it." He was not taking a pot-shot at the behaviourists, then prominent on the skyline of the philosophies. He was thinking thoughts that, as Asquith said, were a genuine part of himself.

For Viola Meynell, the novelist and poet, he had "such shining qualities of youth, such strength and courage and love, that to others who are young he seems like the perfection of themselves." A respected war correspondent and chronicler of the English countryside, Sir William Beach Thomas, saw in him "the supreme type of his race, in body, in character and in mind."

At Balliol, as at Eton, he was at the centre of a group whose appetite for life now seems to have been ravenous because they were to have so few years in which to in-

[1] *Pages from a Family Journal: 1888-1915.*

dulge it. The physical and intellectual excitability of some among them was exceptional if not preternatural. Julian Grenfell's pugnacious vitality, symbolised and perhaps too often reinforced by his Australian stockwhip with its fifteen-foot lash, with which he could produce the highly professional double-crack, was countered by gentler qualities that gave depth and substance to his poetic impulses. His friends could speak of his "great tenderness of heart," and of his "in some ways, very humble disposition."[1] His brother Billy wrote of "the mysticism and idealism, and that strange streak of melancholy, which underlay Julian's war-whooping, sun-bathing, fearless exterior."[2]

His Eton and Oxford contemporary, Patrick Shaw-Stewart, said that "Julian, when leaving Eton, was equally and enormously fired by Keats, a roebuck, a summer's day, and the genius of Ronnie Knox." Recalling that Julian Grenfell and himself and others of the set went up from Eton "with a private philosophy, something between a pose and a creed," Ronald Knox said that for Grenfell physical excellence was a duty, "the noble savage expressing himself, as far as could be, under nineteenth-century conditions." It was a cult that more than once brought him to the edge of a health breakdown. Monsignor Knox remembered him holding forth, "like a missionary," on the glories of the short-arm balance, indicating a certain muscle just above the hip which, he said, was essential to proper physical development. "He had the Greek love of form but not for its own sake. His interests were not athletic; he did not care who won. Strength, speed, and skill were to him the assertion of the dignity of man." (Knox.) There was a story that he gave up playing poker because a

[1] Charles Lister, writing to Julian Grenfell's mother, Lady Desborough.
[2] Letter to Mrs. Harry Lindsay.

man of inferior physique won $14.00 from him.

His abounding vitality could overpower himself as it did others, by whom he was known as "The Rough Man" and sometimes addressed as "Roughers." He was continually putting up his fists. He wrote to tell his mother in the Balliol years about "a fearful row" he had with a cabman who demanded "a preposterous fare." Grenfell pulled him down from his cab and gave him "a good shaking," afterwards wondering why he had been "so passionately angry" at being over-charged a shilling.

From his Oxford recollections, Sir Lawrence Jones wrote of Julian Grenfell "driving Philip Sassoon out of College, cracking the prodigious lash within inches of Sassoon's sleek head."[1] Quoting that account, an historian of Eton ascribes the episode to Grenfell's dislike of Sassoon's "alien blood."[2] That may not be a fair deduction. Sassoon later wrote in admiration of Grenfell, who, it is known, was irritated by Sassoon's sybaritic tastes as exhibited in the furnishing of his rooms in College. "Julian did everything, and shone in them all. He rowed, hunted, read, roared with laughter, cracked his whip in the quad all night, bought greyhounds, boxed all the local champions, capped poetry with the most precious of the dons, and charmed everybody, from the Master of Balliol to the ostlers at the Randolph."[3]

His brother Billy wrote to their mother in 1909: "Julian has been too glorious, and I spend most of my days with him. He is quite madly and splendidly wrapped up in sport, repelling with a savage intensity all feminine overtures. We have the most splendid talks about Free Love, Socialism, and Philosophy . . . He is a splendid creature, as beautiful as a panther, and no woman can resist him for 10 seconds. I wish I did not

[1] L. E. Jones: *An Edwardian Youth* (Macmillan, 1956).
[2] Christopher Hollis: *Eton.*
[3] L. E. Jones: *An Edwardian Youth.*

162

feel such a centipede beside him." Julian told his mother: "Time forces on me the conclusion that Bill is the only man with whom life is always quite perfect."

2

Controversial clashes often entered into the relationship between Julian Grenfell and his mother, a woman of charm, wit and social finesse whom he devotedly admired. They were frequently in argument on more than petty issues. "Madam," he wrote to her with mock *gravitas* in 1909, "on mature consideration, I have come to the conclusion that our differences of view with regard to the moral sanction, Good and Evil, and social conventions, are such as to make further intercourse impossible between us, and I think that such a decision ought, in order to save confusion, to be made public as soon as possible." He developed antipathies to the social round that constantly preoccupied her. It led to what he liked to call "ructions," states of tension in which he would affirm his preference for "half a dozen friends instead of fifty acquaintances."

He was apt to wear the pugilist's frown in company that he did not find congenial. It was said that he disliked people he did not know. Criticising an acquaintance, he wrote: "I liked him very much sometimes when he was a long way off, and I liked being told the things he said. But I didn't like the way he walked, even when he was walking away. I didn't like his hands, or his feet, or his dislike of dogs."

Coming down from Balliol in 1910, he was commissioned in a crack regiment, the 1st Dragoon Guards, and went with them to India in 1911. There were ceremonial goings-on for the visit of the German Crown Prince. Grenfell wrote home: "We were all rather weary

of bowing and scraping. My Democratic principles get
roused at 11 p.m. At 12, I am a Socialist, and at 1 o'clock
I am an Anarchist." He asked his mother in a letter
written to her at Taplow Court, Maidenhead, from South
Africa in 1913: "Did you ever get the misgiving that
'big houses' are a thing of the past?"

He was on overseas duty with his regiment, training
on the veldt, helping to keep the peace when riots
followed labour troubles in Johannesburg. He wrote to
his mother : "Yes, I am glad with all my heart we had
such ructions, but I wish that I had been a little older;
I should have put up a much better game for you at my
maturer age." In another letter to her: "I want to ask
for such a lot of things," he wrote, and made a light-
hearted inventory of them. His sister, Lady Salmond,
remembers that the blanks in the malefic lines were
filled in with the names of "boring or pompous people
he knew."

Faith
Hope
Charity
Someone to buy my ponies
A grand passion
A new face
A beautiful soul
More love of my fellow-men
Death of—
Death of—
$700
Small feet and hands
Gentleness
Quick repartee
Less appetite
Polished manners of a true gentleman
Truth, sudden discovery of the

Boots, Polo, new
Life, theory of, new
Books, old
Books, new
Death of—

He was already a poet, who at that time revealed himself more intimately in his letters. "I hate material books centred on whether people are successful. I like books about artists and philosophers and dreamers, and anybody who is a little off his dot. I agree with what you say about success, but I like the people best who take it as it comes, or doesn't come, and are busy about unpractical and ideal things in their heart of hearts all the time."

The winter before the war, he thought of giving up soldiering and living the life of an artist in Paris. "I strongly dissuaded him from his artistic leanings," Charles Lister told a friend of them both. "He is such an obvious soldier." Most of the soldier poets of the war would have warranted the suspicion of the old canteen woman in Stendhal's *Chartreuse de Parme* when she told Fabrice : "You are no soldier; you have never been a soldier." She would have had no such intuition about Julian Grenfell.

3

The joyous side of his nature appears in a letter that he wrote not long before the war. "I'm reading the 'Brothers Kmarevitchskopdonpskinrenzen;'[1] it's good, isn't it? I love it. I got muddled up between the names at first, so I made a list. Then they all had three names, used alternately, so I made a second list. Then he began

[1] *The Brothers Karamazov* by Dostoievsky.

calling them by pet names, so I made a glossary, with numbers. And now he has started trying all the possible permutations and combinations of the fifteen names, and varying the characters slightly for each new combination, but he cannot trip me, no, not he." And a few days later: "Oh, I *do* love the 'Brothers Pavvalofitch-kop,'—more and more, every page that I read. It makes me love the Russians too. I believe they are really like that, aren't they?"

On July 2, 1914, he wrote to his mother: "I'm thrilled by the scandals in high life. What a far, far better thing it is not to get married. Marriage is such a short-odds gamble."

The regiment was still in South Africa when the war started. "It must be wonderful to be in England now," he wrote on August 6, 1914. "I suppose the excitement is beyond all words? And don't you think it has been a wonderful and almost incredible rally to the Empire, with Redmond and the Hindus and Will Crooks and the Boers and South Fiji islanders all aching to come and throw stones at the Germans? It reinforces one's belief in the Old Flag and the Mother Country and the Heavy Brigade and the Thin Red Line, and all the Imperial idea, which gets rather shadowy in peace time, don't you think?"

The Royal Dragoons reached France at the end of the Retreat. Julian Grenfell still hoped, even longed, to see action as a cavalryman, towards which his military training was directed. "It is horrible having to leave one's horse. It feels like leaving half oneself behind." He had the consolation of his greyhounds, a breed of dog that had "his special fondness," said Ronald Knox, because of "their perfect architecture—no waste of material, no false proportions, a complete coursing-machine." Their kind had been with him at Oxford, in India, in South Africa, Now, Dawn, Dusk, Hammer,

Tongs and Toby were with him in France, looked after by a French farmer's wife behind the lines when their master was at the fighting. There was a memory of him lying "dead asleep" among some straw bales in the sunshine, after coming out of the line, his devoted "long dogs" grouped around him, like a freshly woven Gobelins subject.

Exulting in war, insisting that it suited his "stolid health and stolid nerves and barbaric disposition," Julian Grenfell could agree also that it was hateful. In one of his letters he showed how completely he could steel himself to ruthless action. "I crawled through sodden clay, going about a yard a minute, and looking and listening. I took about 30 minutes to do 30 yards." He was then within ten yards of the enemy position. He crawled right up to the parapet, where he saw a German "laughing and talking. I saw his teeth glistening against my rifle sight and I pulled the trigger very slowly. He just grunted and crumpled up." His reconnaissance enabled an impending attack to be met with confidence and success. "We simply mowed them down. It was rather horrible." He was awarded the Distinguished Service Order.

"I *was* pleased with my troop under bad fire. They used the most awful language, talking quite quietly, and laughing all the time, even after men were knocked over within a yard of them. I longed to be able to say that I liked it, after all one has heard about being under fire . . . I pretended to myself that I liked it for a bit but it was no good." (Letter, November 4, 1914).

On February 15, 1915, he was in trenches where the Germans were no more than fifteen yards away. "The drawback is that in the parapet there are buried very, very shallow, poor dead Huns and French and English, whose bodies are periodically resurrected by the rain, and bombs and bullets . . . You should have seen our men setting out for the trenches. Absolutely radiant with excitement and joy at getting back to the fight again! I do love fighting, even sedentary fighting; but I wish I was a foot-slogger now."

He had been offered a job on the staff. "I should not like it nearly so well as roughing it here with my own friends and my own men." On February 26, he applied, unsuccessfully, for transfer to the Guards. "Just think of the incredible glory of being a Guardee, and being privileged to create an uproar in a box at *Floradora*, and to marry a chorus-girl, not only with impunity, but with added lustre!"

After two days leave in Paris in April, 1915, he wrote: "I do like the French people." Their capital city—"Isn't it gloriously light and gay and beautiful?" He was struck by "the light-heartedness of it all, the complete *joie-de-vivre* of the place and the people," who, he thought, were so much "lighter of heart than ours are and really much more natural; and such artists in fun." Through all the gaiety ran "the tremendous tension of War," writing his fleeting impressions as if he had come fresh from reading *Vanity Fair*: "I saw a bit of everything—High Society, and the artists, and the Racing Set, and the boxers, and the nuts, and the actresses, and all the different very strictly defined classes in their own particular places. Isn't the Sunday crowd good, walking about and watching each other and enjoying each other?"

He had received a Gibbs rifle with its telescopic sight, a present from his father. "What a wonderful thing it is, the telescopic sight. It will be just the thing for loop-hole shooting, waiting till the face appears and drawing a bead . . . I went into one of the forward dressing stations. A tiny hovel of a farm, 5 doctors, and the bad cases coming in and going out on the stretchers, everything chock-a-block. How *marvellously* brave and cheerful the wounded English Tommy is. And what a fine class of men the Territorial Tommies, quite different from our men of course." (May 8, 1915).

4

Just before midnight on May 15, 1915, a telegram was received at Taplow Court from Monica Grenfell who was nursing at No. 7 General Hospital, Boulogne. It told their parents that Julian had been slightly wounded near Ypres two days before. He was in the hospital at Boulogne and likely to be sent home in the next hospital ship. On May 14, he had written to his mother: "We are practically wiped out; but we charged and took the Hun trenches yesterday. I stopped a Jack Johnson with my head, and my skull is slightly cracked. But I'm getting on splendidly. They said I did well. *All, all* love. —JULIAN OF THE HARD HEAD."

His last day's fighting had been on May 13 near the Ypres-Menin road. A hillock, known for two days as "the hill of death," was under constant shell fire from the enemy. Grenfell volunteered for observation duty from that hazardous vantage point. He reported back to his colonel, George Steele. "He was pleased with me. He got me a whisky-and-soda himself." Colonel Steele was killed within a few hours. Grenfell next volunteered to take a message to the North Somerset Yeomanry in the front line, where they and other units of the 6th Cavalry Brigade were holding trenches near Hooge Lake. The 1st Royal Dragoons, Grenfell's regiment, were in support. Troops on the left of the line had been forced back. Grenfell went up the little hill again to try to discover how far the line had been breached and what the Germans were doing about it. One of the yeomanry officers, Wilfrid Ricardo, saw him "walking very coolly, under very heavy fire." Later in the day, he returned to

169

the hill with the brigadier, General Campbell. A shell splinter struck him in the head. He felt his feet go suddenly cold and told the General: "Go down, sir, don't bother about me. I'm done." It went round the regiment that he remarked "quite cheerfully," that he thought he would die. "You see if I don't," he said when a brother officer protested.

X-ray examination revealed fracture of the skull and laceration of the brain; the shell splinter had penetrated one-and-a-half inches. An operation was done under the supervision of a leading Army consultant, Sir Anthony Bowlby. His parents were advised by telegram: "Better come." They were given Admiralty permission to make the crossing in a ship loaded with ammunition. Three of his friends were in the hospital: Edward Horner, desperately wounded; Rex Benson, wounded and badly gassed; Lord Wendover, who died of his wounds in the next few days. Two other friends were killed while he was in the hospital, John Bigge and Clement Mitford.

The head wound turned septic and a second operation was performed. "He prayed a great deal, asked for psalms and hymns to be sung, and George Herbert's poems to be recited. "Am I going off my rocker?" he asked the surgeons. "*I* thought I was." "Why don't you *argue*?" he asked his mother. To his father he said: "It will soon be over now; only two or three days," correctly numbering them. "Hold my hand before I go," he bade his mother and raised hers to his lips with the last vestige of his strength. His "most radiant smile" as he died left them with an unfading memory.

He was buried in the soldiers' cemetery on the hill above Boulogne on May 28. No mourning was worn. His parents went to rest in the forest of Hardelot, near by. There, the next day, their second son Billy suddenly appeared before them like an apparition. His battalion of The Rifle Brigade had landed in France a fortnight

170

before. He had been given three hours' leave from the front. They never saw him again.

<h1 style="text-align:center">5</h1>

Another life of promise was ended on May 26 when Norman Crawford Maclehose was killed at Festubert after holding a trench under attack through a long night. He was the son of an Edinburgh ophthalmic surgeon and a grandson of Alexander Macmillan, the publisher. "A shy but very resolute honesty of mind made him slow to accept any unfamiliar view; he fought against novelties until he was sure of their value. Behind a cautious, sceptical and hesitating manner there was not only a strong will but a large reserve of impetuosity."[1]

His sense of community obligation was unusually strong. After Oxford, he lived for the greater part of a year in Whitechapel, organising evening classes for young workers and starting a social club for them. He sought and secured a post in a department administering the new unemployment insurance scheme and read law to fit himself more thoroughly for that work. It was as an act of social responsibility that he joined the Territorials and gave up his summer holidays to train with them. In the war he served with one of the oldest volunteer battalions, the Post Office Rifles (8th London), founded in 1868 by General Post Office staff men who had been special constables during the Fenian outbreaks of a few years earlier. He was 26.

John Allen, aged 28, was one of the younger members of the Round Table group of political idealists who drew their inspiration from the able intellects that surrounded Milner as High Commissioner in South Africa. A Bar student from New Zealand, he was "set upon learning

[1] *Balliol War Memorial Book.*

above all things how to speak in public." He spent his Sundays in London listening to sermons. He went regularly to the theatre to hear the silver tongues of the great actors. He took elocution lessons at the Men's College in Mornington Crescent, N.W. He played truant from the Temple chambers in which he was a pupil to sit in the gallery of the House of Commons or to hear famous counsel on their feet at the Law Courts. "I wanted to see how it was done and do it—how I wanted to do it!" he wrote. "On London pavements, in the bare countryside, on a rock on a Brittany beach, imitating those masters of the human voice—never for a moment was my discipleship anything but a pleasure." He declared that he wanted to be able to speak more than he wanted food and drink. "Most of us have some secret and sustaining delights; that was mine. Only a convulsion could have ended my preoccupation."

The convulsion of 1914 hit him hard, he said, "not in pocket or position, but it hit me there. The willing sacrifice of it was my little contribution to England." He joined the Inns of Court O.T.C. At the end of the day's drill he went to the Royal Colonial Institute to read biography, preferably of great men who were also great orators. "In the evening I would mount a bus and ride through the Haymarket, Piccadilly Circus, Regent Street, and Oxford Street," to the Marble Arch, where rhetoric was more common than oratory. "The newspaper placards," he wrote, "the recruiting notices, and an unwonted number of figures in khaki, were the only visible comments on the giant grapple of steel and souls less than a hundred miles away."

Through the Inns of Court training battalion he obtained a commission in the Worcestershires and with them he went to Gallipoli in May 1915. "I don't remember ever visualising what trench life was like except that speaking generally it could not be called pleasant. I now

172

know it to be an unimaginable mixture of horror, strain, discomfort, and fineness." (May 28, 1915). He recalled reading casualty lists at home with sympathy but without intense feeling. Now, he found it impossible to describe his emotion at the sight of suffering men—"nothing can convey it to you." He saw a man bend and fall, after giving "two short surprised coughs." Another soldier "darted to him, opened his tunic and said: 'You're done, Ginger, you're done; they've got you'."

He wrote six days before he was killed: "I always was an optimist. I have never lost faith in human nature. Now I know I was right . . . It has been heart-breaking seeing men one had got to like only in a day or so killed —or worse, receive wounds of which they have died. It has been bad enough for me. It is unspeakably worse for those who have been their soldier friends, who have drilled, slept, eaten, worked and now died together. The men have had twelve days in the trenches and are now shaken in morale. A groaning, tortured man lying below you in a trench is not pleasant company. The men talk about wounds and dead men all day. It was getting on their nerves—remember Wellington's observation that every man in uniform is not a hero. When a man is hit, their way of putting it is that he had ceased to reign— so many kingdoms of this sort have been shattered lately."[1]

6

"We have a good line now. The parapet is high, perhaps five feet above ground level, built of sandbags and banked up behind with earth, four feet thick at the top and anything over ten feet at the bottom." Denis Oliver ("Dobbin") Barnett, of The Leinster Regiment,

[1] From *John Allen of the Gallant Company* (Arnold).

was writing to reassure his mother. (The mothers had constantly to be reassured). "It is lovely sitting in the sun, listening to the cock chaffinches and yellowhammers tuning up. There's nothing like spring air to take you away and back," thinking of his home at Yattendon, Berkshire. He could say that trench life in the spring "is really very nice—barring the smells, which begin to get offensive. We've got lots of quicklime now, and are disposing of heaps of old bodies." (May 29, 1915).

He had been Senior Scholar at St. Paul's School four years before, admired for "his fine brain, powerful physique, complete moral and physical courage, charming frankness of manner and absolute straightness of character." In 1914, he was Scholar-elect of Balliol. He enlisted in the Artists' Rifles and went to France with them before receiving his commission with the Leinsters. He was killed at Poperinghe later that year, aged 20.

School magazines, the few that survived, recorded gallantries in action, decorations, casualties, and Old Boys' nostalgia. *The Portcullis*, published for Emanuel School, Wandsworth Common, S.W., printed a letter in 1915 from S.A.G. ("Sag") Harvey, "who was for us all a pattern of upright manliness," killed later in the war. "Dear old Emanuel, what a treasure house of happy memories! There are no Sundays out here but sometimes one suddenly realises that this twenty-four hours is Sunday," and he thinks of Emanuel chapel. "It is all so easy to picture—the mellow light, the choir, the old familiar faces in the old familiar pews, and S——, good old S——, tucked away in his corner, ready to lower the lights when the sermon begins . . . Thus one dreams, but the crackle of the machine-gun brings one back to earth, to remember that this is war, that just over there is the Hun and that between us there is but fifty yards of good French soil." The school was to add 93 other names to its Roll of Honour before the war ended.

174

The Fourth at Eton in 1915 was "like no other Fourth of June that has ever been." (*The Times*). There was no procession of boats, no band in the playing fields, no firework display, and strictly rationed strawberries and cream. The weather was poignantly perfect. Of the 2,210 Etonians who had gone on active service, 321 had fallen.

The fighting at Givenchy in mid-June, one of a series of minor offensives leading up to the disastrous denouement of Loos, produced an extraordinary reaction from a battalion of the subsequently famous 51st Highland Division, recruited from the central regions of Scotland. "An official letter was received from one of the units asking under what terms the Territorials had been enlisted for this war. In other words, when could the men take their discharge?"[1]

[1] Colonel W. N. Nicholson, C.M.G., D.S.O.: *Behind The Lines* (Cape, 1939).

CHAPTER THIRTEEN

"Goodbye . . . Bless You Always"

1

LETTERS FROM the front told of the rising exasperation of the soldiers in the field against the "slackers" at home. Rudyard Kipling wrote in the *Daily Telegraph* that "there is a great gulf opening between those who have joined and those who have not." *Embusques* in politics, in the law, in agriculture, in the arts, were a subject of scathing comment.

> *I wore a tunic,*
> *A dirty khaki tunic,*
> *And you wore civilian clothes.*
> *We fought and bled at Loos*
> *While you were on the booze,*
> *The booze that no one here knows.*
> *Oh, you were with the wenches*
> *While we were in the trenches*
> *Facing our German foe.*
> *Oh, you were a-slacking*
> *While we were attacking*
> *Down on the Menin Road.*[1]

Ramsay MacDonald was denounced as a traitor for political activities with the Independent Labour Party that made the men in the line feel that they were being

[1] Soldiers' song of the First World War, sung to the tune of *I Wore a Tulip*.

shot at from behind. Bertrand Russell, whose pacifism was resented by those for whom fate had reserved a crueller martyrdom than six months in jail, was commended to the attention of *Punch's* indispensable "Near-sighted Old Lady" who was shown poking her umbrella at a life-size cardboard effigy of Charlie Chaplin outside a "bioscope theatre"[1] and remarking: "A couple of months in the Army would make a man of him."

In earlier times, information about Englishmen available for war service was procured by "arraying the nation," the Commissioners of Array being the responsible authority. In 1915, the National Registration Act performed their function by requiring a return from every civilian male between 15 and 65. When the mass of particulars was sifted, it was seen that 1,800,000 men still shrank, for good reason or none, from putting on what William Hazlitt, meeting a soldier on the road between Wem and Salop, described as "the loathsome finery of the profession of blood."

The voluntary enlistment method was criticised with renewed bitterness. "The present system is grossly unfair to public-spirited young men because the shirkers and wasters reap the advantage of the patriotism of those who enlist."[2] Many were accepted whose experience would have been better employed in other branches of the war organisation. One of Rutherford's most brilliant young men at Cambridge, Harry Moseley, was killed as an infantry captain in the Dardanelles. He was the subject of an obituary notice in a German newspaper. Of another conspicuously misplaced volunteer it was said that "to use such a man as a subaltern was economically equivalent to using the *Lusitania* to carry a pound of butter from Ramsgate to Margate."

[1] As the first cinemas were called.
[2] Lord Denman, formerly Governor-General of Australia, where compulsory military service had been introduced.

A War Office order requiring recruits for the Territorials to agree to transfer to other regiments had bad local effects; for instance, in Lancashire. Lord Derby, whose name was about to be perpetuated in a context other than that of horse-racing, telegraphed angrily to Lord Kitchener about "the damned fool who made the order without consulting anybody connected with the Territorial Force." He wrote to Kitchener's private secretary "very confidentially" on July 5, 1915 : "Recruiting is dead as far as this part of the world is concerned. I have been today to see our 2nd line Territorial Units. They cannot get a single man. I confess it makes one despair as to the result of the war."[1]

Family allowance muddles were another unfavourable factor. So was the doctrinaire view that in a democracy every man must be as free to withhold his services as to offer them. It was still being expounded at the National Liberal Club. Not there was heard the far-off cry of Callinus of Ephesus at the approach of the Scythian hordes: "How long will you lie at ease, young men? When will you take courage to your souls?"

The "willing spirit" was by then almost a spent force. It was no longer capable of providing the great numbers of men required to maintain the new British Army as a fighting machine. Military historians recalled that Hannibal, captain of a great voluntary army, perished for lack of recruits, while the Roman legions were replenished with conscripts. A final big-scale advertising campaign was authorised. Its chief effect was to offend those people who considered national prestige to be hardly less important than man-power.

The tone of much of the publicity was deplorable. "Women of England! Do your duty! Send your Man *Today* To Join Our Glorious Army!" Another poster,

[1] *Lord Derby: King of Lancashire*, by Randolph S. Churchill (Heinemann, 1959).

178

"Be A Sport—Join Today!" was indignantly reported to have been seen on the walls of Windsor Castle. Eno's Fruit Salts sponsored a series of advertisements illustrated by a popular picture called *Follow the Drum,* with the text: "The British Empire! The Land of Beauty, Virtue, Valour, Truth. Oh! Who Would Not Fight For Such A Land! In Sad Or Glad Times, or All Times, Take Eno's!" Double-column spaces in the newspapers were filled with no less lamentable bathos.

The Men To Be Pitied!

How sad is the lot of men who cannot go! After the war *they* will be able to hold up their heads. *Their* women and children will be proud of them. But *he* —he who had no part in it—no crowds will cheer *him* in the streets. His lot is hard. He is to be pitied. Are *you* going to be pitied? Enlist today.

GOD SAVE THE KING!

Among the men secured by the relentless pressures of publicity were many who had nothing to give save unwilling obedience. A letter from a commanding officer was read out in a House of Commons speech. "I have any number of misfits, the halt, the lame, the blind, men who cannot march and even if carried to a trench could not see to shoot." It was reliably judged that at the least 200,000 radically unfit men were enlisted during the later recruiting drives of 1915.

Sir Thomas Oliver, M.D., Honorary Colonel of the 20th Northumberland Fusiliers (Tyneside Scottish) complained that medical examinations had become too casual. "Men were passed who had the sight of only one eye, hernia, varicose veins, advanced heart and lung diseases, hammer toes." Miners with weak knee-joints that were easily displaced were enlisted and many more with flat feet. Another commonly overlooked defect was nystagmus, the victims of which eye complaint were

179

likely to make dangerous sentries. For the record, Sir Thomas also stated that among 100,000 recruits who came forward from Tyneside there was remarkably little venereal disease and crime. Thirty per cent of the men aged 45 were rejected. Yet in the Scottish Horse and Lovat Scouts many of the fittest recruits were men of that age.

In *Problems in Eugenics* (1912), Professor Kellogg had stated that "the average height of the men of France began notably to decrease with the coming of age, in 1813 and after, of the young men born in the years of the Revolutionary Wars (1792–1802)." Of the biological implications of the First World War there was little printed discussion in its first years and it was not a foremost public topic at any time. One of the few attempted assessments of the possible physical consequences was ventured by a writer using the *nom de guerre* of "A British Captain" in an American magazine.[1]

"I have read much of the horror and sacrifice, yet the men I see round me prove that there are compensations. We may have lost a couple of hundred thousand men and we may lose half a million more, but against this must be balanced the three million new men who twelve months ago were living the life of cities and the rural life of selfish idleness or ill-paid toil. Some were clerks, others were shopmen, others were rustics not far removed from serfs. For nearly a year they have lived a man's life in the open and are twice the men they were. Striking a balance, it seems to me that with all our losses, past or to be, we British are something to the good and thus in losing we have gained immensely and that out of these present sorrows we may emerge stronger, saner and healthier than we have ever been before." Research would be unlikely to disclose a more speciously objective proposition at a time when so many pursuivants of

[1] *Atlantic Monthly,* July-December, 1915.

moral and intellectual probity were being wiped out.

A Cabinet committee, appointed to study manpower, interviewed the highest authorities, including Lord Kitchener himself, who was clearly confused by the recurring clashes of political opinion. With what was taken to be "ironic tact", he suggested in a speech that shyness was the cause of many young men holding back. He said that he intended to ask Parliament to sanction conscription. Lloyd George, the new Minister of Munitions, suggested that the French example was the model, rendering every man in certain age groups liable to service.

The committee found that enough men were available to provide seventy new divisions, thirty short of what was considered desirable in view of the mounting war momentum. There was no longer a realistic hope of getting them by the voluntary system. Whether the national resolution was failing, whether the people still did not grasp the mighty issues at stake, were unanswered questions. The debate on conscription blazed and crackled like a bonfire in a storm.

One of the opponents of compulsion was Lord Hugh Cecil. Dining in Cadogan Square, he listened to a bishop's denunciation of voluntary recruitment as "the grossest injustice" and answered it with the opinion that "there is nothing fine in killing, but there *is* something fine in being killed and conscription would take that away." Another of the company, Charles Whibley, who wrote *Musings Without Method*, in *Blackwood's*, snapped back at him: "Epicure! Do you want boys of eighteen slaughtered to satisfy your aesthetic greed?"

2

The early summer casualty lists were not so intimidatingly long as those of the spring, a merciful pause that autumn would savagely annul. Aberdeenshire lost one of its most progressive farmers, C. W. L. Fowlie, aged 40, of the 5th Gordon Highlanders (T.F.); All Souls, Oxford, a brilliant young Fellow, Alan Grey Hulton, who gained a First in Literae Humaniores at New College and the Eldon Law Scholarship, aged 29: "he resolved from the first day of the war to qualify as soon as he could for the firing line." Another loss to Oxford scholarship was Edward Giles Romanes, killed in the Dardanelles with the Worcestershire Regiment, aged 22.

Edinburgh Academy added to its Roll of Honour the name of Robert Patrick Haldane, 22, eldest son of the Crown Agent for Scotland and a nephew of Lord Haldane. "No man," it was written of him, "could hold out against his smile." He joined the 6th Black Watch and went to France with the Highland Division in May. A lance-corporal of his battalion wrote home: "The regiment was in a charge and lost heavily through machine-gun fire. Some of the men were caught up in the enemy's wire. He crawled under it, tearing his kilt to ribbons, and with his pocket filled with bombs mounted the German parapet, waved his cap for reinforcements and then threw his bombs. He received many bullet wounds, but not before he had accounted for many Germans."

On June 18, Flight Sub-Lieutenant Warneford, V.C., Royal Naval Air Service, was killed in France in a flying accident. Educated at Stratford-on-Avon Grammar School, he entered the merchant marine. He came home from Canada to enlist in the 2nd Sportsmen's Battalion in September 1914. He transferred to the R.N.A.S. and quickly got his flying certificate at Hendon. On June 7, he attacked a Zeppelin flying at 6,000 feet between the Belgian coast and Ghent. The airship was the largest of its type: 521 ft. in length, with a capacity of 953,000 cubic feet, carrying $1\frac{1}{4}$ tons of bombs. The resulting

182

explosion turned Warneford's Moraine monoplane up-side down, forcing him to land in enemy-held territory. He restarted his engine and escaped with just enough fuel in his tank to carry him over the lines into France.

He was summoned to Paris to receive the Cross of the Legion of Honour from the French War Minister, M. Millerand. During the visit, he was given a bunch of roses by an admirer in a restaurant. "What rejoicings there will be when you go home to London," the donor prophesied. Warneford answered gravely: "I have a strong feeling that I shall not get there." The fatal crash occurred the next day.

Gordon Mackenzie, Vancouver Regiment, a fruit farmer from British Columbia; David Russell, Post Office Rifles, from a solicitor's office in Gray's Inn; John Bolton, 5th East Lancashires, of the Cotton Spinners' Association; W. H. G. Roley, 3rd Yorkshire Regiment, of Barnsley—each had lost a brother in the war and all were themselves killed that month. Norman Victor Holden, 6th East Lancashire Fusiliers, was an assistant master at Manchester Grammar School: "a man of sterling worth who spent his whole powers in the service of his fellows." In that service he died in action, aged 25. Allen G. Tembath, 36, Civil Service Rifles, had played his last voluntary as organist of St. John the Baptist's, Isleworth. Wallace Moir Annand, 28, Collingwood Battalion, Royal Naval Division, would be seen no more at his desk in the offices of the Northern Press Company of South Africa.

Edward Laurence Sprunt, of Berkhamstead, was finishing his second year at Jesus College, Oxford, in 1914. He was offered a university commission. Instead, he chose to enlist as a private in the Honourable Artillery Company and went to France with them in the autumn. He was in the fighting at Messines. In June, 1915, he was again recommended for a commission. The War Office instructed his commanding officer to send him home for officer training. Learning that an attack at Festubert was imminent, he begged his colonel to defer his return to England. "I would like to be allowed, sir," he said, "to go into action with my friends." The colonel answered him: "Since you put it so gallantly, I cannot refuse." He was killed in the attack the following morning. His elder brother, with the 4th Bedfordshires, had already fallen.

"An athlete of some repute, who at Clifton carried off all the honours at long distances," A. V. Clegg, of Littleborough, near Rochdale, was among the Dardanelles casualties. The name of his brother, Frank, appeared in the same list. So did that of Denis Browne, one of Rupert Brooke's Rugby and Cambridge companions, who at the university held classical and musical scholarships. He was a pianist and composer of undoubted gifts and, as a critic writing for *The Times* and the *New Statesman*, "an intrepid explorer of the most modern musical thought." Two days before his death in action, he wrote: "We passed Rupert's island at sunset. Every colour had come into the sea and sky to do him honour and it seemed that the island must ever be shining with his glory that we buried there."

Weeks afterwards, Edward Marsh in London received Browne's farewell letter: "I've gone now too. I'm luckier than Rupert, because I've fought. But there's no one left to bury me as I buried him. Goodbye . . . bless you always for all your goodness to me." He was 27, one of the quiet and ardent spirits who strive to maintain, without ostentation or conceit, the best standards in the arts and social life, and whose non-fulfilment was part of a tragedy played out beyond their time.

> *I, that on my familiar hill*
> *Saw with uncomprehending eyes*

184

A hundred of Thy sunsets spill
Their fresh and sanguine sacrifice,
Ere the sun swings his noonday sword
Must say goodbye to all of this:
By all delights that I shall miss,
Help me to die, O Lord.[1]

[1] *Before Action:* W. N. Hodgson, 9th Devon Regiment, killed in action, July 1, 1916.

CHAPTER FOURTEEN

Lord Kitchener Passes the Port

1

"THIS TIME last year!" The retrospective mood was stronger in August 1915 than in any of the later war years. Never had there been such a period of transition in England's history: in that sense, 1915 was *annus mirabilis*. So much had happened, so much had been done, that was undreamed of twelve months before. The change in the scope and pace of the energies of the nation was stupendous. A great army of the people, composed of every class and type of citizen, had been brought to birth and one of its divisions had recently arrived in the field. Industrially, the country's war potential was developing a magnitude beyond foreseeing.

Although seaside promenades and beaches were populous that August, and the London, Brighton & South Coast Railway, for example, ran excursion services, much of the old hilarity had gone from the holiday crowds. That was not necessarily an effect of the tense propaganda against drink. No white sails graced the summer horizons. Familiar boat names, *Skylark, My Pretty Jane, Shamrock*, had been painted out and replaced by numbers. Up on the cliffs, coastguards kept a watch for drifting mines, a menace inconceivable a year ago. Austerely bandaged men in bright hospital blue, swinging by on crutches, were a more urgent reminder of realities that discounted merriment.

186

"This time last year" who thought that pheasants would nest on rectory tennis courts knee-high in grass, that the next harvest would be got in by young women, old men, and soldiers on leave, that the cost of living would rise by twenty-five per cent, that a Roll of Honour would be seen in every church porch?

> *Across our stubble—across now,*
> *The teams go four and four;*
> *But outworn elders guide the plough,*
> *And we return no more.*

Who imagined then that men of perception would be asking whether the invention of the telegraph was conducive to peremptory decisions and whether, as a means of communication between governments, it had an evil influence on the fortunes of mankind in 1941?[1]

On both sides of the battle line, the anniversary was marked by proud acclaim of "our brave defenders" and lamentations for "our heroic dead." In London, the entire staff of the Bank of England assembled in the courtyard to sing the National Anthem. At St. Paul's Cathedral, the crowded service attended by Their Majesties "was not one to make any palpably emotional appeal. The people were very quiet and not outwardly moved." (*The Times*). The Archbishop's sermon, taken from the text, *Watch ye. Stand fast in the faith. Quit you like men. Be strong,* was considered to have nobly fitted the occasion. "Things which loomed so large last summer," he reminded the congregation, now seemed "insignificantly small." Ulster, suffragette lawlessness, the affairs of Horatio Bottomley, even the shot at Sarajevo, all were forgotten in the hemispheric tumult.

The nation's casualty figures for the twelve months were 75,957 killed; 251,058 wounded, 54,967 missing: total, 381,982. The Duke of Wellington had put the

[1] E.g., Lord Bryce in *The Hibbert Journal,* 1915.

limit of bearable losses in battle at 30 per cent. When in the American Civil War regiments suffered far more, the world was shocked. In the First World War, shock passed into something like numbness after the slaughter of May 1915. "We rather seem the dead, that stayed behind." What the saddened old Oxford tutor felt, that he was near the end of feeling, was becoming a more general sensation. "If I am spared" was already a commonplace in letters from the front, especially in those by junior officers, whose proportionate losses nearly doubled those of other ranks and whose actuarial life was rapidly shrinking.

2

The British trench line at Hooge, east of Ypres, on the Menin Road, made a triangle that had its apex close to the German line near the once famous White Chateau that had been Haig's 1st Army headquarters and was now a ruin. The Germans had possession of its heaps of crumbled stone and brick, reinforced with sandbags. The site of its stables and coach-houses was in British hands. In June and July, 1915, resolute efforts were made to throw the Germans out of the position, a stronghold of machine-guns menacing the British line on three sides. The earlier attacks failed. Valuable lives were lost, among them men of the First Hundred Thousand. For them it was a ghastly baptismal experience. Plagued by lice, they dug for cover in soil in which their entrenching tools cut into corpses buried by shellfire. Enemy trench mortar explosions threw up among the debris arms, legs, heads. Near by were mine craters filled with water overflowing from a lake called Bellewaarde, on the surface of which floated patches of putrescent blood plasma. Human flesh, pulped into the earth, made

188

sand-bag filling a repulsive task.

On July 22, sappers of the 175th Tunnelling Company, Royal Engineers, touched off a mine consisting of 3,500 lbs of ammonal. At the same time, artillery opened up on the German line. The earth shook. British infantry crouched in their trenches as the fearful storm burst ahead of them. "I thought I had been blown to bits," one of the men told Sir Philip Gibbs, the war correspondent. "I was quaking with fear, with my head in the earth. I kept saying, Christ! . . . Christ!"

What had been an enemy redoubt was now a cavity 120 feet wide and 20 feet deep. Immediately, two companies of the 4th Middlesex rushed in and occupied it They lay against the hot earth, gasping for breath in the uncoiling fumes of the explosion. What none could know was that its shattering reverberation had numbered the days of a splendid group of young Englishmen.

On the night of July 29–30 retaliation came. The 8th Battn., The Rifle Brigade held the foremost lip of the crater. To their right were men of the 7th Battn., King's Royal Rifle Corps. They had relieved other battalions of their regiments whose men stumbled back from the line like sleepwalkers, so harassing had been their time as crater garrison. The Germans appeared to be unaware of the change-over, though in places the lines were no more than five yards apart. The men passing in and out of the line could not suppress sounds incidental to such a movement. The enemy gave no sign. Half an hour before dawn silence hung over that part of the Hooge sector.

At a quarter past three a.m., the site of the old White Chateau stables held by the British was sent sky-high by a German mine. The ground rocked under men's feet hundreds of yards away. Chunks of concrete and brickwork, tons of earth, and many human bodies, were flung up as if in a volcanic eruption. After the explosion had

189

died down, a fierce, sibilant noise, like the hissing of many geese, was heard coming from the German side. It heralded long spurts of crimson flame that lashed and licked like dragon's breath. Some of the new young soldiers of the King's Royal Rifle Corps, lying in hurriedly thrown up forward trenches, were set alight and burnt to death. Others, with their clothes smoking, fell back before the weird onslaught, which was designed to succeed where the gas attacks of three months before had failed.

It was the British Army's first taste of liquid fire, the new German incendiary weapon. The flames, projected under pressure from appliances called *Flammenwerfer* strapped to the carriers' backs like portable fire extinguishers, were controlled by flexible tube nozzles producing jets effective up to about twenty-five yards. Each spurt was followed by a cloud of black smoke.

"So I've had a curious experience," Hugh Montague Butterworth, a New Zealand schoolmaster serving with The Rifle Brigade, wrote to his friends in Wanganui. "Everybody in neighbouring trenches wants to know about the liquid fire in my trench, and I can't say if I had it or not. The noise, dust and general tumult were such that anything might be happening . . . I felt absolutely as cool as ice, one was so worked up that one felt that one could stick anything out." He regretted that his letter failed to express his true feelings during the attack, "or to give you a real idea of what Hell is like. We lost two hundred and fifty men. I left Aldershot fifth officer in the company. I am now second in command of it. I am fairly certain of my second star, but we haven't time to think about promotion just now."

"I am sad about King Edward, aren't you? It seems as if the glory has departed; and there will be lots of war, and mothers will have to worry considerably." That was how Billy Grenfell,[1] aged 20, had received the news of the death of King Edward VII in 1910. His notion that a force for good in European affairs had gone was shared by many. Not many expressed it so daringly. A memory remained of him in Westminster Abbey after the king's funeral. "He was standing against the Dryden monument, and a shaft of sunlight came down on his head, and I thought what a beautiful picture of manly youth. He looked like a young knight who would ride into battle with joy."[2]

Flaxen-haired, tall, gauntly graceful, he moved among the crowd with what one of his friends called "a kind of drowsy arrogance." His individuality was clearly outlined. Raymond Asquith, no devotee of rhetoric, said that "there was not a gesture or a phrase of his that could be taken for anyone else's," and that he was "a perfect companion and in every context of life a perpetual joy."

Like his brother Julian, he was a boxer, well-versed in the science. In 1911, he knocked out the reigning Cambridge heavyweight in an inter-Varsity match with his long surprising left hook. "The winner's amiable, cherubic smile," wrote a spectator, "was a curious contrast to the stealthy alacrity of his foot work and his menacing hands." Lady Diana Cooper recalls him in her autobiography as "the titan cherub." He was not naturally pugnacious. His boxing, like his lawn tennis, for which he was given his Blue, suggested that he was

[1] The Hon. Gerald William Grenfell, second son of Lord and Lady Desborough.
[2] *Pages from a Family Journal*

engaged in a ritual rather than a contest. A friend's comparison of him with his brother was that "Julian stood for motion, Billy for mass; Julian for force in action, Billy for force in rest. Julian was like a torrent, Billy like a still, deep lake, having the same inviting serenity."

He shone in the galactic setting of Eton and Balliol in those years with his brother Julian, Edward Horner, Charles Lister and Patrick Shaw-Stewart, a group that combined academic and social athleticism. "Billy Grenfell was the greatest natural scholar of them all," in the opinion of Mrs. Warre Cornish, wife of the Vice-Provost of Eton. In the privately printed Grenfell memoirs there is a delightful record of the effect on the family of his success in winning one of the notable Eton prizes. "After an anguish of suspense, the news came, at 2.45, that Billy had got the Newcastle Scholarship. After all the elaborate arrangements for hearing, his mother and sister were told it on the telephone by Tom Browne, the tailor at Eton! They went to tell Willie [Lord Desborough] but neither of them could speak, so he thought Billy had not got it. The whole family went to tell Lizzie Grenfell at Elibank, who was ill in bed, and then drove straight to Eton, and Billy. It was a day of such wonderful happiness. They had all been sleepless for days, almost weeks, with suspense about it." (April 7, 1909).

After the Newcastle and a First Classical Exhibition at Balliol, he won the coveted Craven Scholarship. His failure, in 1913, to obtain a First in Greats was a disappointment that hit him hard after the previous successes. He had taken on too much, reading for the Ireland as well as for Greats. He went on with his studies, aspiring to an All Souls Fellowship. In August 1914 it was put to him that he could fairly wait for the autumn examination results before taking up military or other war duties. He would not think of it. With an introduction to a member of Lord Kitchener's staff, he went to the War Office and asked for a commission. He was gazetted as a subaltern with one of the New Army battalions of The Rifle Brigade.

Those of his family and friends who said their farewells to him when he left for France in May 1915 were not surprised to hear that he refused the offer of an appointment as A.D.C. to an Army commander. "Nor *could* I really leave the battalion, which is already five officers short," he wrote on July 6. "The men are glorious. I do love them." Five days later, he wrote again:

"Do you know, I had not seen a corpus vile since I was fifteen, at the Morgue, and dreamed of it for weeks afterwards. I guess you could not show me much new now in that line. I had to bury five K.R.R.s one afternoon in a shell-hole in full view of the Germans. I longed to signal that we were making a sepulchre and not a fort. However, we got it done somehow, and read the burial service. That same evening we collected 28 British rifles in a little wood in front of my trenches, mostly tightly clasped by their late owners." On July 14, he wrote to his sister Monica (Lady Salmond): "I take the opportunity of writing to you in the intervals of the most boring cricket match I have ever played in. I feel we should be a stronger and braver people if cricket had never been invented."

His glancing humour was not long subdued by the death in action of his brother Julian on May 26. "Darling Julian is so constantly beside me and laughs so debonairly at my qualms and hesitations. I pray for one tenth of his courage," he wrote, having told his parents in the same letter: "My servant is ex-footman to Lady Beecham. The other day he was getting me some afternoon tea, when a 'crump' crumped most effectually the dug-out in which he reposes 18 hours out of the 24. I have forbidden him to mention his 'providential escape' to me again, under pain of being returned to duty."

In another letter, asking for novels to read, "*Clayhanger* or *Hilda Lessways*," by Arnold Bennett, "and some of Thomas Hardy's," he referred to Rupert Brooke's poems. "What a fiery poignant spirit, and how unassuaged by this life; I do not remember anything so nakedly personal since Catullus. His sonnet to the Dead is lovely." He thought that Brooke had never been in love, "but had drained 'love's sad satiety' to the dregs . . . God, how he *felt*." Cast down by news from the home front, he wrote as if Great Britain no longer merited the prefixing adjective. "What a sad, disgraceful, unennobled, burglarious huckster among nations we are. I am glad not to be in England now." The next day the battalion was to move up into reserve trenches at Ypres, "a unique opportunity to study the ruins. You cannot imagine how tawdry unvenerable ruins are, fragments of chests of drawers and housemaids' cupboards, instead of skeleton oriel windows. It looks like a spring uncleaning . . . The Tiptree jam is awfully good. I like the strawberry and blackberry best." (July 20, 1915).

On the afternoon of July 30, after the liquid fire attack, he drew the men of his platoon together to speak to them as they waited for the order to go over the top near Hooge. In a low voice he bade them: "Remember, you are Englishmen. Do nothing to dishonour that name." They thought he would not survive the day, "because of his fearlessness." Those who came out of the action remembered how he often joked about his height, his habit of exclaiming: "Oh, I think my head must be showing," when the bullets sang past him. It became a catchphrase in the company.

The rest was told in a letter written on July 31 to Lord Desborough by Lieut.-Colonel R. C. Maclachlan, commanding the 8th Battn., The Rifle Brigade, one of the

194

first New Army battalions to go into action. "Billy was killed yesterday afternoon about 3 p.m. when gallantly charging over the open at the head of his men. It is all too tragic and I dare not think what this double shock can mean to you. I've but a few minutes to write. We were fighting for exactly 24 hours yesterday and I've just marched into billets with a casualty list of 19 officers, and one's only inclination is to sit and sob. I can't grasp the magnitude of the loss." Billy Grenfell had fallen within a mile of the spot where his brother Julian was fatally wounded two months before.

In London that night, Mrs. Asquith ("Margot"), the Prime Minister's wife, sat at dinner next to Lord Kitchener. They spoke together of Billy Grenfell's death, agreeing that he and Julian "combined all that life can give of courage, brains and good feeling." Mrs. Asquith thought that faith "should be rewarded in this world with more knowledge." She said that she "longed for one glimpse of God's purpose— if only a gleam of hope as to our sure immortality." She recalled in her autobiography that "the expression on Lord K's face was one of puzzled kindness and he handed me the port. To hide my emotion, he turned abruptly to the table and, changing the subject, said we had only ourselves to blame for the failures in the war."

"Like Castor and Pollux, they are together, shining in some other place. Glorious sorrow is as necessary, is as priceless, as the nightingale or the evening star." Maurice Baring, poet and man of letters (1874–1945) was applying his powers to the distillation of essential comfort for the Grenfell family. More imposing minds were set to discovering the elusive formula. A. J. Balfour to Lord and Lady Desborough: "For myself, I entertain no doubt whatever about a future life. I deem it at least as certain as any of the hundred-and-one truths by which I and all mankind direct our actions. I am as sure that those

195

I love and have lost are living today, as I am that yesterday they were fighting heroically in the trenches."[1] Hilaire Belloc to the same: "That we cannot in this world seize immortality troubles me not at all. Neither can we, on the globe, grasp the system of the universe. I believe in the Resurrection of the Body; not as a figment of desire, not as a drug of consolation, but as truth arrived at."[2]

> *Like clouds that rake the mountain summits,*
> *Or waves that own no curbing hand,*
> *How fast has brother followed brother,*
> *From sunshine to the sunless land . . .*[3]

4

The return of The Rifle Brigade men from the fighting area that day was the subject of a letter written by Captain Arthur Grenfell, 9th Lancers. "I have seen the saddest and I think the noblest sight of my life—the remnants of a regiment of gentlemen—splendid heroes —dragging themselves back with heavy hearts through Ypres. The battalion was practically wiped out." The dead, he wrote, were laid out in No-man's-Land, "in perfect rows, the dressing as correct as on parade."

Once again, German machine-gun supremacy had been savagely proved. Besides 19 officers, the 8th Battn., The Rifle Brigade, lost 462 other ranks; the 7th Battn., King's Royal Rifle Corps, 12 officers and 289 others, the 7th Battn., The Rifle Brigade, 12 and 240, the 8th Battn., K.R.R.C., 12 and 190. The 9th K.R.R.C. lost their colonel killed, 16 other officers and 333 other

[1] *Pages from a Family Journal.*
[2] Ibid.
[3] Wordsworth.

196

ranks. When the day was done, the enemy still held 500 yards of the ground that had been fought for. The fighting had no strategic significance. "It was only an incident in the eternal struggle of small losses and small gains to which the policy of holding the Ypres salient condemned us."[1]

Among the fallen were John Hyland Fosdick, aged 20, of Ipswich, a Cambridge football blue who in 1914 went with the Corinthians to the Argentine; John Douglas Henderson Radcliffe, M.A., B.C.L., of Widdecombe-in-the-moor, Fellow of All Souls, aged 30; Harry Noel Leslie Renton, who was head of his house at Harrow and was going up to Oxford; Richard Selby Durnford, of Basingstoke, Captain of Oppidans, 1904–5, Scholar of King's College, Cambridge, an assistant master at Eton, aged 30; John Frederick Lascelles, of Woolbeding, Sussex, who played cricket for Winchester and was attached to the Royal Flying Corps, aged 30; Meaburn Staniland, Town Clerk of Boston, Lincolnshire, a pre-war Territorial; Cecil Faber, head of his house at Eton, aged 19; Alan Crawhall Challoner, of Ealing, public school swimmer, boxer and footballer, and winner of natural history prizes; and H. W. Goldberg, who took a first in jurisprudence at University College, Oxford, and was newly called to the Bar.

Bryan Osmond Dewes, of Blackheath, had left Repton to become a medical student at St. Thomas's Hospital, London. He was a Henley oarsman. He enlisted in the Artists' Rifles, afterwards being commissioned in the Middlesex Regiment. "You would have found him considerably changed," his company commander wrote in a commiserating letter. "He came out here a delightful, high-spirited, healthy boy. He suddenly became a man. Today he has left us and we have lost a very gallant officer and a very gentle gentleman." He was 21.

[1] John Buchan: *History of the War*, (1922).

197

A. S. Knight won a London County Council scholarship to Dulwich College when he was 16. With further scholarships, he went to Magdalen College. He was a school and college athlete who excelled in cross-country running. Going down from Oxford with an honours degree, he was given a university commission in the Royal Fusiliers. He was 24 when he died in the shambles at Hooge.

Robert Brandt, of the Rifle Brigade, was shot down that day as, leading what remained of his platoon, he reached the parapet of a German trench. In his last letter to a friend in England, he wrote: "It is very difficult to think of anything beyond tomorrow." On the morrow he was killed. Streatham born, he was an old Harrovian who was always first in his form, captained the school football eleven, kept wicket for Oxford against Cambridge in 1907. By contemporary report, "all the gifts of the gods were his," boundless energy, high spirits, a penetrating intelligence, "a nimble and often fantastic wit," and a phenomenal memory. With his sharp-cut profile, close-lying black hair, well arched eyebrows, he was likened to a greyhound waiting in the slips. He had a controlled delight in existence. He would discuss Meredith into the small hours and, after a short recuperative sleep, would rush off into the hills with a geological hammer.

Going down from the university, he settled in Bermondsey with the Oxford Mission to study what was implied by the "social problem." He was understood to have had public service in view as his ultimate career. No one, knowing him, doubted his ability to make a notable success of it. Among the 45 Balliol men killed in 1915, he is on record as "one of the heaviest losses."[1] He was 27.

[1] *Balliol War Memorial Book.*

5

Small lust to spill man's blood had he,
Small thirst for battles' joys.

The lines are from verses composed memorially for
Keith Rae, aged 26, of Courthill, Birkenhead, another
Rifle Brigade subaltern who faced the liquid fire onslaught at Hooge. He had written with uplifted heart
a fortnight before: "I cannot express what I mean, but
it was the happiest moment of my life," referring to his
being with wounded men under heavy shellfire. "We
were all just on the brink of the Next World. Suddenly
everything seemed to become clear, and one no longer
'saw through a glass darkly'; one felt certain about what
one hardly understood at all. And fear and nerves and
egoism all vanished in the joy of just being there. I am
not mad, and I will one day try to explain to you."[1]
Not long before the war, he was at a private gathering
of Oxford men addressed by a leading Labour speaker,
who told them: "The fact of the matter is, you fellows
are only 'alf-educated'." In the audience were Craven
and Hertford Scholars and other vintage intellects. Keith
Rae was doubtless not alone in seeing the point. According to his friend, the Rev. Eric Crosse, he was "tremendously impressed," the more so, possibly, because his
mind was not grooved by public school concepts. The
speaker had lately served on a parliamentary committee
concerned with slum clearance and re-housing. "Some
of the best men in Parliament," he said, were his colleagues on the committee. "I was confronted at every
meeting with the fact that those men of genius, though
sympathetic, had no understanding of the problems before us." After that, academic argument had little interest
for Keith Rae. He threw himself into the work of the

[1] *Keith Rae, A Memoir,* by E. C. C. (privately printed, 1926).

Balliol Boys' Club, a willing apprentice to labours by which he hoped to be inducted into wider fields of social usefulness.

After Oxford, he was for some time undecided whether to go to work among the poor of South London or to make the Bar his career. He chose teaching one of the lowest forms at Marlborough, though he had reservations about public schools, "regarding them," said the Rev. Eric Crosse, himself later a public school headmaster (Ardingly), "as vast machines governed by the forces of tradition and conventionality, which left little scope for the play of individuality or personal influence." Before exercising his power to order canings, never having himself been caned, Rae persuaded a fellow form-master to give him "three of the best" with a thicker cane than was normally used. His short teaching career was as invigorating for some of his fellow form-masters as for his pupils, among whom he constantly raised laughter during lessons.

To prepare for promotion, he spent some time in Germany in 1913. He went to a football match between England and Germany, curious to see whether the German crowd had the same enthusiasm for games as the British. "The behaviour of the English players was simply disgusting," he wrote to tell his father. "They lost their tempers, as they were obviously losing the match, and played as foul a game as you can imagine, tripping the Germans and swearing at the referee. One could not help feeling heartily ashamed." To add to his embarrassment, "the Germans, though not beyond reproach, were far less unsporting. They gave the English players quite a gentlemanly reception, and nearly destroyed one fellow who clapped when an English player was hurt."

He was oppressed by the Germans' "stupendous lack of genuine humour. *Verboten* is written everywhere, even on the seats of men's trousers." The more he saw of the Germans, he wrote, the less he feared them. "All the social causes which are shoving old England down the hill are operating here too—among the rich, luxury and blasé indifference to everything; among the poor, increasing poverty and unemployment. Man for man, the English troops would give the Germans the soundest of thrashings."

Receiving his commission in The Rifle Brigade in 1914, he made it known that he wanted to be sent to the front soon. At the end of his first month's training, he was writing: "I am beginning to love some of my men very dearly. They are priceless fellows on the whole. They have given up good homes and well-paid jobs, and have a terrible lot of hardship to put up with in K's army. They seem at times to be mere children, and helpless without advice. You will gather that there is a plentiful supply of the last-named from a distinguished ex-president of the Balliol College Boys' Club." He was shaken by the death in action of Ronnie Poulton who had worked devotedly there with him. "You felt better for merely living near him."

Keith Rae had been two months in the deadly Ypres salient when his company was sent into the line at Hooge. Their trench was lost. He was last seen on the parapet, firing his revolver as the Germans came on, "splendidly regardless of his life and fighting against fearful odds."

> *Oh, never shall I forget you,*
> *My men, who trusted me:*
> *More my sons than your fathers'—*
> *For they could only see*
> *The little helpless babies,*
> *Or the young men in their pride:*
> *They could not see you dying*
> *Or hold you, while you died.*

> *Happy and young and gallant*
> *They saw their first-born go;*
> *But not the strong limbs broken,*
> *And the beautiful men laid low,*
> *And the piteous writhing bodies*
> *That screamed: "Don't leave me, sir!"*
> *For they were only your fathers,*
> *And I was your officer.*[1]

6

A voice that might have been heard in the highest councils was stilled for ever in the counter-attack that followed the *Flammenwerfer* assault at Hooge. Gilbert Talbot was one of the instinctive leaders. "He would have been on the threshold of the Cabinet by now," a friend of his wrote two years after the war. Another, no less admiring, wished for him that he would attain his ideal of service as a Christian statesman "while avoiding the murk of politics." It was said of him that whatever society or club he joined, he became at once its secretary or chairman. If he was not one of the prize winners, he was a born prize giver, courtly, humorous, engagingly sympathetic.

The son of a bishop of Winchester, piety and politics converged when he became president of the Oxford Union. Both Balfour and Lloyd George received him into their private circles. At the Canning Club, in 1912, he had spoken on the loss of the *Titanic* that year. "It seems to me that this giant ship was built and fitted out on a scale of luxury which is absolutely indefensible. Paying $2,200 for a single suite for a five days' voyage is, without any qualification whatever, utterly indefen-

[1] From *A Highland Regiment and Other Poems*, by Ewart Alan Mackintosh, Seaforth Highlanders; see footnote, page 91.

sible and morally wrong. The greatest social reform which the Tory Party can give to the nation is a decrease of luxury and a more intimate knowledge of the working classes. That has now become a platitude. The sinking of the *Titanic* has enormously added to its force. What is absolutely intolerable is that this luxury should become a habit and a necessity."

The moral enthusiasm echoes over the years that have occluded so many memories of "the valiant, infectious urgency" which John Murray, the Christ Church tutor, cited as a chief mark of Gilbert Talbot's personality. Sir Victor Mallet, retired from diplomacy, has recalled "the warm smile of welcome," and the vigour of mind and body "which made one think of Gilbert as eternally young and alive." Viscount Monckton has written that Talbot had "the most vigorous, fresh and noble mind of any man I ever knew." Some saw him as a potentially great advocate. Some thought that he would be Prime Minister. He had the air, the habitude, the *panache*, that predicates more than personal distinction. Canon Scott Holland, who knew him from boyhood, said that "he would certainly have gone far. He had high political ambitions. He saw visions of a better social order." Others would say that he was aspiring rather than ambitious, that for him attainment had a deeper meaning than achievement. He could relish what is meant by the Cecilian temper and at the same time be a devoted admirer of Lloyd George.

Late in July, 1914, when he was 22, he went off joyfully with a friend, Geoffrey Colman, on a world tour. The ship was met at Quebec by a band and cheering crowds. It was their first intimation that war had broken out. Talbot and Colman had only twelve hours ashore. They caught the next ship back to England, intent on offering their services. Both joined The Rifle Brigade. On September 3 Talbot wrote from a training camp:

203

"I can't imagine wanting to be a peace soldier, but it's wonderful to be doing it now. And I still can't help reading the war news and the casualty lists without a sense of wondering whether some day one's turn will come, and whether it is possible to imagine a finer thing happening to me, and which at the same time would deal for ever with all troubles and difficulties in this world." There had been an unsuccessful love affair. His frank attitude to the life of prosperous idleness made him enemies and cost him, according to one of his seniors, "more than quite as honourable but less brave a man could have endured." He seems to have welcomed the discipline of Army life, as if it were a means of grace, rescuing him from a tendency to untidiness in his daily living.

His battalion of The Rifle Brigade went to France in the middle of May 1915. At home, the shells crisis was the topic of the day. Talbot reported effects of the shortage in one of his first letters home: "Those infernal labour people must buck up with the shells. I saw a Battn. yesterday, 200 strong only, which had been in and out of the same trenches for over 6 months, and for the time being they are really beat, done. It's heart-breaking. And with the ammunition everybody's confident we could bang right through tomorrow." (May 31). Longing for home was an undertone of most of the letters that followed.

"At times one's thoughts fly back to all the precious things in England, a thousand times more precious now. I think of Farnham, Winchester, Oxford in summer. What Winchester meads are like on a $\frac{1}{2}$ holiday in June —or Magdalen cloisters on a May evening. And one thinks of all the family and the happy times we've had —the love that binds us all, and Mother and all she is to me, and I don't feel ashamed of wondering fairly often if I shall see them again, and if so when." (June, 1915).

Again: "Death is not so formidable or awful in a way here. Soldiers put it in its right place somehow. I know it's not the end—only an incident—and that the love that unites us lives through and will triumph over all. But I do long for home sometimes." (July 22, 1915).

He wrote a week later to his brother about "the hell of a time" the company had had in the Hooge crater— "the deuce of a place . . . Very trying, and we've had a lot of nervous breakdowns." On July 28, he wrote to Lloyd George, Minister of Munitions, "a delightful and intimate letter," according to Canon Scott Holland, "telling him of the deep gratitude to him that was going up from the hearts of the soldiers in the trenches who once had hardly been able to bear the sound of his name; and recalling again the visions of national welfare which he had opened out for him to follow."

Forty-eight hours after the letter was written and sent off, the 8th Battn., The Rifle Brigade was relieved in the Hooge sector, having endured shelling and machine-gunning that went on without a break for the whole of one day and most of a night. Talbot marched his platoon eight miles, half-way back to their billets. Meanwhile, the Germans launched their liquid fire attack. Two companies of the 8th Rifle Brigade, including Talbot's platoon, were ordered back into the line for a counter-attack. The men had only two hours' sleep. With mugs of tea, nothing more, to sustain them, they moved through a communication trench into Zouave Wood, which was under heavy artillery fire. "I don't suppose many of us will come back," Talbot said to his batman. During the forty minutes' wait several of the men were killed or wounded. Talbot's colonel told him: "Remember, you are responsible for fifty-two lives. Your own doesn't count." Before the wait in Zouave Wood was over, the platoon was reduced to sixteen men.

As zero hour drew near, Talbot looked repeatedly at

his wrist watch. The German artillery fire drummed the air with an intensity that made speech inaudible. Up till then, Talbot had been going from man to man, talking with brisk cheerfulness. The tumult growing, he went and sat apart from the others. He was seen with his head bent, as if in prayer. With a final glance at his watch, counting the seconds, he sprang up, calling to the remainder of his platoon: "Come on, lads, this is our day."

They advanced through the wood and out into the open, "in one straight line, just as if they were on an Aldershot parade ground, although under terrible shell, rifle and machine-gun fire." (Sergeant J. L. Chumley). Talbot was the first to reach the part of the crater that was to be recovered from the Germans. He was hit in the neck and fell on the barbed wire. His batman, Nash, rushed to his aid and was himself wounded as he did so. Talbot gazed at him with what Whitman called "man's enduring astonishment at his own position," then smiled and died.

A week later, his body was recovered by his brother Neville, later Bishop of Pretoria, who crawled out between the lines to find it. A grave was dug in Sanctuary Wood, which was soon afterwards blown out of existence as a recognisable landmark. At the end of the year, a resthouse for the troops was opened in Poperinghe, the small boundary town through which marched, back and forth, the myriad men who fought in the Ypres salient. The house in the Rue de l'Hopital, next to the chemist's, was dedicated to the memory of Gilbert Talbot and named after him. It was made the headquarters of the priest-in-charge of the newly created Army parish of Poperinghe-cum-Ypres, the Rev. P. B. ("Tubby") Clayton, chaplain of the 16th Infantry Brigade. Talbot House was soon known to the soldiers as Toc House, an abbreviation from the Army signalling code. The stairs to its consecrated Upper Room were climbed by "perhaps 100,000 men" during the next three years. "Certainly some 20,000 in all have there received the Sacrament."[1]

I came to a halt at the end of the road;
I reached for my ration and loosened my load;
I came to a halt at the end of the road.

O weary the way, Lord, forsaken of Thee,
My spirit is faint—lone, comfortless me:
O weary the way, Lord, forsaken of Thee.

And the Lord answered, Son, be thy heart lifted up,
I drank as thou drinkest, of agony's cup:
And the Lord answered, Son, be thy heart lifted up.

For thee that I loved, I went down to the grave,
Pay thou the like forfeit thy country to save;
For thee that I loved, I went down to the grave.

Then I cried, "I am Thine, Lord; yes, unto this last!"
And I strapped on my knapsack, and onward I passed.
Then I cried, "I am Thine, Lord; yes, unto this last."

Fulfilled is the sacrifice. Lord, is it well?
Be it said—for the dear sake of country he fell.
Fulfilled is the sacrifice, Lord! Is it well?
                                        —from the Flemish, 1915.

[1] The Rev. P. B. Clayton, M.C., in *Plain Tales From Flanders* (Longmans, Green, 1930).

CHAPTER FIFTEEN

"Fun Has Left the World"

1

DOMINATING THE Allied strategic situation in the
West that summer was the fact that French manpower,
between the ages of 18 and 48, was stretched to its limits,
and that British manpower was not fully mobilised or
even fully realised. The French, disabled by 2,700,000
casualties, including a minimum of 600,000 men killed,
and by the loss of a large productive region of their
country, favoured Joffre's project of a large-scale offensive in the Champagne, between Rheims and Verdun.
It might be the beginning of the end of the war. The
British were still counting heads. In Paris, hardly a man
of military age was to be seen who was not in uniform.
In London, as in other centres of population in England,
great numbers of unenlisted men still walked the streets.
Against that rhomboidal background, the British
took over another fifteen miles of line south of Arras;
conferences of extreme importance to munition supplies
were held at Boulogne under the chairmanship of Lloyd
George; and a minor sharp counter-attack was undertaken at Hooge, where the Germans still held the
notorious crater. They were dislodged on August 9, a
date that provided two other footnotes of interest to
military historians: British soldiers wore experimentally
their subsequently familiar tin hats and some were fired
on by their comrades who, in the early morning light,

mistook them for Germans; and for the first time, too, British artillerymen went into action without restriction on the number of rounds they could fire. The fight for the crater, culminating in man-to-man combats with bayonets and bombs, resulted in the recapture of 700 yards of lost ground and 1,328 casualties.

Among them were young men who could be expected to contribute to the mental and spiritual grace of our time—John Kenelm Digby, of Fakenham, for example, who was preparing for ordination in Canada when the war started and who at once enlisted as a private and trained with the first Canadian contingent on Salisbury Plain before being commissioned in the 7th Norfolks. He was 25 when he was killed in the fighting that August. Others who fell were Roger Wentworth Watson, Senior Commoner Prefect of Winchester and scholar of King's College, Cambridge, "where all his tastes were literary," aged 22; James Colin Taylor, of the Honourable Artillery Company, who after leaving Rugby gave much of his leisure and energy to working for social betterment, aged 28; John William Reynolds, of Kirkley, Lowestoft, Major Scholar of Trinity College, Cambridge, and Lecturer in History at Sidney Sussex College; Hugh Anthony Crookham, only son of the vicar of Wisbech, and a Cambridge classical scholar, aged 22; and Edwin Gerald Venning, aged 32, an actor who was educated at the Clergy Orphanage School, and who had terrible tales to tell of the fighting at Second Ypres, where he had been in the thick of it with the Royal Sussex Regiment. "Good Lord, my dear," he wrote to his sister from the trenches, "there'll be people so glad when it's all over that some, I think, may drop dead for sheer joy and others from heartbreak with the despondency of what has been . . . It's a dirty, repulsive and utterly foolish game."

Also named in the August catalogue of death were

209

Ronald Raw, of Albert Court, South Kensington, an amateur boxer who was champion of the middle-weights in the Public Schools competition; Kenneth Falshaw Watson, of Leeds, well-known in Rugby Union football; John William Ashley Maude, aged 29, a barrister who, known to the golfing public as a distinguished amateur, perfectly exemplified the volunteers who had no "faculty for storm and turbulence" and who gave their fullest energies to mastering the soldier's business. Photographed in uniform, he looked engagingly embarrassed. His commanding officer wrote that he had been "too careless of his own comfort and safety" when in the line. "He loved life but went cheerfully to his death, of which he had a premonition."

Horace Annesley Vachell, the novelist, lost his only son Richard, serving with the Royal Flying Corps. From the Dardanelles came news of the death in action of Lance-Corporal Gilbert Ramsay, aged 35, Superintendent of Glasgow Art Galleries and Museums, who had succeeded Charles Aitken as director of Whitechapel Art Gallery, London, and whose Glasgow appointment was to take effect from August 1, 1914. He enlisted as a private in the 6th Highland Light Infantry.

Also killed in the Dardanelles that month, two sons of William Thomson, shipowner of Leith, both serving with the Royal Scots; two brothers Morgan, of the Royal Field Artillery and the South Lancashires, respectively; and Howard Field, of the 4th Worcestershires, an old St. Paul's School boy who had lost two brothers in the war. In the Hooge fighting, two brothers Linnell, from Mill Lane, Lincoln, standing side by side in a support trench, were killed by the same shell. At Hooge, it seems that prestige was as much in the minds of the planning staff as strategic necessity. In the Dardanelles, it was already clear that men were dying uselessly.

2

"One felt all the time: he will be a great man." Viola Tree, annotating her friends' letters for publication between the wars,[1] was calling up in memory the presence of Charles Lister, "who would have looked like his father had he survived but not so magnificent." His father, the last Lord Ribblesdale, was fixed in the public mind as a magnifico by Sargent's portrait of him as Master of the Buckhounds, painted in 1902 and hung in the National Gallery.

The question was whether Charles Lister's predicted greatness would have been manifested in performance or whether it would have been finally revealed as the emanation of his personality, which was by all accounts unusual and by some remarkable. He was tall and stalky, as if he had been reared under a top light. Sir Rennell Rodd, British Ambassador in Rome, said that he had "a certain constitutional disability of harmonious movement," a nervous habit of twisting himself into ungainly postures as he walked and talked. He was awkward with his hands, lacking deftness, so that he could hardly strike a match without fumbling. His large head, often rocking on his wide sloping shoulders with his readily induced laughter, was covered with close-curled hair that defied his persistence in parting it. His face was a patrician ellipse, delicately pale. His well-arched eyebrows were more expressive than his blue eyes.

Women fell for his "melting smile." Men envied him for his easy disregard of sets and class differences and of what others thought or said of him. He had no borrowed attitudes. All liked him for his contagious gaiety and excellent humour. He was attractive to many types of person, from Philip and Ethel Snowden to A. J. Balfour. They did not represent the extremes of his friend-

[1] *Castles in the Air* (Hogarth Press, 1926).

ships, which reached out to the back streets of West Ham. One of his closest Eton and Balliol companions, Patrick Shaw-Stewart, spoke of his "incomparable personality." It ensured him success even with those who did not understand him.

As a preparatory school boy at Rottingdean, he developed a precociously censorious attitude to "property," and at Eton he advocated the nationalisation of the raw materials of industry as part of the reconstruction of society. His adolescent intelligence extended well beyond the range of the ordinary preoccupations of his years, establishing him as "a most unusual boy."[1] He took up as subjects of interest if not of close study the repatriation of the Boers and the teaching of English in South Africa; Franciscanism in the twentieth century; Ruskin's financial theories; and the policies of the Independent Labour Party, which he joined when he was 18. He seized every chance in debates of championing oppressed peoples. He raised money in College for the relief of victims of Russian ruthlessness in Siberia and organised a public meeting in Windsor for the same object. Compassion ruled his heart.

At Oxford, "meetings seemed to spring up at his feet." (Ronald Knox). He founded two local trades union branches, organised an anti-sweated industries exhibition, increased the membership of the Oxford branch of the Fabian Society fourfold, obtained lecturers for Ruskin Hall which the university tended to patronise, and actively supported a strike of girl workers at the Clarendon Press; in doing so, coming into conflict with the university authorities.

Co-existent with those activities, which Balfour said were "probably better than keeping racehorses or running an actress," was a frank enjoyment of the pleasures of place and privilege, of shooting over moors in the

[1] Mrs. Warre Cornish, wife of the Provost of Eton.

Highlands, of week-ends in great houses, of the masquerades of "the season." He never had any difficulty in detaching himself to attend a Socialist conference, where he would be seen in the liveliest converse with leaders and delegates. As much as anyone, he enjoyed Ronald Knox's affectionate satire:

> *A rescue-the-poor young man,*
> *A waiter-look-sharp young man...*

Sir Lawrence Jones, an Oxford contemporary, said that "he was at once the most serious and the most frivolous of us all." Sir Rex Benson remembers the mock funeral given him at Balliol when he was sent down for the fag-end of a term for "undue familiarity" with a university senior with whom he insisted on waltzing round a bonfire. Patrick Shaw-Stewart delivered an oration enlivened by impromptu references to "lice in donnish whiskers" as the bearded Dean passed by. Sir Rex says that Charles Lister was "always ready to try anything," ride a difficult horse, dispute with experts, face up to unruly elements at an East End boys' club. At a Birmingham circus he leapt from his seat and mounted Louis de Rougemont's giant turtle in its tank.

His First in Greats, in his third year at Balliol, was no surprise intellectually. It was perhaps something of a triumph of self-management in a life that was lived too much in the moment, that defied Marcus Aurelius's dictum: "Do not be whirled about." Monsignor Knox said that Lister "threw himself into everything . . . as if that was all he lived for." He told Viola Tree, with whom he kept up a lively pre-war correspondence: "I should make a first-class unbelieving ecclesiastic."

3

"My colleagues are appreciative, and I'm very fond of them; but their vitality at times is rather low. Of course I've always been used to living with tremendously vital people." Lister was writing from his embassy post in Rome (1912). Experience abroad brought about a readjustment of his Socialist ideas, without shaking his belief in first principles. "I feel the Labour grievance as strongly as ever," he wrote to tell a friend, "Tommy" (Alan) Lascelles, "but I've lost faith in most of the remedies I used to believe in. If only they could get back to the old sober trade unionism and to collective bargaining on the same lines."

Militant trades unionism offended him. It could become a challenge to the law and order which, projected by him as a basic premise of human progress, was essential to his effective functioning as a Tory Democrat. He now seemed to see the Empire as the surest and widest guarantee of stability and he went on leave to India to study the workings of "the Imperial machine." He wrote during that time: "Between ourselves, I'm afraid I'm getting a slight distaste for our race when I see them collectively and super-British."

He was at the Constantinople embassy in August 1914. Seeing friends leave for England was a depressing experience. Going aboard one of the home-going ships to say farewells, he stayed behind until after sailing time. At Smyrna, he repented his impulsiveness and hurried back to Constantinople, where he did not rest until he had secured his release from the diplomatic service to join the Army.

His letters annotate events in the Near East at that critical time. "The *morale* of the French is at this moment very high, but one must at least be prepared for their failure." He did not think that any Germans were "worth English tears," nor did the tears of the departing German ambassador in London, Prince Lichnowsky, stir him to regret. "Ever since the 1st of July Germany had decided on aggressive war against France and Russia, and the feigned innocence of the Lichnowskys should not find any believers."

On August 20, he wrote to the Hon. Irene Lawley: "I can hear the beating of the wings of the Angel of Death very near." He referred more than once to the possibility of England's decline into a second-class power, reflecting on "the tranquil existence" of her people in that state. "I shouldn't like it myself, because I feel my life very much bound up with my flag."

He had a close view of the Sultan of Turkey at a reception. "He is like a great egg, and sits half-right or half-left as the case may be, on the edge of the throne, with his hands tightly crossed in his lap. His whole chest and tummy are gold lace." He resented German behaviour in the Turkish capital. With his scowling face and duelling scars, the German Ambassador was "running round to the hotels and shouting victory in the streets—the ungraciousness of their whole way of looking at things makes one feel very bitter. These cads—I cannot reconcile them with the Germans I have really liked."

He contrived his return to England at the end of September 1914. Rennell Rodd regretted it, "for men of his ability and sense of duty are rare, and can ill be spared." His example, the ambassador wrote, would have been followed by nearly all the younger members of the diplomatic service, "but authoritative steps were taken to prevent them from volunteering. Alas! he found the means."

He joined the 1st County of London Yeomanry as an interpreter. The regiment was sent to the Norfolk coast for training and defence duties. Soon he was given a commission, a change of status that made him impatient

215

for action. He wrote on December 1: "Last week we were rather hopeful as to our prospects of going out. We alternate between hope and despondency." Looking ahead, it seemed to him that "nothing will be the same," after the war, that "fun has left the world." He felt that his khaki was "a sort of fancy dress. I am very much of a civilian all the time."

By the end of February 1915 his "fancy dress" combined khaki with navy blue. Presumably with influential help, he transferred to the Royal Naval Division, which Patrick Shaw-Stewart said "he caught as one catches a last train." On March 5, he wrote from the troopship *Franconia* that it was "most exhilarating to be again on the sea of the ancient civilisations and dream of the galleys of Carthage and Venice—or farther back still—of the raft of Odysseus." In April, as a result of what he referred to as "my intrigue," he became a subaltern of Hood Battalion, having in the meanwhile declined "special and interesting work" at the Foreign Office in London and been appointed temporarily as interpreter to the Royal Naval Division staff.

"He pulled as many strings to get off the Staff as others do to get on it," Shaw-Stewart said, "and in about three days he had a platoon." His fellow subalterns in the company were Rupert Brooke, Shaw-Stewart, F. S. Kelly, Bernard Freyberg and John Bigelow Dodge, a young American, ardent for England's cause. "My platoon is fine material," Lister wrote, "nearly all Naval Reserve men: hard nuts. I feel a sort of baby among them." It was a stimulating experience, "marching in front of a line of strong men in step, their bayonets bright in the sun and the great adventure in their eyes." He added: "I hope I shall be brave. I am sure they will."

Denis Browne, the young Cambridge musician, who was in another company but a member of the "very jolly

216

family party," (Shaw-Stewart), wrote of Lister: "He has the kindest heart imaginable." Brooke and Lister were much together. "A sad end to such dazzling purity of mind and work," Lister wrote after helping to erect the marble cairn over Brooke's grave on Skyros: "clean-cut, classical, and unaffected all the time like his face, unfurrowed or lined by cares. And the eaglet had begun to beat his wings and soar."

After a series of feints, Hood Battalion landed on the Gallipoli Peninsula on April 29. Shaw-Stewart wrote an account of their arrival in the firing line on May 2. "That day every one who saw him says Charles was superb: he was hit by a shrapnel bullet in the retirement and tried to conceal it, till he was given away by his breeches being filled with blood—so his sergeant told me. That meant a long dreary blank for me, especially as Oc. [Arthur Asquith] was wounded on May 6th and Denis [Browne] on May 8th." He was sent to hospital in Malta. "I should like to get back quick," he wrote to his father, "because I have seen just enough to tantalize. It is rather like love-making in this . . . I had a feeling of great peace as I lay on my back and looked at the blue overhead."

In hospital, he read Thackeray. "I spare much needless pity on Becky, and I'm sure I should have married her if she would have married me." He was amused by Arthur Pendennis's insistence, after having been most affectionate the whole evening to poor little Fanny, that she "must always call him 'Sir' or 'Mr. Pendennis,' as their 'stations in life were so different.' " Reproach seems to radiate from afar as we read Lister's comment on "deep gulfs of class differences." It was his hope that "the dead of the war, side by side, may fill these up."[1]

Hearing of Julian Grenfell's death, he wrote to Lord

[1] Letter to Mrs. Warre Cornish, June 11, 1915.

Ribblesdale: "God, how sad it is—the bitterest blow I have had since this war and am likely to have," and to Lady Desborough: "The void is so terrible for me and the thought of it quite unmans me. I'd so few ties with the life I left when I went abroad—so few, that is to say, that I wanted to keep, and I always felt as sure of Julian's love as he did of mine . . . How much worse it must be for you and yours. All of us loved him so." And to his aunt, the Hon. Beatrix Lister: "Julian is an appalling loss to me. He was the most perfect of friends and heartening of examples."

Lister returned to a battalion much reduced by the fighting at Cape Helles between June 4 and 28, when 10,300 officers and men were killed and wounded in attacks that yielded negligible gains. At Malta, on the way back to duty, he had been invited to celebrate the battle of June 4, in which the Hood and Anson Battalions advanced 250–500 yards on a mile-wide front. "I didn't, as I was not for organised guzzles at a time when better fellows were celebrating it in a very different way." He returned to a battalion that was down to "about sixty men with four officers or so."

Middle East morale began to sag. Success seemed far off. The men of Gallipoli realised that a new plan of campaign was needed. They had no conviction that it would be produced in time to save the situation, or at all. They felt isolated from the hub of events and from national sentiment. By the testimony of Kelly, Lister's influence in checking pessimism at that time "was, by universal consent, invaluable. The heat, the flies, the horrible stench in the trenches, seemed to have no effect at all on his cheerfulness, and, above all, he did not know what fear was." Kelly said that he never knew "a more original character, nor one of more sterling worth, nor one with a more exquisite sense of humour."

218

Another Hood Battalion officer, Ivan Heald,[1] wrote that "Charles Lister was a tower of strength" and that "his wonderful personality" greatly aided "the task of rebuilding a battalion of fighting men out of the salvage from the disaster of June 4th." Heald wrote further that Lister's "willingness to sacrifice himself seemed part of some high secret religion of his own. Throughout the war, I have never met a man in whose heart there burned so steadily that first fine flame that sent us all out soldiering."

On August 23, Lister wrote to his father: "I almost dread my home-coming. So many of our old joy-places will be full of ghosts." He was then acting company commander, "a giddy position, with three subordinate officers. I feel rather embarrassed." Two days later he was hit by shrapnel again, "struck in the pelvis and my bladder deranged," he wrote from a hospital ship. The shell had killed one man and wounded others. "My doctor is quite happy at the way things are going," he wrote in his last letter to his father. The Commander-in-Chief had recommended him for a decoration, "for brilliant deeds of gallantry throughout our operations." He died of that third wound on August 28, 1915, at the age of 28. Not long before, he had written: "I know now that I shall live. I do not mean that I may not be killed."

His death sent waves of grief across the world. "It really is heartbreaking," Robert Palmer[2] wrote from Amarah, Mesopotamia, to Ronald Knox. "All the men one had so hoped would make this world a little better to live in seem to be taken away. Charles was a spirit no country could afford to lose."

[1] Ivan Heald, from Fleet Street, was later killed in action on the Western Front.

[2] The Hon. Robert Stafford Palmer, Hampshire Regiment, killed in action, January 21, 1916.

To C.A.L.

To have laughed and talked—wise, witty, fantastic,
*   feckless—*
To have mocked at rules and rulers and learnt to
*   obey,*
To have led your men with a daring adored and
*   reckless,*
To have struck your blow for Freedom, the old straight
*   way:*

To have hated the world and lived among those who
*   love it,*
To have thought great thoughts and lived till you
*   knew them true,*
To have loved men more than yourself, and have died
*   to prove it—*
Yes, Charles, this is to have lived: was there more to
*   do?*

—C.A.A.[1]

4

Charles Lister's death reduced to two the group of scholar-soldiers who, six months earlier, had sailed to the Aegean with Argonautic pride. Of those who formed the exclusive mess known as the Latin Club, Patrick Shaw-Stewart and F. S. ("Cleg") Kelly remained. Arthur Asquith's seniority in years had caused him to be moved up in rank. Kelly was an Eton and Oxford alumnus whose life was dedicated to music. Those two were among the last of the subalterns who had gone out with the Hood Battalion to Gallipoli. Like his friends, Shaw-Stewart was deeply dismayed (rather than shocked) by

[1] By Dr. C. A. Alington, from *Charles Lister: Letters and Recollections* (1917).

Charles Lister's death. "I suppose it's the the same for everyone, and yet, you know, it's an odd fact that all the people I really care about are dead, and all the people I used to say 'Hullo!' to and see when there was nothing better to do are absolutely intact."

Frederick Septimus Kelly was an Australian who had lived most of his thirty-three years in England when he joined the Royal Naval Division in 1914. Brother-in-law of a non-related namesake who became Admiral Sir John Kelly, he had "ample means," and kept establishments at 29, Queen Anne Street, London, W., and at Bispham, near Marlow. He was a none the less serious musician who worked devotedly at improving his technique as a pianist and at realising his best powers as a composer. At the same time, he was socially active, with his name on the invitation lists of many leading hostesses of "the season."

Publicly, he had a reputation in a different *milieu*. He won the Diamond Sculls at Henley three times. He rowed in the Oxford University Eight in 1903, in the Leander Eight which won the Grand Challenge Cup three years running, and in the English Olympics Eight of 1908. Like Ronald Poulton, the Rugby footballer, the excellence he had attained in his branch of sport led to his being cherished as a national exemplar. It was music that possessed his soul.

He had been secretary of Balliol College Musical Society. He composed songs, lyric cycles, a string trio, a serenade for flute and orchestra, organ preludes. In the Dardanelles, he composed an Elegy for String Orchestra in memory of Rupert Brooke. "I am writing a violin sonata for you—I mean, violin and piano—in G major, which I hope you will accept." He was writing from Cape Helles to Jelly d'Aranyi, then a very young but already distinguished violinist who was later acclaimed by the concert audiences of Europe and

221

America. "I began composing it $3\frac{1}{2}$ months ago. Of course there are many interruptions. It is all there in my head but not yet on paper."

Arriving on the Western Front, he wrote again to her: "The scream of howitzers would be the despair of Richard Strauss, though it would be amusing if he tried to write a battle symphonic poem! I have had thoughts of writing an Overture 1914 *à la* 1812 . . . but that sort of work isn't really in my line." He played the piano in public as soloist and accompanist. Musically, it seemed that a career of interesting and possibly exciting fulfilment lay before him. It all came to naught at Beaucourt-sur-Ancre on November 13, 1916.

Ten days later, Jelly d'Aranyi was lying awake in the dark early hours when she heard violin music. The notes played were those of the sonata that Kelly composed for her. Though "sounding from a distance," they were "clear and real." She has no theory to offer, no prejudices to air. "I heard them. That is what happened." The experience was repeated. She took up again the violin practice which, in her grief, she had for the time being abandoned.

5

Patrick Shaw-Stewart was the son of a retired major-general of the British Army whose modest means were said to have been an embarrassment to the boy when the time came for him to go to Eton from a day school. From then on, he seems to have been money-conscious, though he had no talent for finance. At Eton, he professed indifference to the classics, a branch of scholarship in which he excelled. He often referred to himself there as "a mere sap," but he won the coveted Newcastle Scholarship.

At Balliol, he was regarded by some as "a Scotchman on the make,"[1] possibly because of his resolute disclaimer of ideals. "I have only worldly ambitions," he would say. He chose to be thought a Philistine, a preference in which he was sustained by few of his friends. It was part of a self-depreciation that was apparently intended to be socially entertaining, a passport to good will, rather than masochistically gratifying. "All Stewarts are pretenders," Raymond Asquith remarked cheerfully, "just as all Shaws are charlatans."

There was no pretence in Shaw-Stewart's scholastic brilliance. He carried off some of the supreme prizes: the Ireland and Hertford Scholarships, and took a First in Mods and Greats. He was disqualified for the Derby Scholarship by his election to a fellowship of All Souls, "a brilliant and beguiling youth who never failed in anything."[2]

Conversationally, he never missed a point and his fiercely acute intellect kept him to the fore in any argument. At the Union, he fell short of the first-rate as a speaker, appreciated for the subtlety of his wit. Though his voice was habitually pitched too low, what he had to say was invariably enjoyed by those with ears to hear. In spite of Charles Lister's almost hypnotic powers of persuasion, Shaw-Stewart obstinately remained a Tory who, while having little taste for politics and asserting no platform principles, staunchly upheld the old virtues of family loyalty, duty as an obligation, respect for one's elders.

As secretary of a College society for which he failed to summon a meeting throughout one term, he was required to convene a special session at which he was to be censured. Forgetting the appointed hour, he arrived early and carried off two jugs of claret cup under the

[1] Evelyn Waugh: *Ronald Knox* (Chapman & Hall, 1959).
[2] Ibid.

impression that his fellow members were not sufficiently keen to attend.

He was an admirer and correspondent of Lady Diana Manners and Viola Tree. To the latter, he wrote in a scolding vein from Balliol: "I am not going to be retained on sufferance as a court jester, or a thinking machine, or a whetstone of the mind, or an *Enquire Within Upon Everything*. I am not going to have you take me as hens take grit, to promote your mental digestion, and assist you to lay intellectual eggs. So there you have it, and this is deadly earnest."[1]

Viola Tree said that he was "comparatively ugly. He had a dead-white face with pale red freckles and red hair, straight and shiny." She recalled his "extremely expressive eyes" and that he was "given to laughter." Acquaintances, rather than friends, thought him conceited; others, according to Viola Tree, regarded him as recklessly ambitious; some decided that "he had no heart." Ronald Knox could recite an act of academic chivalry by Shaw-Stewart that diminished such criticisms to pin-pricks.

There was a general expectation that his fine brain would bear him up to heights of which, it appeared, he had himself as yet no clear view. His friends considered that by putting on uniform he sacrificed more than most others of that generation. For the time being, the two or three years before the war, he engaged himself in the City. Billy Grenfell wrote to his mother in 1912: "Patrick came down here (Balliol) last night, and was charming but infinitely depressed, poor old Shylock, at the idea of banking in the dog-days ahead, and through the autumn equinox and to the end of all time. However, I was a good Job's comforter and heartened him with the prospect of being a merchant prince, which is surely as good as or better than most things in this untidy world."

[1] Viola Tree: *Castles in the Air.*

He had no business habits, and "his acceptance of a job with Baring Bros. seemed farcical."[1] When his friends hinted at cynicism, he retorted: "It's such fun to say eight when one means eight thousand!" No doubt, compared with the schools, mental effort in the service of Mammon was so much play to him, who had known what it was to study to the point of breakdown and, incidentally, to lose temporarily much of his hair from the same cause.

His sense of duty strong upon him, he easily adapted himself to the amphibious life of the Royal Naval Division. He joined with no repining for things past, delighted as he was to be with the companions of other days. He took his regimental work seriously. For him, efficiency was part of his obligation as a patriot. He was smart on parade; in the line, cool and brave. He wrote to Lady Diana Manners after the burial of Rupert Brooke: "I commanded the firing party, in so much terror for the correctness of my ceremonial drill that I was inaccessible to sorrow or grandeur. It's very like Byron, really."[2]

After Gallipoli, he was attached to the French Army staff at Salonika, which the Germans derisively called "the Allies' biggest internment camp." Feeling "out of it" and desperately bored, he at last succeeded in getting himself returned to the Royal Naval Division, by then on the Western Front. When he heard of the death in action of Raymond Asquith, he wrote: "It makes me more inclined than anything that has happened yet to take off my boots and go to bed."

Kelly was killed; then Edward Horner, who had been one of Shaw-Stewart's intimates at Oxford. Sorrowfully, Shaw-Stewart wrote to Edward Marsh: "I continue to believe that the luck of my generation must change. Nowadays, we who are alive have the sense of being old,

[1] *The Times*, January 12, 1918.
[2] *The Rainbow Comes and Goes*

225

old survivors." Edward Horner's death was thought to be his greatest blow. Friends of both believed that he had lost the will to live on.

He was killed on December 30, 1917, at the age of 29. *The Times*, in an obituary note, suggested that he would have attained to "power and eminence." For himself, the rest was stark silence: "I am sure that there is nothing to be looked for from the dead."[1]

[1] In a letter to Lady Hermione Buxton, November 7, 1915.

CHAPTER SIXTEEN

A Fearful Price to Pay

1

ON THE afternoon of September 24, 1915, orderlies of the Royal Army Medical Corps were seen bending to a strange task in fields behind the line between Lens and the La Bassée canal in the French Black Country. They were marking out routes with wooden arrows bearing the direction: *Walking Wounded.* The signs were pointers to succour and safety for survivors of the coming battle.

Casualty clearing stations were ready to deal with a record influx of cases. Ammunition dumps had grown to mountainous size, welcome proof of the new production assiduity at home. There was low-voiced talk of an intention to use gas, less as a reprisal for the enemy's introduction of it at Ypres in April than as a demonstration of the British resolve to drop at last the cricket metaphor in war. Not necessarily for that reason, the enemy reported it as "an absolute surprise."[1]

After pursuing a policy of strategic inaction while the first of his new armies finished their training, Lord Kitchener had decided that the long-planned French offensive in Champagne, between Rheims and Verdun, must be supported because of the alarming situation on the Russian front. It was thought unlikely that the Germans

---

[1] *Official History of the War*, quoting German records.

could bring back from the east enough divisions to forestall Joffre's impending large-scale attack. Kitchener's order was issued in ominous terms. "We must do our utmost to help the French in the offensive, even though by doing so we may suffer very heavy losses."

No phrase in the grammar of modern war had come to be more mistrusted by the rank and file than "preliminary bombardment." To the headquarters' staffs it was still an indispensable prelude to success. When nine hundred British heavy guns and sixteen hundred field guns opened up on September 22, many hearts shuddered at the remembrance of the costly and futile operations earlier in the year at Neuve Chapelle, Second Ypres and Festubert. "Behind our lines, in scores of villages where our men were quartered, there was a sense of impending fate," wrote Philip Gibbs, the war correspondent. To one of the R.A.M.C. orderlies it seemed that the sun that day was going down in anger at what portended below. Black clouds were edged with wrathful red. Away to the east, a different symbol proclaimed itself, a perfect rainbow shedding its mystery on a landscape as tenuous as a vision. It was not difficult to match the smouldering western sky with coming events. The contrasting scene, arched by the sublime emblem of peace, was a poignant reminder of a choice that man had lost the power to make.

Among the mass of troops moving up from the base camps to the battle area at Loos were two divisions of Kitchener's Army, the 21st and 24th, both raised from the "third hundred thousand" who volunteered in the early autumn of 1914. The 21st Division consisted mainly of men from Northumberland, Durham and Yorkshire. The battalion commanders were ex-Regular officers, mostly retired from the Indian Army. Otherwise, only 14 Regular or ex-Regular officers were serving in the division, all the other officers being newly commissioned.

228

The ranks were stiffened by a small number of ex-Regular N.C.O.s. Trained at Aylesbury and Tring, the division had moved into the Aldershot Command at Godalming and Frensham in July. Equipment shortages hindered training up to the end of April. The troops had to wait another three months for their rifles.

That was the story also of the 24th Division, drawn from 13 regiments of the Home Counties, the Midlands and East Anglia. None of its battalions had more than one Regular or ex-Regular officer, apart from the C.O. Its training on the South Downs at Patcham, near Brighton, and at Shoreham, had been similarly handicapped all through the spring. Both divisions were sent forward as part of the general reserve for Sir Douglas Haig's 1st Army which was to supply the assault forces at Loos. They had been in France only three weeks. None of the men had seen a shot fired in action. They were to have a shattering initiation into the realities of war.

2

On September 20, they began a series of four night marches from St. Omer to their appointed positions along the Béthune-Lens road (21st Division) and the Vermelles-Hulluch road (24th Division). The hours of darkness were chosen to avoid enemy air observation; in daylight, the men rested in billets. The marches were made needlessly tiring by bad transport organisation leading to congestion of the roads. From corps headquarters, the divisional commanders had been informed that their troops would not be put in the line of fire "unless the Germans are absolutely smashed and retiring in disorder."

It happened that the two divisions arrived at their

thousand-yard frontages at a moment when Haig was being misled by reports suggesting that his 1st Army was about to achieve a break-through at Hulluch. That expectation was communicated to the men of the 21st and 24th divisions, who welcomed the prospect of being sent in pursuit of a beaten and demoralised enemy. A corps order that they were to carry packs, greatcoats and extra rations was taken as assurance that they faced an advance in which they would meet little or no resistance.

Instead, they were sent forward to secure and entrench a line from Hill 70, east of Loos, to the west side of Hulluch, one of two villages on the skyline of the slag-tip disfigured plain that was the battle arena. They moved up in discouraging conditions of pouring rain and more traffic congestion that again and again severed the column of marchers slogging along under their heavy kit loads. The mud on the men's greatcoats flapped like lead against their legs, making the going even more wearisome. March discipline suffered and was unfairly criticised by professionals of the brigade staffs. Many of the men ate not only their extra ration but the iron ration that was for use only in extremity. Some drained their waterbottles dry. Desperate tiredness was obvious in many of the battalions as they filed into the communication trenches. There, almost at once, they came under heavy shelling.

Extraordinary confusion ensued. The order to move into the area of attack had come as a surprise, to some a shock. None of the officers had maps, none knew the terrain, and there was uncertainty about objectives. Instead of concentrating on Bois Hugo, as was intended, the 21st Division "sheered south-east towards Hill 70." (*Official History*). Subalterns, acting independently, tried to lead their platoons forward but their bewilderment was as obvious as the men's. Shrapnel lashed down

230

on them while high explosive smashed the crowded trenches.

By dusk on the first day of battle groups that had gone forward unled straggled back to the broken support lines, where, by the account of a war correspondent, there were hysterical scenes in which frustrated men smashed their rifles. Officers cursed, some wept, fearing disgrace. The correspondent saw the 21st Division return to billets. "They walked with bent heads. The young officers had a blanched and beaten look. The sight of those dejected men was tragic and pitiful."[1] The two divisions lost a total of 385 officers and 7,844 other ranks.

As the *Official History* was careful to say of the stories subsequently circulating about the retirement of the 21st and 24th Divisions at Loos: "It was as 'old campaigners' that the divisions failed, and this, seeing how few experienced men they contained, can be no reproach to them." Twelve of the twenty-six battalions showed that they were not lacking in dash and courage in trying to carry out a nearly impossible task. Many of those men would be found fighting with the tenacity of seasoned soldiers in the months to come.

Meanwhile, the "walking wounded" were following the paths that had been marked out for them before the battle. They stumbled back in a steady stream that continued for a day and a night and another day. Before the climax of the battle, there were diversionary attacks that cast dark shadows. Basil Hoyle, son of the vicar of Stoke Poges, was killed at Festubert, aged 23; a Radley exhibitioner and gold medallist whose delicacy of temperament made it harder for him than for most men to be a soldier. He was modest and retiring, happiest in pursuit of the pleasures of music. His lack of self-emphasis, and a certain inner radiance, brought him the best kind of popularity. "He was absolutely beloved by

[1] Sir Philip Gibbs: *Realities of War.*

231

every man in the company and not one but would have saved him had it been possible," a private soldier wrote after the battle. "Indescribable bravery" was a phrase used about him in another letter. He fell within twenty yards of the German front line, leading his platoon of the 9th Royal Welch Fusiliers.

"He was lost in his uniform and George Meredith," a friend wrote of Arthur Innes Adam, casually met at Abbeville in 1915. Aged 21, Adam had been as it were baptised by total immersion in classical learning. His father was Platonic Scholar and Tutor of Emmanuel College, Cambridge, his mother a Classical Lecturer at Girton. He was Senior Scholar at Winchester, where he gained a variety of prizes and almost as many nicknames, including "The Mouse" and "The Scarecrow." In the Army he was "Parson Snowy" because of his extremely fair hair. Music was his passion, too. He was a devoted member of the Bach Choir. He is remembered for his unusual energy, whimsical wit and fluting laugh: "the life and soul of his circle, the one and only Adam." He joined the Cambridgeshires from Oxford and vanished in one of the preliminary actions before Loos, reported wounded and missing or captured. No further news of him was ever received.

Charles Francis ("Frank") Purcell, from County Cork, fell in an engagement on September 15 in which practically all his brother officers of the Irish Guards and all but one of the men of his machine-gun section were killed. At Oxford, where he took a history degree, he helped to start the St. Patrick's Society and he was one of the promoters of a movement for "a reasonable Irish nationalism." He proved an admirable leader of men.

"His good nature made him universally liked. His death was a real loss, for he was just the man who might have done great things for Ireland."[1]

[1] *Balliol War Memorial Book.*

The main attacks in the battle of Loos came on September 25–26, 1915. The first casualty lists were published on October 1, while a series of sub-offensives was in progress. On one day, *The Times* filled a page and a half with the closely printed names and regiments of the dead, wounded and missing. Every day, the newspaper published memorial notices of those killed in action or who died of wounds. In four days 236 names appeared on the front page, one hundred of them young men between 18–25, forty-one of them only sons. The mournful recital of the carnage at Loos continued through most of the month.

Of 106 officers killed in the first week, 102 were under thirty years of age and all but 22 of those were under twenty-six. Five were only 18 years old, ten were 19, fifteen were 21, nine were 22, eight were 23, nine were 24 and eleven were 25. Among them were the sons of clergymen, barristers, naval and military officers, medical men, missionaries and members of both Houses of Parliament. The final figures of losses in the battle were 2,013 officers and 48,367 N.C.O.s and men. "Of the grand total, some 800 officers and 15,000 men were killed or missing and never heard of again." (*Official History*). It was a fearful price to pay in support of an ally who required British troops to fight over a region far more difficult than his own selected battlefield of Champagne.

Smoke hung over the field of Loos for some time after the guns had ceased to fire. It was the shroud of many of the young men of the 47th London Division who had crowded into the recruiting centre at Great Scotland Yard the previous autumn. Now they lay with their fellow volunteers of the 15th Scottish Division who were foremost in the advance on Loos village and Hill 70, close by.

Some of the wounded were not picked up for several days. Two crawled in on their sixth day in no-man's-land, where they had kept themselves going by sucking grass stems and eating iron rations taken from the dead men around them. They reported having seen German stretcher-bearers bandaging slightly wounded British soldiers and sending them back to the lines.

One of the familiar landmarks of the battlefield was the tall pithead wheel house known to the troops as Tower Bridge. It was the objective of the 12th Highland Infantry, whose nineteen-year-old adjutant, Kenneth Gordon Campbell, fell in the advance. He had been head of his house at Winchester and was a classical scholar of Trinity Hall, Cambridge. Lawrence Vaughan Chapman, B.A., LL.B., was killed in one of the subsidiary attacks, a prizeman, medallist and exhibitioner of London University, and a member of the legal staff of the City & Midland Bank.

Of the 17 officers and 650 other ranks of the 2nd Royal Warwickshires who were in the action of September 25, no officer and only 140 others came out unscathed. One of those who fell was Rex Elderton, aged 23, an all-round athlete who competed in international events. When the war started he was working as an engineer in Switzerland. He returned at once to join the Army. Robert Bruce was serving with a Territorial battery of the Royal Field Artillery when he was killed on September 25, aged 33. He joined the Army & Navy Stores as a boy and was secretary to the Board at the time of his enlistment in 1914. John Owen Iles was the only son of H.M. Divisional Inspector of Schools at Wolverhampton. He won an open mathematics scholarship at Caius College, Cambridge, and took honours in the first part of the Mathematics Tripos and the Law Tripos. He represented his university at chess. He was "a fearless boy who combined considerable judgment with his boldness," they said of him in the Royal Welch Fusiliers in which he was serving when he was killed at Loos, aged 22. Another scholarly soldier killed that day was Julian Richards, son of the rector of South Luffenham, Rutland, scholar of King's School, Sherborne, and Wadham College, Oxford. He was in the Civil Service, employed as an assistant surveyor at the General Post Office.

Edward Worrell Carrington, M.R.C.S., L.R.C.P., of Reading, medical officer of the 2nd Worcestershires, was killed in the close fighting near the La Bassée Canal; aged 26. He had trained for medicine at King's College Hospital, London, after Marlborough and Keble College, Oxford. Arthur Ernest Bullock, who had held house appointments at St. Mary's Hospital, London, was also killed in the battle, aged 26. At St. Paul's School he won the Public Schools' Championship Shield for gymnastics. He represented his hospital at football and swimming. Another loss to the medical profession was Edgar Faulks, M.R.C.S., of Loughborough, house surgeon at Guy's Hospital, London; aged 38.

Leonard Righton Burrows, 27, Northumberland Fusiliers, was shot through the head going to the rescue of one of his men under fire. The second son of the Bishop of Sheffield, he had gained high academic honours at Oxford, after which he went to work in India, his special subject education. He returned to England in October 1914 and joined the Inns of Court O.T.C. He was buried on the field by his brother, the Rev. H. R. Burrows, a chaplain of the Forces.

William Cadge, of Loddon, Norfolk, was a Ceylon tea planter, home on leave in August 1914. He joined the London Rifle Brigade before being commissioned in his county regiment, in which he was serving at Loos. Raymond Scott Dickinson, Queen's Westminster Rifles, was the only son of Sir John Dickinson, chief magistrate at

Bow Street police court. Geoffrey Murray Smith, Royal Fusiliers, aged 19, was a grandson of George Smith, founder of the *Dictionary of National Biography*. His elder brother had died of wounds in November 1914.

Dr. George Adam Smith, Principal of Aberdeen University, lost his son in the battle. So did Principal Morris, of the North Wales Baptist College, Bangor; his son, Henry, was head of Rugby School, 1912–13. Rudyard Kipling's only son, John, a wartime subaltern in the Irish Guards, was killed. Sir Max Pemberton, novelist, lost a nephew, Leigh Pemberton, aged 18½, an all-round athlete and champion shot of Watford Grammar School.

> *Yours seemed an easy part*
> *To construe, learn some trivial lines by heart;*
> *Yet to your hands has God assigned*
> *The burden of the sorrows of mankind.*[1]

The founder and publisher of *Everyman's Library*, Joseph Malaby Dent, noted that month: "I saw one of my girls in the office here with red eyes, and I found that she had just been weeping for a second brother she had lost." He wrote from a full heart. Two of his sons had been killed.

William Frederick (Wilfred) Sheridan was the great-grandson of R. B. Sheridan, the dramatist, and grandson of John Lothrop Motley, historian of the Dutch Republic and sometime United States Minister in London. James Campbell Henderson-Hamilton, younger son of the rector of St. Mary's, Hamilton, was an advocate who joined the 9th Black Watch, a battalion that was well to the fore in the fighting at Hulluch on September 25. He was 31. His brother had been killed at Gallipoli.

[1] *To My Pupils, Gone Before Their Day*, by Guy Kendall, M.A., Headmaster of University College School, London, 1916–36, in *The Spectator*, October 2, 1915.

Denis Donaldson, a doctor's son from Harlington, Middlesex, was studying at the City & Guilds of London Engineering College. In August 1914 he enlisted in one of the London battalions. He was soon promoted sergeant. He fought at Loos with the 47th Division, which was manned by Territorials and wartime volunteers like himself and had a leading role in the battle order for Loos. He was gazetted second-lieutenant of his battalion the day before he was killed, aged 19. Edwin Mawby, 36, of Spalding, Lincolnshire, was a Cheapside solicitor who enlisted as a trooper in the Westminster Dragoons before being commissioned in the Welsh Guards. Gerald Moyna, Royal Scots Fusiliers, was head of the modern side at Rugby and an exhibitioner in Modern Languages at New College, Oxford, where he took first class history honours. He was a university boxer and represented Oxford against Cambridge. After extensive travel in the Far East, he became a leader writer on the *Morning Post*. At the outbreak of war he enlisted as a private in the London Scottish. He was 35.

Lord Reading said of Norman Lindsay Mackie, 23, an Oxford history and law student, that he would "one day be a leading theoretical jurist." He went to France with the London Scottish in 1914 and was killed in the Loos fighting. Robert Whyte, 23, one of the founders of the New Liberal Club at Oxford, had trained as a chartered accountant, though his personal interests spanned the wide range of natural history, poetry, politics and philosophy. He enlisted in the 9th Black Watch. His colonel urged him to apply for a commission. He did so after more persuasion and as a junior officer he was in and out of the trenches at Vermelles through most of the summer, until he fell at Loos.

Clement Aubrey Symons, 22, The Gloucestershire Regiment, became a schoolmaster after leaving King Edward VI School, Bath. He wrote to his brother three weeks before his death in action on September 25 describing the effect of a bomb dropped by a German aircraft on his battalion headquarters. "Two fellows near by saw the plane coming and one said to the other, 'Wouldn't it be a blighter if they dropped a bomb here!' The bomb was dropped and the man who had spoken had his left leg blown off." Lieutenant Symons saw the severed limb lying across the man's body. "It looked like a leg of beef—awful! All he said was 'Dear me! dear me!' about 100 times, and said the Lord's Prayer over and over. He died in the night. It was the first thing I had seen of the kind, and it upset me badly and it then dawned on me what war was."[1]

Another schoolmaster, Hugh Butterworth, on the staff of Wanganui College, New Zealand, was killed the same day at Loos. Serving with The Rifle Brigade, he was in the liquid fire attack at Hooge.[2] He wrote to his fellow masters at the College: "Our part of the line was a wild place to send a new regiment to; only all regiments are new nowadays," and noted nuances in the art of leadership: "If one takes out a party of men somewhere they don't know—in the open, probably—to dig, they'll go like lambs as long as they've got an officer with them. The curious thing is in civilian life they've probably cursed us as plutocrats, but here they fairly look to us." When he ordered a digging party to go out with a sergeant in charge, the sergeant told him: "I wish you were coming, sir. I don't know the way." Butterworth replied: "My dear man, nor do I." The sergeant said: "Very likely not, sir, but the men will think you do and they know I don't."

O England, I heard the cry of those who died for thee
Sounding like an organ voice across the winter sea;

[1] *Letters of Fallen Englishmen* (Gollancz, 1930).
[2] See page 190.

*They lived and died for England, and gladly went
their way.
England, O England—how could I stay?*

Those lines, printed in an Australian newspaper, were
a reminder of sacrifices being made farther afield.
Corporal James Burns, who wrote them, was fighting
with the 21st Battn., 6th Brigade of the Australian
Forces in Gallipoli, where he was killed in action that
September.

4

American-born Harold Chapin joined the Royal Army
Medical Corps in September, 1914. Because he lived and
worked in England, he considered that he owed her a
duty, while holding to his American citizenship. After
six months' training at St. Albans, he went to France
with the 6th Field Ambulance attached to the 6th
Brigade, 2nd London Division (Territorial). When someone, remarking on his volunteering gesture, spoke of
"King and Country," Chapin said: "I'm fighting for no
King, and the best of this King is that he knows we're
not fighting for him."

His mother, an American actress, brought him to
England when he was very young. She was engaged to
play in a Benson production of *Coriolanus* at Stratford-
on-Avon. The boy was given a walk-on part. It was
his first taste of the stage life. He never lost his appetite
for it. He went first to North London Collegiate School
as a day boy, and then to Norwich Grammar School as
a boarder. His education was rounded off by two "very
happy years" at University College School, London.
After that, he set about learning the actors' trade. He
joined a touring company. He appeared in Drury Lane
pantomime. He was assistant stage manager at the

239

Shaftesbury Theatre, London. It was the best possible apprenticeship for a dramatic writer who was filling his notebooks with ideas for plays.

He was sensitive, intelligent, humorously observant and hard-working. They said he "might have become a dramatic Dickens. It was genius beyond question." He wrote a full-length play, *Art and Opportunity*, for Marie Tempest and the Prince of Wales's Theatre. It brought him money and reputation but little satisfaction. He suffered vexations of the spirit, feeling that he had betrayed his best powers. It was a relief to him to be engaged by Granville Barker as stage director for a series of Shakespearean revivals at the Savoy Theatre. Another full length play of his, *The Marriage of Columbine*, was reviewed as "good drama but not good theatre."

He became an understudy while continuing his stage direction work. He was seen in plays by Jerome K. Jerome and Israel Zangwill, his virile voice and personality making their mark without raising him to the heights. Always there was the suggestion of powers maturing in a mind enriched by sympathies and insights acquired behind the scenes. His one-act plays were hailed as small masterpieces.

Identifying himself with England's cause in 1914 may have had a more recondite meaning for Chapin. Americans at that time had extraordinarily little standing in Europe and rather less in England, where the sanctions of history were more intimately involved. In spite of heiresses who came over to acquire titles and husbands, sometimes in that order, Americans were of little social or political account. As a nation, they had no great place in the world, like Englishmen in their small island. In the glare of later history it is laughable to reflect on the bland general indifference to America then prevailing. "What does American opinion matter?" asked Si

Reginald Brade, Secretary of the War Office, in 1916, when facilities for American war correspondents were being discussed.

Having supposed that the war would be over by the end of its second year, Chapin wrote to his wife on May 29, 1915, that "it won't be November twelvemonth unless England drops attacking Kitchener, attacking the *Daily Mail*, attacking defenceless Germans in London, striking, and all the rest of it, and devotes all its attention to attacking the German Army out here." He wished those at home realised the enormous concentration of force required to take a mile of trench; "the terrific resistance we have to put up to hold it; the price we have to pay for every little failure."

As an R.A.M.C. man, Chapin had a wider acquaintance with wounds and suffering and death than the soldier in his trench who was normally aware of them only in his own limited sector. Chapin saw them on the battlefield, in the ambulances, at the casualty clearing stations, in the field hospitals. "I can stick anything but depressed fracture of the skull," he wrote. "A man died in one of the wards here of that. He had a ward to himself (they make such a noise) and a mouse came out and ran back and forth under the stretcher he was tied to. These things almost *please* one by their perfection of eeriness and horror. Do you understand? They are like some gigantic supernatural artist in the grotesque and horrible. I shall never fear the picturesque in stage grouping again."

He had never seen "such perfect grouping," he said, as when, after a shell had fallen, "the light of an electric torch lit up a little interior 10 ft square, with one man sitting against the far wall, another lying across his feet and a dog prone in the foreground, all dead and covered thinly with the dust of powdered plaster and masonry brought down by the explosion. They might have been

241

grouped so for forty years. That they were dead seemed right and proper—but that they had ever been alive—beyond all credence." He had recently seen those same men mount guard—"another department of experience altogether."

He pondered the problems of perception that had often occupied his mind. The war, he said, "lit up" such problems, which recurred as he watched the effects of partial anaesthesia: "just what feeling is and what consciousness; how can there be degrees down from our normal to zero and if there can be degrees up as well—you follow?—to some zenith of apprehensiveness to existence. Of course, the normal capacity for perception fluctuates a little. Has it any limits up as it obviously has down?"

One of his last letters told how he and others went into a small French mining town in July, 1915, to recover wounded after heavy shelling. "Horses, men, women, and children blown to pieces by huge high explosives. Amusing, ironic contrasts abounded: within five minutes of each other came in a self-possessed young woman of about ten to have the remains of her arm cut off—perfectly calm—walked in, never cried or showed the least excitement, *and* a man of fifty on a stretcher with a mangled leg, who roared out in an enormous mad voice for his *Maman* over and over again till he was anaesthetised." He described a scene in a house to which he was called:

"A huge woman dead on her face across the threshold, a little child also dead at her feet, the legs of her menfolk (husband and son?) straggling across the foot of the way outside (I am keeping back the hundreds of horrible details, hard though it may be to believe it), and her remaining daughter, a child of about twelve—leaping back and forth over the bodies struggling to get a chain from the neck of the woman. *'Souvenir!'* I tried

242

to get her away—she was half mad—but was assailed fiercely by neighbours on her behalf. While I was being suppressed, another shell came over and we went to earth in a heap." Afterwards, "the child returned to the chain—armed now with a carving knife—and I left her to it."[1]

He had brought in a number of wounded to the regimental aid posts in September 1915. He was seen to go over the parapet in search of others lying in the open. He did not come back. His body was found and buried under the great smoke pall at Loos the next day.

After attending a memorial performance of his best one-act plays at the Queen's Theatre on December 14, 1915, William Archer, distinguished as a critic and successful as a dramatist, wrote an appreciation for *The Nation* (New York.) "It was no mere respectful solemnity: the audience vividly enjoyed every word of it. Something was due to the excellent acting; for many of our best artists had come forward to do honour to their lost comrade. But what one realises most keenly in retrospect is the abounding vitality of Chapin's talent. There was not a moment when one did not feel one's self in touch with a living spirit, bounteously endowed with thought, observation, humour, craftsmanship. It filled one with a sort of dumb rage to think that such rare promise had been extinguished, on the threshold of fulfilment, by the brute hazard of the battlefield. It was a youth in his twenties who had done all this fine work—what might we not have expected from the ripened man?"

[1] Harold Chapin's letters were published in *Soldier and Dramatist* (John Lane, 1916).

5

Culture bearers of the European tradition were being extinguished every day; lamps that could never be lighted again. Who could measure the loss to the civilised life of man by the destruction of so much refined mental energy, so many dedicated intelligences? On every field of battle there were casualties that devitalised the republics of learning and letters, the creative arts and crafts, constructive thought, the sanity of nations.

Charles Peguy, leader of a new school of French poets, killed; Bertheim, of the Physiological Institute at Frankfort, whose chemistry researches benefited international medicine, killed; Joseph Dechelette, Franco-Roman scholar, killed; Max Strack, Professor of Ancient History, Kiel University, killed; Alfred Druin, French writer, killed; Herman Lons, German novelist and folk song authority, killed; Paul Gret, Professor of Architectural Design, University of Pennsylvania, killed; Albert Magnard, composer, killed; Jean Pierre Barbier, French writer, killed; Richard von Gizychi, Berlin Seminar for Oriental Languages, killed; Ernest Psichori, poet, killed; Ernst Stadler (B.Litt., Oxon.), Professor of Philology, Strasbourg, killed; Henri Gaudier-Brezska, sculptor and painter, killed; Robert d'Humières, translator of Kipling, killed.

6

"It is the eve of our crowning hour." Charles Hamilton Sorley, aged 20, was going into action with the Suffolks in one of the minor offensives that were reverberations of the thunder of Loos. "And I think exultantly and sweetly of the one or two or three outstandingly admirable meals of my life." One, he remembered, was in Yorkshire, at a moorland inn before a log fire, "with ale and tea and every sort of Yorkshire bakery." Another was at Mecklenburg-Schwerin, in a farmhouse, "utterly at peace" amid its fields. There was a tureen of champagne on the table, "to which we helped ourselves with ladles!" Fish fresh caught, duck fresh killed: "It was Homeric and its memory fills many hungry hours."

He ended his letter with an "Adieu!" and the prayer "that I ride my frisky nerves with cool and steady hands when the time comes." The time came eight days later, on the afternoon of October 13, while leading his company to the attack at Hulluch after his company commander had been wounded. A bullet struck him in the side of the head; and one more joyous heart ceased to beat, one more gifted tongue would sing its songs no more. Of the war poets, he was one of the two or three most promising and the least fulfilled: the most promising because he was also the most self-forgetful, largely unfulfilled because poetry was not for him the inescapable vocation. Rather, it was the casual expression of a classically disciplined mind which, for his years, was remarkably alert to the false note in life and in art. His modern spirit, asserted in a relentless respect for truth, impenetrates the slim volume, *Marlborough and Other Poems*,[1] in which are embalmed his poetic remains.

> *We do not see the vital point*
> *That 'tis the eighth, most deadly, sin*
> *To wail "The world is out of joint"—*
> *And not attempt to put it in.*
> —A Call to Action: 1913.

"What would have been the career of such a boy? Whenever his house-master came to see me on business, that being disposed of, we always found ourselves discussing Charles Sorley and his future, was it to be

[1] Cambridge University Press, 1916.

245

literary, or social, or political? Well, God knows! But anyhow he would have been a great and true man, who would have served his generation and made a big name."[1]

A craftsman whose works declare that he had a fineness of more than the hand also came to his end in one of those minor engagements at Loos. George Elton Sedding was "a gentle and peaceful man" whose life was dedicated to the making of beautiful things. After a public school education (Radley) and training at the Royal College of Art, South Kensington, finishing at Heatherley's and the L.C.C. School of Arts & Crafts, he set up as an art metal designer in Noel Street, Soho. He wrought Communion plate and processional crosses for the Church. He designed and made settings for every kind of precious stone. His crucifixes and patens still grace African altars. His pendants and brooches gleam in famous jewellery collections. Everything he put his hand to was touched by his quiet excellence. He belonged to the now rare order of men who, in our era of proliferating machine-shops, seem to be like monks of the Middle Ages guarding the flame of human culture.

When in August 1914 he went to join a Public Schools battalion of the Royal Fusiliers he found the recruiting officer temporarily off duty. The next nearest recruiting officer was taking men for the Norfolk Regiment. Sedding enlisted as a private in the 7th Battn., and went with it to France, where he was made a lance-corporal. At Loos, severely wounded by shrapnel, he lay in the open for several hours before attracting the attention of stretcher-bearers, who pulled him into the comparative safety of a shellhole on a waterproof sheet. His wounds became septic. He died on October 25, a creative worker who enriched life by being as well as by doing. He was 33.

[1] Dr. Wynne Willson, former Headmaster of Marlborough College: see *Letters of Charles Sorley* (Cambridge University Press, 1919).

That year, England lost about 90,000 of her young men, half as many again as from tuberculosis, then called consumption and the deadliest endemic scourge. As Sophocles had noted, it is not disease but war that takes the best. In terms of the nation's vital statistics, 1915 was a year for deep concern. Only birth can make good the ravages of death and the birth rate was the lowest on record—21.9. The civilian death rate was rising too, largely because of infant mortality. Clio, the muse of history, had cause to wear an ironic smile. Hundreds of thousands of square miles of new territory were being added by overseas conquest to the Empire of a people bereft of more young male adults than at any other known time.

In October, Lord Derby, hailed by Lloyd George as "the best recruiting sergeant in England," was given the post of Director-General of Recruiting, a role cynically interpreted by critics of the Asquith leadership as a device for delaying conscription. On that overriding issue, the Coalition Government was still deeply divided. Liberals remained unconvinced that a case had been or could be made. Conservatives pressed for conscription as the only means of military salvation.

Up to that time, rather more than 3,000,000 men had voluntarily answered the call to service. It was an imposing and even inspiring response. The battle of Loos gave no more comfort to the realists than the earlier costly offensives of the year, Neuve Chapelle (March), Second Ypres (April–May), and Festubert (May). The terrible losses of the French continued. It was impossible that they could go on holding five-sixths of the line in the West with a casualty list averaging 150,000 a month. The British would be required to take over more trenches—and how, without conscription, were they to be manned?

Resisting the pressure of Lloyd George, Winston Churchill, and others, to resign his appointment and so force Asquith's hand, the seventeenth Earl of Derby set about his business of administering what came to be known as the Derby Scheme. It was based on the recently compiled National Register and required that men between 18 and 41 should be asked to attest in age groups for armed service if and when called upon, single men to go first. Every man who pledged himself was given an armlet to wear; incidentally, protection against the "white feather" campaign of women in the grip of impulses perhaps not always derived from patriotism, which is not a feminine emotion.

Door-to-door canvassing of householders was part of the Scheme. It produced a number of converts to the idea of voluntary service without much affecting the recruiting averages. A critic and essayist, A. Clutton Brock, wrote of his experience as one of a team engaged in that form of organised persuasion. "You find a man sitting in his parlour with his wife and children on a Sunday evening and you feel guilty towards the wife if not towards the man. If she tells him not to enlist, how are you to oppose her?" The canvasser explains the Prime Minister's pledge to married men and how the group system operates. "They either listen out of politeness or tell you politely that they have read all about it. Then you take out your card and say that you have to ask the man if he will enlist and to write his answer on the back of the card, and often he surprises you by saying at once, 'Well, I suppose I shall have to go,' and his wife surprises you still more by smiling at you quite cheerfully, although there may be a baby in the cradle close beside her." Nothing, the canvasser notes, is said about patriotism or the crimes of the Germans. "Sometimes the wife says the war is a dreadful thing with so many young men being killed on both sides. Sometimes the women would say that the German women were suffering more than the English. No one has any thought of glory or revenge."[1]

In the last weeks of the Derby Scheme, which ended in December 1915, there was a rush of enlistments comparable to that of August 1914. An illustrated paper published a drawing of the tired-out staff of a London recruiting centre sleeping on the office floor as they had done then. The new wave of recruits soon fell away and by the New Year the Scheme was being spoken of in accents of disappointment. It had yielded under 350,000 men. Married men, whose group certifications were the more numerous, could not fairly be held to their undertaking while single men hung back to the number of over 650,000. The burden of separation allowances was a new element in the debate. For the resulting chaos there could be only one solution. Parliament met in its first secret session to consider it.

A Bill embodying the principle of compulsion for unmarried men was put through both Houses in January 1916. Sir John Simon, Home Secretary, saw in it the beginning of "an immense change in the fundamental structure of our society." He would not be a party to it and resigned office. The Archbishop of Canterbury wholeheartedly supported the Bill, pleading the next day for the exemption of the clergy. Bertrand Russell published his views. "The response to voluntary effort has been magnificent . . . To abandon so recklessly that great glory, and to admit that our citizens have to be driven and compelled to fight for freedom is to my mind a national dishonour and a deep disgrace."[2] Under the new bill, nearly 60,000 single young men failed to report for duty.

[1] *Country Life*, October 1915.
[2] *New Statesman*, January 22, 1916.

Early in May 1916, the Military Service (General Compulsion) Bill was given its second reading in the House of Commons. Weakening opposition to it was virtually swept away by Lloyd George, Minister of Munitions, who was soon to step up to the topmost pinnacle of British politics. The historical parallels he cited were shown to be dubious by a later speaker, who could not prevail against the Welshman's mesmeric fervour. By the end of the month, conscription had come at last to the "Land of Hope and Glory, Mother of the Free."

CHAPTER SEVENTEEN

"Flocks Sent to the Slaughter"

1

THE NEW ARMY of 1915–16 was a spontaneous growth
which escaped the blight of bitter controversy, the
evasions, and the political and other manoeuvres that
beset its replacements. The coming of compulsion in
1916 disclosed the existence of more conscientious
objectors than had been heard of before. After seeing the
worst of the Western Front, a much travelled observer
whose contacts with the East might have been expected
to incline him to tolerance, wrote: "The superhuman
egotism of it is what so appals me, that anybody should
trouble about keeping his lily-white hands clean when
there is a question of damming back this unspeakable
tide of filth in which the Boche is trying to submerge
the world. After seeing the misery they have taken no
share in stemming, I do not see how one is ever again
going to feel comfortable towards a conscientious
objector or take his hand. Self-righteousness is its own
damnation."[1]

The so-called First Hundred Thousand (they numbered many more), approaching the critical hour of
their brief appearance in history, were beyond the pale
of internecine debate and special pleading. "The thought
that is uppermost on seeing the New Army in the field
is that these are the men who must complete what has

[1] Reginald Farrar: *The Void of War* (Constable, 1918)

251

been begun, the men who must carry on the torch so bravely upheld by the old Army."[1]

Expressing the race-personality more explicitly than the old Army ever did, the New Army men accepted the torch-bearing role without proclaiming, and perhaps not feeling, any peculiar pride in it. Though they were less susceptible than the recruits of another day to the appeal of tattered regimental colours in cathedrals and painted drums in county museums, they were responsive to the *esprit de corps* of the famous regiments in whose satellite battalions they served. For the men of Kitchener's battalions of the Berkshires, whose colours bore the names of every battle of note fought by the British Army through two hundred years, it was something to say that the regiment's first battalion had been "out from the beginning, in every engagement, and always in the front line," since the Sunday afternoon in August 1914 when they dug themselves in at Givry.

The Lincolnshires never doubted that one of their officers fired the first shot of the war from the British side. The regiment had an undisputed claim to have been the first to capture German guns. It also gained one of the first V.C.s of the war, awarded to Corporal Sharpe and celebrated by a peal of bells at Lincoln Cathedral.

Those in the 7th Royal Fusiliers could flaunt the privilege of marching through the City of London with fixed bayonets, like the Brigade of Guards. The King's Own Scottish Borderers could retort that they had a similar right when marching through the streets of Edinburgh, "for services rendered at Killiecrankie."

Newcomers to the Coldstreams wrote to tell their folks at home that when the five regiments of Foot Guards paraded as a brigade, theirs took fifth place although entitled by seniority to the second place, to which they

[1] Valentine Williams: *With Our Army in Flanders* (Arnold, 1915).

had been relegated by Charles the Second, favouring the Grenadiers. "A regiment whose motto is *Nulli secundus* cannot take second place anywhere, so we march fifth."

Those were chiefly personal satisfactions. The New Army had little sense of being invested with the duty of cherishing its predecessor's traditions and customs. It was not always highly sensitive about its own panache. Although over eighty per cent of it was English, representing the oldest, wealthiest, most populous and most influential unit of the Commonwealth, the New Army let the credit go where it listeth. In June 1916 it listeth heavily westward to Canada, whose volunteers holding a sector in the Ypres Salient came suddenly under fire from German heavy guns that pulverised the trenches in five minutes and was maintained for five hours. Ordered to retire, the survivors formed a second line of defence which met a mass assault by German infantry and sent them reeling back under withering machine-gun and rifle fire.

During the bombardment and the subsequent fighting, the Canadians had terrible losses. Their 8th Brigade of 3,000 men came out of the line minus 2,200. The 1st Canadian Mounted Rifles, serving as infantry, had 151 survivors, the 4th, 130. Massacre figures were reported from other battalions. A little more than a week afterwards, the Canadians in a dashing attack regained their first-line trenches and the soil of the Salient was drenched once more with blood.

Heedless of the censorship, the news went forth to the world of a Canadian success. A publicity machine was set up by the diminutive and dynamic young politician, Max Aitken (afterwards Lord Beaverbrook), who had been acting as official "Eyewitness" with the Canadian Corps. Interviewers, artists, photographers, were commissioned to record the Canadian exploit. That seventy per cent of the men who took part in it were

United Kingdom born was unnoted or conveniently ignored. As a result of the skilfully managed propaganda, "Canada believed her men made up the British Army and did all the fighting."[1]

"Canadians Recover Lost Ground." "Gallant Charge by Anzacs." "Splendid Stand by Scottish Troops." "Welshmen's Haul of Prisoners." "Irish Gallantry at Arras." The headlines lauded, praised and magnified the arms and accomplishments of all but those of the country that was doing four-fifths of the British fighting on land and sea, keeping the seas, transporting nine-tenths of the sea-borne supplies to the Allies, financing them, and spending up to five million pounds a day on its own account. *"Vivent les Canadiens!"* cried the French. *"Vivent les Australiens!"*

The Englishmen of the New Army were content in their illusion that what they would never give utterance to as "the English spirit" had permeated the Scots, the Welsh, the South Africans, the Canadians and the Antipodeans, inspiring them to the grand decisions and splendid deeds for which they were gaining so much renown. There may have been an added tincture of pleasure in knowing that foreigners in general, and the Germans in particular, referred to all troops of United Kingdom provenance as English.

Woven into the self-depreciation, that English cast of mind, was the humour that could not be denied. H. G. Wells drew attention to "the English disposition to treat the war as a monstrous joke." The Englishman, he said, "refused to see anything magnificent or terrible" in the German adversary. Rudyard Kipling, given War Office facilities for visiting New Army training centres, came back confirmed in his belief that "for all our long faces, we are the only genuinely humorous race on earth." He could have cited as an illustration a front line inci-

[1] Sir Philip Gibbs.

dent of a day or two after the Battle of Jutland, May 31, 1916. Germans at St. Eloi in the Salient displayed a notice board on their parapet: "Where is your bloody Fleet now?" The next morning it was facing them from the British trenches opposite with "Fleet" struck out and "board" written over it. The "better 'ole" humour of Bairnsfather had depended for its success on the public image of the 1914 old soldier sticking it out in the mud of 1915. By 1916 it was beginning to lose its grip. The New Army made it seem insipid.

The old Army never dared to laugh at its generals or to use their names familiarly, far less criticise their leadership. "Bobs" for Lord Roberts was about the limit. To the New Army, General Allenby was "Bull Allenby," General Byng, "Bungo," General Birdwood, "Birdie." The old Army, going into battle, seldom knew or asked the reason why. The New Army discussed policy and strategy and those responsible for both. The old Army was naïve enough to mistake wisps of smoke for angels at Mons. Had the New Army seen angels it would most likely have written them off as smoke.

Debrett for 1915 recorded 800 "members of the peerage, baronetage, knightage and companionage of this country," killed in action or died of wounds. Distinguishing persons by rank and place in the context of calamity seems invidious now. The men of the old Army saluted earls, baronets and knights serving as their officers with more punctilio than any others, except generals.

The new race of soldiers destroyed the myth of essential class superiority. At every level, they proved that the "inferior" often displayed attributes that put the "superior" to shame. "The men are splendid and convince me more and more that we are all exactly the same, and that one so-called class is as good as another."[1]

[1] Lieutenant A. W. R. Don, The Black Watch; medical student, died on active service, Mesopotamia, 1916, aged 26. See page 93.

Lord Crawford and Balcarres, whose ancestors fought at Flodden and Marston Moor and who enlisted as a private in the Royal Army Medical Corps, may have made the same discovery. As on the social plane, so on the physical. There were New Army battalions composed of men whose physique was as good as that of the Guards and above that of the average of the Territorials who preceded them in the field.

Marching songs, slang, nicknames: the men of the New Army were prolific innovators in every direction. They put up "No Hawkers, No Circulars" and "Ici On Parle Billingsgate" signs over their dug-out entrances. Wire entanglements were "the zoo," a trench exposed to snipers a "picture gallery," machine-guns in action "bloody typewriters." They minted or popularised words that passed from the military vocabulary into the language: "dope," "wangle," "stunt," "dud," "gadget," "click." Though they endowed bawdy music-hall songs with the gravity of national anthems, they rarely set their patriotism to music and would have derided the dismal chant of the war to come, *There'll Always Be An England*. They marched up to the line at night singing *Kitchener Loves Me, this I know, 'cos the Bible tells me so*, and *The Bells of hell go ting-a-ling-ling, For you but not for me*. The sound of distant shellfire rending the darkness would change their mood abruptly to *Onward, Christian Soldiers,* sung with the reverence of men awed by a fate that had set their feet on the road to Calvary.[1]

A letter from a New Army subaltern still has the power to chill the heart as a reminder of what had to be endured. "Last night, turning a traverse sharply, I almost stepped on a Horrible Thing. We can afford to laugh at corpses, if we did not know them when alive, because with them it is a case of what the men call

[1] A personal recollection.—R.P.

'nappoo fineesh.' We can joke with badly wounded men who are going to recover. But when a German bullet strikes a man in the head and takes away his scalp and a lot of his brains clean away, and still lets him live for two hours, the joke is there no more."

2

They surged into the tumult of the first Somme battle on July 1, 1916, those battalions of English and Scottish volunteers, the West Yorkshires, the York and Lancasters, the Berkshires, the Norfolks, the Royal Scots, the Durhams, the Manchesters, the Liverpools, the Gordons, the Northumberland Fusiliers. Along a great sweeping crescent, the German front line rose and fell and broke apart under a bombardment that had the effect of a cataclysm originating in the nether depths. From Thiepval, through La Boiselle, down to Fricourt, gigantic spouts of earth shot skyward as if some leviathan was about to surface with even more terrifying results. "Nothing like it has been seen or heard on our front before," and the war correspondents, unanimous in that verdict, ransacked their stock of adjectives in describing the events of a day that was to be for ever black-edged in the annals of the Western world.

Counterpointing the thunder of the big guns were the staccato explosions of trench mortars, bombs and grenades. It was an orchestration of destructive power that seemed certain to fulfil the intention of its manipulators, which was to dislodge the Germans at last from their seemingly impregnable positions, and in doing so to bring relief to the hard-pressed French at Verdun. This was *it*—the "Great Push" that was to decide the course and duration of the war, the turning of the tide. Facing the world's finest professional soldiers, who were defending positions of enormous depth and strength, the New Army was at last put to the test of battle on a large scale. From that day, the British bore the major burden of the fighting in the West.

Fricourt was captured by the 21st Division, gallantly retrieving its reverse at Loos. The 18th and 30th Divisions carried Montauban, where Germans shrieked for mercy on their knees and received it at the hands of pitying Englishmen of Lancashire, Surrey, Kent, Essex, Bedford and Norfolk battalions. The Gordons took Mametz at heavy cost to themselves. Advancing on the ridge of La Boisselle, "a splendid and memorable thing," (Gibbs) Tyneside pipers played the Northumberland Fusiliers into action through machine-gun fire that swept No-man's-Land like a scythe. "They threw everything at us except the kitchen sink," said a Royal Scotsman who was also in the charge, meeting the enemy head-on with the bayonet. English county regiments were in the heavy fighting in Thiepval woods. The wounded, many lying helpless, called out words of encouragement as their comrades went forward, like the drowning men of the *Warrior*, sunk at Jutland, who almost with their last breath raised a cheer for a sister ship that was racing past them into the fray.

The task of taking Gommecourt was given to a London Territorial division, the 56th, which included the London Scottish, the Rangers (1/12th Battn., London Regiment), the 4th Londons (Royal Fusiliers), the Kensingtons (13th London), Queen Victoria's Rifles, the London Rifle Brigade and the Queen's Westminsters. The *Official History* states that "the assault by the 56th Division was carried out with the greatest dash, and the failure to capture the Gommecourt salient cannot be attributed to the gallant regiments composing it, for they did practically all that was asked of them." Some of the battalions pushed forward to a point at which they could be given no lateral support, with the result that they were enfiladed and heavily shelled and machine-gunned. Towards sunset, the Germans sent over a low-flying aircraft which dropped a message of truce while the stretcher-bearers of both sides went about their errands. Acceptance was signalled on the spot, with no reference to higher authority.

Despite the setbacks, men spoke with relief at taking part in a war of movement. The long stalemate had been broken. They were exhilarated even though the hazards were multiplied. Many battalions suffered such heavy losses that their morale might have failed but it never did. Formations were in a state of almost continuous flux, yet *esprit de corps* was maintained.

3

The series of offensive operations officially designated "The Battles of the Somme 1916," informally referred to as "the Battle of the Somme," and known by old soldiers simply as "The Somme," covered the period July 1 to November 18. It consisted of twelve separate battles with names that still toll mournfully in many memories: Albert, Bazentin Ridge, Delville Wood, Pozières Ridge, Guillemont, Ginchy, Flers-Courcelette, Morval, Thiepval Ridge, the Transloy Ridges, the Ancre Heights, and the Ancre 1916. In those furnace fires that blazed for five desperate months was consumed the best of a generation in fineness of spirit, in physical and mental soundness, in courage, skills, aptitudes and promise.

The Times printed, under the heading "Roll of Honour," sixty-eight columns of names of private soldiers, "unless otherwise stated," killed and wounded in the first four weeks of the Somme fighting. Through the next four months the columns appeared daily and by the end totalled many pages of the newspaper. The senselessness that has been the recurring theme of criticisms of the battles is borne in on one afresh by the sight of those appalling close-set lists. William John Mason, of the Gloucestershires, a lecturer at Bristol University who was killed on the third day of the opening battle, aged 27, had written in a letter: "The sufferings of the men at the Front, of the wounded whose flesh and bodies are torn in a way you cannot conceive; the sorrow of those at home . . . all that is being piled up day after day in France, England, Germany, Bulgaria and Turkey! What a cruel and mad diversion of human activity!"[1]

The *New Statesman* was moved to comment that "in the present war men go voluntarily to death in a manner that has amazed all who held that the European races had grown decadent and had lost their courage. Obviously, thousands of young men are living in the spirit of the choice of Achilles. There is nothing in the records of human warfare—no, not in the story of Marathon or Thermopylae—to surpass this epic of courage and self-sacrifice that is being written all over the face of Europe today . . . War reveals the noble man as nobler than we had guessed."[2] To Beach Thomas, war correspondent of the *Daily Mail*, "it was almost unbearable to watch our troops going forward into the gloom of night on July 1, 1916, so terribly did they resemble the numbered flocks being sent to deliberate slaughter. Before the next sunset sixty thousand of our men were dead or wounded."[3] The finally corrected figure for the day was 57,470. It included 993 officers and 18,247 other ranks dead.[4]

[1] *Letters of Fallen Englishmen.*
[2] *New Statesman,* vol. October-March, 1916.
[3] Sir William Beach Thomas: *The Way of a Countryman* (Michael Joseph, 1944).
[4] *Official History.*

Hark the roar grows . . . the thunders reawaken—
We ask one thing, Lord, only one thing now:
Hearts as high as theirs who went to death unshaken,
Courage like theirs to make and keep their vow.

Then to our children there shall be no handing
Of fates so vain—of passions so abhorred . . .
But Peace . . . the Peace which passeth under-
*   standing . . .*
Not in our time . . . but in their time, O Lord.[1]

[1] R. E. Vernede, poet and author, killed in action, 1917: *War Poems* (Heinemann).

CHAPTER EIGHTEEN

"We Will Remember Them . . ."

1

IN THOSE great waves of casualties, as the war correspondent noted, "distinction of personalities was drowned." Confronted by so much suffering and sacrifice, one particularises the loss of individuals with discomfort. It is a dilemma that troubled the Oxford fellow and tutor who wrote on hearing of the death in action, earlier that year, of Robert Stafford Palmer, son of Lord Selborne, serving with the Hampshires in Mesopotamia: "Tonight the bell tolls in the brain over one of the noblest—if it be not treason to discriminate—of all the dead one has known who have died for England." He saw it as an occasion "for thanksgiving that God has made men after this manner."

Of Robert Dennys, a young Bart's man who qualified in medicine and did not practise, it was said that he was "a man to *know* and to be thankful for having known." He worked for a time at Gordon Craig's theatre school at Florence. He wrote good verse. He was a true amateur, a type less well known, and certainly less well understood, in England now. It implies the many-sided intelligence that is in regrettable disrepute in our age of specialists.

"Ben" Keeling, from Colchester—his first name was Frederic but H. G. Wells said that there was "not a trace of 'Freddiness' in him"—had gone into the wartime

Army with Rupert Brooke. He might not have cared to be proposed as one of Carlyle's "living light-fountains." He was none the less a natural luminary who would have shone in the world had he lived beyond his thirty years. Arthur Greenwood, sometime Labour Cabinet Minister, insisted that Keeling was "one of the first six of his generation." The direction of his career and the development of his intellect are amply, sometimes touchingly, and always most readably documented in *Keeling Letters and Recollections.*[1] A number of times recommended for a commission, he loyally remained to the end in the ranks of a New Army battalion, the 6th Duke of Cornwall's Light Infantry. He was killed in a bombing raid on German trenches on August 18, 1916, "a great man in the making. Had he survived, the world would have been enriched by the fruits of his fertile mind, his intimate knowledge of social and economic problems, and his passion for truth." (Greenwood).

Brian Brooke, from Lickleyhead Castle, Aberdeenshire, might have been one of the architects of the postwar Commonwealth, John Macfarlan Charlton almost certainly a top ornithologist. William Noel Hodgson ("Smiler" to his brother officers of the 9th Devons), who wrote one of the finest war poems, *Before Action,* was another of those rare men who impress as much by being as by doing. Henry Dundas, who left Eton in 1915 to join the Scots Guards at Wellington Barracks, is remembered for "the remarkable fusion and unity of spiritual and physical qualities that made his friends think of him as Greek." Restless, witty, full of pluck, quick in movement, he reminded his memoir writer, Horatio F. Brown, of "the worrying puppies of the Platonic dialogue." It was another twenty-year-old Guardsman, Stephen Christy, of Emsworth, Hampshire, who inspired the published heartcry:

[1] With an introduction by H. G. Wells (Allen & Unwin, 1918).

263

Yet in these ears, till hearing dies,
One set slow bell will seem to toll
The passing of the sweetest soul
That ever looked with human eyes.[1]

They were part of the "torrent of young life" poured out in the bloody cataracts of the Somme. Some, like Vere Harmsworth,[2] were more than half resigned to what seemed a sentence of death. He wrote on the eve of battle in October: "Somehow I have never imagined myself as an old man with the infirmities and limitations of old age. At school and in the later years I have tried to imagine myself at 50 or so. I do not seem to fit in. At business in the years to come I shall never be any good." The future, he continued, had always been "rather vague, far away and unreal" to him. "I may have been born just to live my 21 years and then fade away." A fellow officer serving with him in the Royal Naval Division on the Western Front wrote that "Harmsworth was the despair of adjutants and colonels. He did as he liked and said what he thought, which often sounded foolish enough. He might have become an eccentric, a millionaire, a saint or a dictator."[3] His last written thoughts were set down in a postscript. "I am leaving all I have for the betterment of those who have suffered through the war. Most of it for the men of my Battalion. My whole being is bound up in my men, heart, body and soul. Nothing else seems to matter."

Donald Hankey, whose book of collected articles originally contributed to *The Spectator* under the *nom de guerre* of "A Student in Arms" was one of the publishing successes of the war, went "over the top" with the memorable remark to his men: "If wounded,

[1] *The Times*, July, 1916.
[2] One of the two sons of Lord Rothermere, chief proprietor of the *Daily Mail*, lost in the war.
[3] Douglas Jerrold: *Georgian Adventure*.

Blighty—if killed, the Resurrection." The son of an English father and an Australian mother, he chose a military career from Rugby School because of the death in action during the Boer War of his eldest brother, to whom he was greatly attached. He entered the Royal Military Academy, Woolwich, as a gunner cadet. After two years he left to go to Oxford, where all his vacations were spent in working for the Oxford and Bermondsey Mission. He interested himself in the future of boys who emigrated from south-east London to Australia and when it seemed to him that too many of them failed to strike root in that country, he went out at his own expense to discover why, travelling steerage as they had done. At what point, but for the war, his life would have expanded in accord with his exceptional capacities none could tell. It was governed, consciously and constantly, by an entirely self-effacing ambition to leave the world better than he found it. He was in the fullest sense a good man whose deep religious insight and theological explorations went with a robust taste in wine, cigars, boxing, wide open spaces and 'cello music.

He enlisted as a private soldier in a Kitchener battalion and soon gained a sergeant's stripes. A long and detailed letter based on his New Army experiences, written to his brother, Colonel Maurice Hankey, of the Cabinet secretariat, was put before Lord Kitchener, "who read it with much interest." He was commissioned in the Royal Garrison Artillery but having no liking for that branch of the Army he tried to rejoin the ranks. Failing in two attempts to do so, he was satisfied to be transferred as a subaltern to his dead brother's old regiment, the Royal Warwickshires.

In the trenches, it distressed him that to be a good soldier a man must have experienced "the blood lust." He could imagine nothing more horrible, he wrote to his sister, "than suddenly to feel the primitive passion for

265

slaughter let loose in one, and to know that one was more than at liberty to give it full rein." To him, "it is that, more than anything perhaps, which brings home what an abominable thing war is." On September 23, 1916, writing again to his sister, he looked into a future in which he was to have no part. "I should not be surprised if, when we are old, we see a repetition of this war . . . A depressing thought, isn't it?"

He fell, leading his men in an attack, three weeks later, a loss to letters, possibly; a loss to Christian apologetics, presumably; a loss to the civilised comity, undoubtedly.

2

Guy Dickins, of Hopefield, Manchester, was working at the British School of Archaeology at Athens before coming home to enlist. John Gulliland, of North Foreland, Broadstairs, was a medical student. Edgar Haselden was secretary of the City Temple Literary and Debating Society. Gerard Garvin, public schools fencing champion, 1913, was the son of J. L. Garvin, editor of *The Observer*. Arnold Bradley Taylor was working at his father's bell foundry at Loughborough. Noel Edinborough was an Associate of the Institute of Electrical Engineers. Charles Kingsley Howe was a member of the teaching staff of Goldsmith's College Art School. Geoffrey Burney had been working in Siberia for the British Museum. Thomas Heathcock had gone from a Grangetown, Yorkshire, council school with scholarships that took him to Pembroke College, Cambridge, where he gained first class honours in Part 1 of the Natural Sciences Tripos and the special prize awarded to the best man of his year. E. E. Polack was the son of the housemaster of the Jewish House at Clifton College and the winner of a cluster of academic prizes. Francis Saxon

Snell was a private tutor; Raymond Vevir one of the founders of the New Tory Club at Oxford; his co-founders had already fallen in battle.

Charles Burdett was a Durham University theological student who was about to be ordained curate at St. Thomas's, Stepney. John Hartley, from Stonyhurst, Eton and Merton College, Oxford, was an athletics "blue" who represented his university against Yale and Harvard. Douglas Warner was training as an engineer at Gainsborough. Stephen Hewitt, one of the youngest Balliol men of his year and one of the most affectionately remembered, had an exceptionally distinguished college career. Oswald Blunden, a former York Minster chorister, worked in the offices of the Gresham Life Assurance Society. Evelyn Herbert Southwell and Malcolm Graham White were masters at Shrewsbury. John William Streets was a Derbyshire miner; his war poems showed a fine sensibility. Henry Cholmeley, son of a partner in the law firm of Frere, Cholmeley & Co., of Lincoln's Inn Fields, intended taking Holy Orders. Alan Smiles, grandson of Dr Samuel Smiles of *Self-Help* fame, was a young Belfast lawyer. W. Thornton Wetenhall, barrister, was a generous giver of his professional services to the Working Men's College, Crowndale Road, North London. Alfred Victor Ratcliffe, student of the Inner Temple, was one of Rupert Brooke's Cambridge friends of whom it was written that "he seemed to live in a higher sphere than the rest of us and to breathe a purer air."

The long grey lists of the New Army's dead contain what appears to be a disproportionately large number of names of young men of the law. Its significance was not apparent to the new Commander-in-Chief. An artillery officer wrote in his diary on December 23, 1916: "I had the honour of being introduced to Sir Douglas Haig yesterday morning. We were told that he would inspect a certain gun of ours at noon . . . He shook hands with me and said: 'Well, young man, how much service have you got?' I answered, 'Commissioned service, since October 1914, and before that a year in the ranks of the Inns of Court.' He asked me if I intended taking up law, seeing that I had joined the Inns of Court. I replied, that had been my intention. 'Well, I hope you won't,' he said. 'Lawyers are a curse to our country.' "[1]

3

Which of the lofty expectations of his gifts Raymond Asquith would have fulfilled, not even his closest friends would presume to suggest. He was 38 and a family man and therefore only marginally qualified to be considered a member of the war generation. The gifts were sincerely celebrated in the tributes that fell as thickly as leaves of Vallambrosa when his name appeared in the "Killed in Action" list that September.

By seniority and example he was reckoned a leader, though leadership may not have been his forte. He had a strong distaste even for the mildest arts of the demagogue. "He never did homage to the deities of the crowd." (John Buchan). As a member of a political family, he could speak of "the bleak futility of politics." Keeping his diary for January 28, 1916, Maurice Baring, who had a job at Royal Flying Corps headquarters in France, wrote that when Raymond Asquith came to dinner he asked the C.O. what the truth was about some air incident concerning which questions were asked in Parliament. The C.O. replied that the facts had been accurately given. "Oh," said Asquith, "so it was true! I thought that as it was stated in the House of Commons, it couldn't possibly be." As a barrister, he

[1] From the unpublished diary of Captain Neville Grahame Chamberlain, R.G.A.

could speak of the law as "a lean, casuistical business."

During the summer of 1915 he was attached to the Queen's Westminsters (T.F.), then under canvas in Richmond Park, where one of his fellow subalterns was Harold Macmillan. "We revelled in the dry humour of Asquith's conversation. Off duty, too, he was excellent company and he knew just where, at that time, to obtain in Soho the best dinner and the best wine. His men in the company knew him to be the son of the Prime Minister, but he was utterly devoid of 'side.' He was respected for his intellect and maturity and his unemotional friendliness."[1] To some of his friends it seemed, surprisingly, that in the Army he found "a natural place for his spirit." He transferred by his own wish to the Grenadier Guards.

In the opinion of Lord Chandos (Oliver Lyttelton), "England lost in him one of its rarest men. Even a stranger could have seen that his good looks and noble profile disclosed a man of the finest character and powers."[2] By the testimony of the same admiring friend, "the death of the Prime Minister's son in action at last convinced the French that we were with them to the very end." One of the last of Raymond Asquith's letters from the trenches was written to J. H. Thomas, the railwaymen's leader, with whom he was on terms of genial accord. He shrank from facile acquaintance and his fastidiousness in that and other matters sometimes exposed him to criticisms of aloofness. Not seeking the suffrages of the mass, he seemed at times a lonely figure. A just appraisal of his gifts and their potential was perhaps made in after years by a Balliol contemporary: "He would, I think, have been a stern and authoritative guardian of good things."[3]

[1] R. R. Calkin, in a letter to the author.
[2] *Memoirs of Lord Chandos.*
[3] L. E. Jones: *An Edwardian Youth*

Visiting an observation post at Ploegsteert in 1916, Winston Churchill was "charmed by the extraordinary fund of wit and gaiety" of a young Californian serving with the Royal Field Artillery. "His conversation was delightful . . . A whole table could sit and listen to him with the utmost interest and pleasure." The subject of a eulogy that went on to refer to him as "a great 'character' " was Harry Butters, the son of an American mining and railway magnate whose fortunes and health were adversely affected by the San Francisco earthquake of 1906. Between father and son there was a felicity of understanding so complete that they were described as being like "mutually enraptured friends." Young Butters was sent over to Beaumont College, Windsor, for the main part of his education, which otherwise was desultory. J. L. Garvin, editor of *The Observer*, retained a firmly imprinted memory of him after the school years: "When he went back to America he was a young man of mark, framed to excel both in sport and affairs. He was very tall, supple, active, frank, and comely of face, as gay as he was good-looking. You saw by a glance at his hands that he had a born instinct for management and technique. He had been a good deal at sea. He knew all about horses and motor-cars. He was a crack shot and a fine polo player. His business acumen was shown as soon as he took over the management of his father's estates . . . To talk with him was to receive a new and promising revelation of the mind of young America."[1]

When the news of war was flashed to San Francisco, in Garvin's words, young Butters "put aside as fair a prospect of wealth, success, happiness and long life as could well open before a young man, and determined

[1] E. B. Osborn: *The New Elizabethans* (John Lane, 1919).

to throw in his lot with the old country and the Allies in the fight for civilisation." He had dismayed the family lawyers by declining to benefit from a will that practically disinherited his step-brothers and sisters and left him in sole command of his father's affairs and wealth. As soon as he had ordered that and other business matters satisfactorily, he sailed for England and joined the Royal Warwickshires, transferring afterwards to the Royal Field Artillery, where he thought there would be more scope for his technical aptitude. He told Churchill: "No, sir, I've not taken any oath of allegiance—but I'm just as loyal." He soon decided that he was "a born gunner," his efficiency such that an inspecting British officer wished that there was an American in every battery. He took part in various engagements, small and great, emerging from them with pride in his fellowship with the men of the battery.

In the Somme offensive, he and the battery moved up to the reserve lines, "to find the bravest sight that ever gladdened my eyes . . . the finest body of fighting troops I verily believe in all the world—the whole division of Guards, 12,000 strong, the first pick of the whole British Army. Not a man under five feet ten inches, magnificently disciplined and with the unbeaten tradition of five centuries behind them. They had been pushed up in the night and were now cooking their breakfast; in high spirits, clean and dry and in the very pink of fighting condition, their shining rifles with bayonets fixed bristling over the parapet. And our Divisional Artillery were to have the honour of reinforcing them."

His gay vitality sustained him through various crises and he appeared to be dismayed at finding himself vulnerable to shell shock. He suffered concussion when a cluster of 5.9 shells fell on his observation post and, although urged to take leave, he rested for no more than a week, writing home to say: "I reckon I've always had

271

too damn much vanity and low-down selfish ambition in my nature. That last week has certainly served to knock out a large portion of both." He grieved deeply for Gerard Garvin, his school friend killed with twenty machine-gun bullets in his body. Soon, a wooden cross was lettered with Harry Butters' name. He was 24, a prototype of the young Americans who helped to beat down tyranny in two world wars.

5

As the Somme battles flared to their climax at the Ancre, it began to appear all too starkly that the New Army was shrinking in quality as the old Army had, two years before. Many high-grade young men, who were as eager as those others to discover signs that wars would become extinct, had yet to fall: the valiant air fighter, Albert Ball, V.C., from Nottingham, and Eric Waterlow, M.C., D.F.C., who trained with him; Basil Hallam, a popular young West End actor; Arthur Graeme West, post-graduate student at Oxford; Bernard Lewis Strauss, from New College; Adrian Consett Stephen, from Sydney University, New South Wales; Theodore Cameron Wilson, schoolmaster and writer; Edwin Leonard Wood, cartographer and naturalist; Henry Lamont Simpson, poet; Arthur Charlwood Turner, Fellow of Trinity College, Cambridge, one of the founders of the Anglican Fellowship, "who seemed to have more than any man of his years the qualities of a prophet and a saint"; Isaac Rosenberg, poet and painter; Bernard Pitt, tutor at the Working Men's College, London; Eric Fox Pitt Lubbock, Eton, Balliol; Norman Clayton, M.A., a master at Dollar Academy; Edward Wyndham Tennant, the Guardsman poet; Thomas Michael Kettle, Professor of Economics,

272

Dublin; T. E. Hulme, "one of the most influential thinkers of his generation";[1] Arnold Howe, "popular with all ranks" of the 1st Battn., Artists Rifles; G. K. Chesterton's brother, Cecil, in the opinion of Sir Desmond MacCarthy "the best pugnacious journalist since Cobbett"; a fanfare from Valhalla that rings down the years.

Yet, while the conscript divisions that filled the widening gaps in the New Army were doomed to fight at muddier and bloodier Passchendaele, a graver injury may have been done to the race of Englishmen in 1916 than at any other time in the war. On the Somme there came to an end the tradition of voluntary military service that had been England's pride and was now her salvation. By the time the smoke had drifted from the wastelands of that terrible battlefield, "little of this splendid material was left to leaven the barrel scrapings of 1917 and 1918. There was never to be such an army again."[2] Although life at home went on with what often seemed extraordinary detachment from events "over there," few families escaped loss.

The United Kingdom casualties alone during the five months' fighting, some of it the fiercest of the war, came to not far short of 400,000, a desperately high proportion of them killed and seriously wounded. They included the men who in the normal way would have been leaders in politics, the arts, the sciences, commerce and industry. For sagacious minds, the sacrificial blood-flow was a source of misgivings about the future. In racial terms, every subaltern killed could be deemed worth any number of generals; and in the New Army a great many young men had the qualities but not the rank of leadership. The mortality rate among junior officers on the Somme was higher than ever. Among the young pilots of

[1] See *The Life and Opinions of T. E. Hulme* by Alun R. Jones (Gollancz, 1960).

[2] J. A. Terraine: *The Observer*, July 1, 1956.

the Royal Flying Corps it would later become catastrophic.

Lord Bryce, formerly British ambassador at Washington, had already asked in the *Hibbert Journal* whether, as a consequence of war losses, the physical and mental energy of the generation to come would "show a decline." He stressed the fact that "those who are perishing now belong to the most healthy and vigorous part of the population, from whom the strongest progeny might have been expected." A professorial writer in the *Eugenics Review* thought that England would be better off with a population level of about 24,000,000. The *New Statesman* asserted that "the losses could be remedied and decisively remedied by any nation with the will to do it," an early intimation perhaps that racial repair might be accomplished by bulk-purchased orange juice and pre-natal clinics.

It has been suggested that the biological victory, such as it is, may belong to the side that loses a war.[1] The theory that war wastes the best life of nations was challenged by Professor Sir Arthur Keith, F.R.S., who would not concede that "the bravest are the best," and who maintained that "the brave are relatively valueless in an industrial age and an industrial community." There was also the argument that military training was conducive to better health and physique for great numbers of town-dwelling men. Another leading anthropologist held that the vascular and muscular systems of young men may be damaged by military training at the age of 18 or 19.

In the biological context, probably the most realistic pronouncement to be made regarding the two great wars of our era is that the flaying of a generation in 1914–18 averted that fate for another in 1939–45. The clamour for a Second Front in 1942 crassly ignored the lessons

[1] See *The Trend of the Race:* S. J. Holmes (Constable, 1921).

of the Somme, which, fortunately, had been branded on the sensibilities of the nation's leaders in the later cataclysm. "Too much blood had been spilt," Winston Churchill had written in *World Crisis: The Aftermath,* "too much life-essence consumed."

Setting aside the innumerable personal tragedies, the real losses of the First World War were no doubt cultural. The author of a recent study of culture in private and public life suggests that the battles that had their climax on the Somme were "an especial disaster for Great Britain," which lost in them "almost all the young men morally and physically qualified to become leaders of their generation, and the fathers, guides, tutors and leaders of the next generation." As a result of the "universal slaughter," the same authority maintains that Europe has continued to suffer from "a deficiency of first-class talent and character."[1]

There was no estimating the extent to which creative thought was depleted, or the cost to learning, literature and science of the destruction of so many strong and cultivated intelligences. Would they have resisted the Satanic forces that have invaded the arts? Could they have seen to it that their second-rate would not become our first-rate, or have arrested the decline of moral indignation into unheroic tolerance? Such questions persist, though they trail away into infinity and may seem profitless to pursue.

After a College feast at St. John's, Cambridge, the then Chancellor of the University, Stanley Baldwin, referred in conversation to his difficulty in filling certain posts within his competence as Prime Minister, and ascribed it to the losses of the First World War. Reporting the occasion, a later Master of St. Catharine's College, Cambridge, who was present, wrote: "Some of us who survived that blood-bath must be all too conscious

[1] Richard Cowell, B.A., B.Sc.: *Culture* (Thames & Hudson, 1959).

that we have risen beyond our normal ceiling, due to the casualties among men who would have been better qualified than ourselves."[1]

Leaders of stature are a missing factor in many departments of the national life, which presents as never before the embarrassing spectacle of men of minor powers wrestling with major responsibilities. There is impoverishment at all levels, though at some it is obscured by the rampant publicity that deifies mediocrity. It is undeniably true that the volunteers of 1914–16 helped to save freedom in the world. Who can say whether "by all the sacrifice of blood and tears, by all the broken hearts and lives laid down, by all the glory and the pain . . ." they saved the England of their dreams?

[1] Donald Portway, D.L., J.P., M.A.: *Militant Don* (Hale, 1964).

276

Some Sources

Raising and Training the New Armies: Captain Basil Williams (Constable, 1918)

The Fighting Territorials: Percy Hurd (Country Life, 1916)

Realities of War: Sir Philip Gibbs (Heinemann, 1920)

Francis and Riversdale Grenfell: John Buchan (Nelson, 1920)

The Struggle in the Air: Major Charles C. Turner (Arnold, 1919)

A History of the Great War: John Buchan (Nelson, 1921)

War Letters of Fallen Englishmen (Gollancz, 1930)

Everyman at War: edited by C. B. Purdom (Dent, 1930)

The New Elizabethans: E. B. Osborn (John Lane, 1919)

For Remembrance: A. St. John Adcock (Hodder & Stoughton)

Ordeal by Battle: F. S. Oliver (Macmillan, 1915)

Official History of the War: Military Operations, France and Belgium (Macmillan, 1927)

An Autobiography: Richard Burdon Haldane (Hodder & Stoughton, 1929)

Moments of Memory: Herbert Asquith (Hutchinson, 1937)

Charles Lister: Letters and Recollections, edited by Lord Ribblesdale (Fisher Unwin, 1917)

The Rainbow Comes and Goes: Lady Diana Cooper (Hart-Davis, 1959)

Various Regimental Histories and privately printed Memoirs

Files of *The Times, The Graphic, Country Life, Illustrated London News*

Index

Index

Birmingham, enlistments in, 27

Black Watch, The, 93; at Hulluch, 236; at Loos, 237; at Neuve Chapelle, 98; in Mesopotamia, 255 n.

Blatchford, Robert, warns Britain about German aims, 16

Blunden, Oswald, death of, 267

Bolton, John, death of, 183

Border Regiment with B.E.F., 47

Bowlby, Sir Anthony, with B.E.F., 170

Brandt, Robert, death of, 198

Brignall, Frank, death of, 135; on a day in the trenches, 134-5

British Army, *passim*; change in officers' dress (1915), 147-8; condition of in 1914, 31-2; deterrents to recruitment (1915), 178; drop in enlistments (1915), 129; effect of discords in Britain on recruitment, 131-2; lack of supplies (1914), 32-3; musketry supremacy of, 46; pay (1914), 129; radically unfit men recruited (1915), 179-80; recruiting campaign (1915), 178-9; reforms, 60; Reserves mobilised, 25; voluntary system criticised, 177-81. *See also* B.E.F.; Kitchener's Army; Territorials

Brooke, Brian, death of, 263

Brooke, Rupert, 8, 120-4, 184, 194, 263, 267; articles for *Westminster Gazette*, 51—2; at Antwerp, 89; at Cambridge, 51; at Port Said, 121; death and burial of, 123, 225; declines Staff post, 121; describes retreat from Antwerp, 54; dines with H. H. Asquith, 54; in London, 51, 54; in Tahiti, 122; in U.S.A., 51-2; joins Inns of Court training battalion, 53; letter to John Drinkwater, 89-90; mental malaise of, 52; music in memory of, 221; on Skyros, 122; patriotism of, 52-3; physical appearance, 50; with Royal Naval Division, 49-55, 216, 217; works of, 54-5

Brown, Philip, death of, 154, 155

Browne, Denis, at burial of Rupert Brooke, 123; death of, 184; *en route* for Gallipoli, 121; farewell letter to Edward Marsh, 184; on Charles Lister, 217; on Rupert Brooke, 184; with Royal Naval Division, 216-17; wounded, 217

Bruce family, 77

Bruce, Robert, death of, 234

Buckinghamshire Hussars, 37

Buffs, *see* East Kent Regiment

Bullock, Arthur Ernest, M.R.C.P., death of, 235

Burdett, Charles, death of, 267

Burney, Geoffrey, death of, 266

Burns, James, death of, 239; poem quoted, 238-9

Burrows, Leonard Righton, death of, 235

Butters, Harry (American), 270-2; death of, 272; English education of, 270; joins Royal Warwickshire Regiment, 271; on the Guards, 271; on the Somme, 271-2; transfers to R.F.A., 271

Butterworth, Hugh Montague, at Hooge, 238; death of, 238; on action at Hooge, 190; on the art of leadership, 238

Cadge, William, death of, 235

Calkin, R. R., 8; on Raymond Asquith, 269

Callinan, Thomas William, death of, 134

Cambridgeshire Regiment at Loos, 232

Cameron Highlanders at Neuve Chapelle, 98

Cameronians, *see* Scottish Rifles

Campbell, Kenneth Gordon, death of 234

Canadian Expeditionary Force with B.E.F., 131, 134

Canadian Mounted Rifles at Ypres, 253; casualties, 253

Canadian 8th Brigade at Ypres, 253

Carington family, 77

Carrington, Dr. Edward Worrell, death of, 235

Cathcart family, 77

Cavendish family, 77

Cecil family, 77

Challoner, Alan Crawhall, death of, 197

Chapin, Harold (American), 8, 239-43; at Loos, 243; death and burial of, 243; education in England, 239; in the theatre, 239-40; joins R.A.M.C., 239; memorial performance of his plays, 243; on dissension in Britain (1915), 241; on effects of shell-bursts, 241-3; on problems of perception, 242; on wounds and the wounded, 241; plays by, 240

Chapman, Lawrence Vaughan, death of, 234

Charlton, John Macfarlan, death of, 263

Chaworth-Muster family, 77

Chaytor, Hugh Clervaux, death of, 87

Cheesman, G. L., death of, 154

Cheshire Regiment, 30

Chesterton, Cecil, death of, 273

Index

Index

282

Index

Grenfell, Julian Henry Francis, D.S.O., 37, 159–71, 191; as boxer, 159; at Oxford, 159, 160–3, 192; awarded D.S.O., 167; burial of, 170; commissioned in 1st Dragoon Guards, 163; death of, 80 n., 107, 159, 170, 193, 217–18; declines Staff job, 168; desire for physical excellence, 161–2; dislike of Philip Sassoon, 162; compared with Billy Grenfell, 192; fondness for greyhounds, 166–7; in India, 163–4; in South Africa, 164–6; letters to his mother, 163–4, 166, 169; list of things he wanted, 164–5; love of fighting, 167–8; on books, 165; on character, 160; on marriage, 166; on *The Brothers Karamazov*, 165–6; on the Territorials, 168; on the trenches, 168; on war, 80, 166, 167–8; on visit of German Crown Prince to India, 163–4; relationship with his mother, 163, 164; with B.E.F., 166–71; wounded, 169, 170, 195

Grenfell, Riversdale, death of, 38, 144; with B.E.F., 37–8

Gulliland, John, death of, 266

H.A.C., 32, 82–3, 132; as source of commissioned officers, 82; at Ypres, 83; with B.E.F., 47, 183–4, 209

Haig, Sir Douglas, 72, 97, 100, 145, 188; appointed C.-in-C., 267; at Loos, 229, 230

Haldane, Lord, 15, 60, 182, 277; Army reforms of, 23–4; on Lord Kitchener, 62

Haldane, Robert Patrick, death of, 182; heroism of, 182

Hallam, Basil, 155; death of, 272

Hallamshire Rifles, 88

Hamilton family, 77

Hamilton-Fletcher, Gareth, death of, 92

Hampshire Regiment at Aubers Ridge, 141; in Mesopotamia, 219, 262

Hankey, Donald, 264–6; death of, 266; joins Kitchener's Army, 265; with Royal Warwickshire Regiment, 265–6

Harmsworth, the Hon. Vere, 8; death of, 264; on his future, 264

Hartley, John, death of, 267

Harvey, S. A. G., 174; death of, 174; on Emanuel School, 174

Hawley family, 77

Heald, Ivan, death of, 219 n., on Charles Lister, 219

Heath, Arthur, 148–51; at Loos, 150–1; death of, 151; letters to his mother, 149–50; on war, 149

Heathcock, Thomas, death of, 266

Hedderwick, C. S., death of, 105

Hellyar, Sidney, death of, 140

Henderson-Hamilton, James Campbell, death of, 236

Hewitt, Stephen, death of, 267

Highland Light Infantry, at Gallipoli, 210; at Loos, 234

Hitler, Adolf, at First Ypres, 66

Hodgson, William Noel, death of, 185 n., 263

Holden, Norman Victor, death of, 183

Hooge, Battle of, 30, 188–90, 194–8, 201, 202, 205, 210; casualties at, 209; counter-attack at, 208–9; German lines mined, 189; Germans use liquid fire, 190, 202, 205, 238; opposing trenches at, 188

Hornby, A. H., 20

Horner, Edward, 107–9; at Neuve Chapelle, 108; at Noyelles, 108; at Oxford, 192; death of, 108, 225–6; letter to his mother, 108; wounded, 170

Howe, Arnold, death of, 273

Howe, Charles Kingsley, death of, 266

Howele, Brigadier-General Philip, death of, 80 n.; on war, 80

Hoyle, Basil, 231–2; at Festubert, 231–2; death of, 231, 232

Hughes-Onslow family, 77

Hull Rifles, 88

Hulme, T. E., death of, 273

Hulton, Alan Grey, death of, 182

Hunter, Leslie, death of, 154

Hutt, Harold Vernon, death of, 92

Iles, John Owen, 234–5; at Cambridge, 234; at Loos, 235; death of, 235

Irish Guards, 154; at Loos, 232, 236; casualties at Loos, 232

Jameson, Maurice Gurney, death of, 93

Jarvis, W. D. Powell, death of, 134

Jenkinson family, 77

Job, Bernard Craig, death of, 117

Keeling, Frederic ("Ben"), 53, 262–3; death of, 53, 263

Kelly, Frederick Septimus ("Cleg"), 8, 220, 221–2; as oarsman, 221; at Beaucourt-sur-Ancre, 222; at burial of Rupert Brooke, 123; at Oxford, 221–2; compositions of, 221–2; death of, 222, 225; describes artillery fire, 222; *en route* for Gallipoli, 121; on Charles Lister, 218; on Rupert Brooke, 123; with Royal Naval Division, 216

Kemp, Hugh, death of, 134

283

Index

Kennedy, E. V., memorial to Malcolm Proctor-Dilworth, 79

Kensingtons, The, at Aubers Ridge, 140; at Neuve Chapelle, 102; on the Somme, 258

Kerr family, 77

Kettle, Professor Thomas Michael, death of, 272

Keyser, Sister Agnes, 114

King Edward VII's Hospital for Officers, 9, 114

King, Lucas, death of, 140

King's Liverpools at Second Ypres, 138; on the Somme, 257

King's Own Regiment at Aubers Ridge, 141

King's Own Scottish Borderers, 252; at Aubers Ridge, 141

King's Shropshire Light Infantry at Aubers Ridge, 141

King's Royal Rifle Corps at Aubers Ridge, 140; at Hooge, 189; casualties at Hooge, 196

Kinnaird family, 77

Kipling, John, death of, 236

Kipling, Rudyard, 18, 31, 57, 61, 236, 244; on Englishmen, 254; on "Slackers," 176

Kitchener, Lord, 25, 26, 27, 32, 61, 89, 178, 193, 265; advocates conscription, 181; appeals for recruits (1915), 129; objections to war correspondents, 39; on failures in war, 195; on recruitment failure (1915), 181; on Territorials, 61–2; orders for Loos battle, 227–8

Kitchener's Army, 47, 84–5, 112, 251–61, 263, 273–4; at Hooge, 188–90, 194–5; at Loos, 227–43; baptism of fire, 188–90; billeting of, 28–9; casualties, 259–60, 196, 273; compared with Regulars and Territorials, 255–6; effects of losses on, 272; enlistment in, 86–9; formation of, 26–8; humour of, 255–6; in Mesopotamia, 255 n.; joins B.E.F., 186; lack of supplies for, 32–3; marching songs of, 256; on the Somme, 257–61; recruiting for, 33; recruitment figures (1914), 86; response of to regimental *esprit de corps*, 252–3; slang of, 256; training of, 29–30, 32–3, 228–9; 21st Division, 228–43; 24th Division, 228–43

Knight, A. S., death of, 198

Knox, Monsignor Ronald, 107, 219; on Charles Lister, 212, 213; on Julian Grenfell, 161, 166; on Patrick Shaw-Stewart, 224

Lahore Division at Neuve Chapelle, 98

Lambton family, 77

Lascelles, John Frederick, death of, 197

"Latin Club," 220

Lee, Brigadier-General Noel, death of, 63

Leete, Alfred, recruiting cartoon, 25

Legard family, 77

Legge-Bourke family, 77

Leicestershire Regiment at Neuve Chapelle, 98

Leicestershire Yeomanry at Aubers Ridge, 141; at Second Ypres, 138

Leighton, Lord, with Artists' Rifles, 81

Leinster Regiment at Poperinghe, 174

Ley family, losses of, 77

Life Guards with B.E.F., 88

Lincolnshire Regiment at Neuve Chapelle, 98; war record of, 252

Liquid fire used by Germans, 190, 194, 202, 205, 238

Lister, Charles, 33–4, 211–21, 223, 277; at Constantinople Embassy, 214–15; at Eton, 211; at Gallipoli, 217; at Oxford, 192, 212–13; at Rome Embassy, 214; commissioned in County of London Yeomanry, 215; death of, 107, 220; *en route* for Gallipoli, 121; in hospital at Malta, 218–19; in India, 214; on death of Julian Grenfell, 217–18; on French morale, 214; on Germans, 214–15; on his Royal Naval Division platoon, 216; on Julian Grenfell, 161, 165; on Prince Lichnowsky, 215; on Rome Embassy staff, 214; on Rupert Brooke, 217; on Sultan of Turkey, 215; on Thackeray, 217; on trade unions, 214; transfers to Royal Naval Division, 216; wounded, 218

Liverpool, dockers' strike at, 16; recruiting in, 26

Liverpool Scottish, 117

Lloyd George, David, 16 n., 202, 203, 205, 208, 248; becomes Prime Minister, 139, 250; favours French recruitment method, 181; on Lord Derby, 247; supports conscription, 250

Loder-Symond family, 77

Lody, Carl Hans, executed, 74–5

London Rifle Brigade, 93, 203–7, 235; at Aubers Ridge, 145; at Hooge, 189–90, 194–5, 198, 199, 205–6, 238; at Loos, 238; at Neuve Chapelle, 98; at Ypres, 138, 194; casualties, 190, 195, 196; on the Somme, 258; with B.E.F., 170, 193, 204–7

284

Index

London Scottish, 67–73; at First Ypres, 68–73; in Lord Mayor's Show, 72; losses at Ypres, 71–2; on the Somme, 258; with B.E.F., 47, 68, 237
Lonsdale, Arthur, death of, 105
Lovat Scouts, 180
Lubbock, Eric Fox Pitt, death of, 272
Lukis, T. S., death of, 104
Lumley family, 77
Lyons family, 78

Macfarlane, Alastair Hunter, death of, 140
Mackenzie, Gordon, death of, 183
Mackie, Norman Lindsay, death of, 237
Mackintosh, Ewart Alan, death of, 91 n.
Maclehose, Norman Crawford, death of, 171
Macmillan, Harold, in Queen's Westminsters, 269
McNab, Captain Angus, death of, 71
Magnard, Albert, death of, 244
Makant, Angus V., death of, 105
Malet, Hugh Grenville, death of, 117
Manchester Regiment on the Somme, 257
Manners family, 77
Manners, Lord John, death of, 38 n.
Marsh, Edward, 53, 184, 225; on death of Rupert Brooke, 123
Marsham-Townsend family, 77
Martin, Charles Robert Herbert George, death of, 140
Mason, William John, death of, 260; on suffering at the Front, 260
Maude, John William Ashley, death of, 210
Mawby, Edwin, death of, 237
May, Harold Gostwych, death of, 105
Meerut Division at Neuve Chapelle, 98
Melland, Brian, death of, 140
Mercer-Nairne family, 77
Middlesex Regiment, 21; at Aubers Ridge, 141; at Hooge, 189, 197; at Neuve Chapelle, 98
Millais, Sir John, with Artists' Rifles, 81
Miller, Alexander Lorimer, adventures of, 84; death of, 84
Military Service (General Compulsion) Act, 1916, passed, 250
Milne, T. Baxter, on First Ypres, 69–70, 71; on London Scottish, 67; on London Scottish journey to Ypres, 68
Mitford, Clement, death of, 170
Monckton family, 77
Monkhouse, J. T., death of, 134

Mons, Angels of, 42; Battle of, 38, 46, 80, 103; Retreat from, 38, 40–1, 42, 103, 166
Montague, C. E., on burial of British soldiers, 118–19; on Walter Dixon Scott, 58
Montgomery, William Sprott, death of, 104
Morgan-Grenville family, 77
Morris, Francis St. Vincent, 128–9; death of, 129
Morris, Henry, death of, 236
Moseley, Harry, death of, 177
Moxley, J. K. S., death of, 105
Moyne, Gerald, death of, 237
Murray, Professor Gilbert, on Arthur Heath, 148–50; on scholars from New College, Oxford, 148–55

Nash (Gilbert Talbot's batman), at Hooge, 206
Neuve Chapelle, Battle of, 96–109, 140, 228, 247; bombardment at, 99–100; casualties, 102, 104–9; failure of bombardment, 100
New Army, see Kitchener's Army
New Zealand Engineers with B.E.F., 134
New Zealand offers troops, 26
9th Lancers at Aubers Ridge, 145; on the Marne, 43
Noble, William Black, death of, 134
Norfolk Regiment at Loos, 235, 246; on the Somme, 257; with B.E.F., 209
North Somerset Yeomanry at Second Ypres, 138; at Hooge Lake, 169
North Staffordshire Regiment at Neuve Chapelle, 98
Northamptonshire Regiment at Aubers Ridge, 141
Northey family, 77
Northumberland Fusiliers (Tyneside Scottish), 179–80; at Aubers Ridge, 140; at La Boisselle, 258; at Loos, 235; on the Somme, 257
Northumberland Yeomanry with B.E.F., 47

Official History of the War, 46–7, 227 n., 277; gives Somme casualties, 260; on attack on Gommecourt, 258; on Battle of Loos, 230; on Battle of Neuve Chapelle, 97, 100, 101; on British Army's successes, 66; on First Ypres, 66; on Loos casualties, 233; on retirement of 21st and 24th Divisions at Loos, 231
Ogilvy family, 77
Orde-Powlett, William, death of, 87

Index

O.T.C. as source of officers, 83–4
Owen family, 77
Oxford University, recruiting at, 55
Oxfordshire Hussars with B.E.F., 47
Oxfordshire Yeomanry at Ypres, 73

Pace, T. Andrew, death of, 93
Palmer, Robert Stafford, death of, 219, 262; on Charles Lister, 219
"Pals" Batallions, 26, 84–5
Parliamentary Recruitment Committee formed, 26
Paterson, S. G., death of, 104
Payne-Gallwey family, 77
Pemberton, Leigh, death of, 236
Pemberton, Sir Max, 236
Pitt, Bernard, death of, 272
Pleydell-Bouverie family, 77
Polack, E. E., death of, 266
Post Office Rifles with B.E.F., 171, 183
Poulton, Ronald, 142–4, 221; at Reading, 144; at Oxford, 143; death of, 142, 144, 201
Pound, John, death of, 134
Prince of Wales' Own Yorkshire Regiment at Ypres, 87
Princess Patricia's Canadian Light Infantry at Aubers Ridge, 141
Proctor-Dilworth, Maclean, death of, 79
Public Schools, recruitment from, 57
Public Schools Battalion, 32, 33
Purcell, Charles Francis, death of, 232

Queen Victoria's Rifles at Second Ypres, 130, 138; on the Somme, 258
Queen's Westminsters, 93, 269; at Loos, 235; on the Somme, 258
Quiller-Couch, Sir Arthur, on Cambridge University (1914), 56; with B.E.F., 153

Radcliffe, John Douglas Henderson, death of, 197
Rae, Keith, 199–200; as master at Marlborough, 200; at Oxford, 199–200; commissioned in London Rifle Brigade, 201; death of, 201; in Germany, 200–1; in Ypres Salient, 201; on being under shellfire, 199; on Kitchener's Army, 201; on Ronald Poulton, 143, 201; work for Balliol Boys' Club, 200
Ramsay, Gilbert, death of, 210
Rangers (London Regiment) on the Somme, 258
Ratcliffe, Alfred Victor, death of, 267
Raw, Robert, death of, 210

Rawlinson, Lieut.-General H., on importance of Neuve Chapelle action, 97–8
Reading, Lord, on Norman Lindsay Mackie, 237
Redmond, John, M.P., 166
Renton, Harry Noel Leslie, death of, 197
Reynolds, G. F., death of, 43
Reynolds, John William, death of, 209
Rhodes-Moorhouse, William Barnard, V.C., 136–7; death of, 137
Ribblesdale, Lord, 217, 218, 277; Sargent's portrait of, 211
Richards, Julian, death of, 235
Rifle Brigade, see London Rifle Brigade
Roberts, Lord, 38, 255; campaign for national service (1914), 15
Roley, W. H. G., death of, 183
Romanes, Edward Giles, death of, 182
Rosenberg, Isaac, death of, 272
Royal Army Medical Corps at Loos, 227, 228; with B.E.F., 239–43, 256
Royal Berkshire Regiment, 40–1; at Neuve Chapelle, 98; on the Somme, 257; war record of, 252
Royal Engineers, 29; at Hooge, 189; at Neuve Chapelle, 102
Royal Field Artillery, 38, 115; at Gallipoli, 210; at Loos, 234; on the Somme, 271
Royal Flying Corps, 129, 197; mortality rate, 273–4; with B.E.F., 46, 210
Royal Fusiliers, 90, 113, 252; at Neuve Chapelle, 103; on the Somme, 258
Royal Marine Light Infantry, 48–9
Royal Munster Fusiliers at Aubers Ridge, 140
Royal Fleet Reserve mobilised, 48
Royal Naval Air Service, 182–3; in 1914, 25
Royal Naval Division, 48–9, 140, 183, 216–20; at Cape Helles, 218; at Gallipoli, 120, 220–6; embark for Dunkirk, 48; on Western Front, 225
Royal Naval Reserve mobilised, 48
Royal Naval Volunteer Reserve mobilised, 48
Royal Navy, 48, 128; casualties (1914), 80; in 1914, 24–5
Royal Scots at Aubers Ridge, 140; at Gallipoli, 210; at La Boisselle, 258; at Loos, 237
Royal Sussex Regiment, 27; at Aubers Ridge, 140–1; at Neuve Chapelle, 98; at Second Ypres, 209
Royal Warwickshire Regiment, 271; at Loos, 234; with B.E.F., 265